FIRST
to
FALL

FIRST
to
FALL

Elijah Lovejoy and the Fight for a Free Press in the Age of Slavery

Ken Ellingwood

PEGASUS BOOKS
NEW YORK LONDON

FIRST TO FALL

Pegasus Books, Ltd.
148 West 37th Street, 13th Floor
New York, NY 10018

First Pegasus Books paperback edition June 2023
First Pegasus Books cloth edition May 2021

Interior design by Maria Torres

Library of Congress Cataloging-in-Publication Data is available.

ISBN: 978-1-63936-461-9

10 9 8 7 6 5 4 3 2 1

Printed in the United States of America
Distributed by Simon & Schuster
www.pegasusbooks.com

For Monique;

and in memory of journalists around the world
who have given their lives in pursuit of the truth

CONTENTS

INTRODUCTION

T HE PEOPLE'S REPUBLIC OF China might seem a strange source of inspiration for a book about American freedom of the press. Or maybe it makes perfect sense. After a long career as a reporter for the *Los Angeles Times*, I was teaching journalism at Nanjing University when the idea for this book came to me, kindled in part by my Chinese students. We covered the history of journalism in the United States, and Elijah Lovejoy came up during a segment on the press and the antislavery movement. My students were fascinated and moved by the story of Lovejoy—a white newspaper editor on the American frontier of the 1830s who insistently raised his pen against slavery and, when enemies circled, raised it again to defend his right to print. He would become the first American journalist slain for his work, and his martyrdom would outrage many compatriots and provide a shot of energy for the antislavery movement in the North.

The Chinese university students seated in front of me expressed admiration for Lovejoy, and I was energized by their reaction. There was something universal in this tale of a man's righteous struggle against larger, hostile forces, for people with little individual power of their own. Yet it was also distinctly American in the two weapons he chose to wield: liberty and a newspaper. I began to dig into Lovejoy's fight.

The story told here of Lovejoy and his press-freedom crusade is that of a hero, if an imperfect one. Like many people during his time—more than two decades before a civil war loomed as an apparent inevitability— Lovejoy came to antislavery through his faith, as a preacher's son and

Princeton-trained minister in his own right. Lovejoy found a parallel calling as a newspaper editor as a way to carry out God's work. Alongside the usual moral causes that consumed so many evangelical Protestants—such as temperance and strict observance of the Sabbath—the issue of slavery assumed an increasingly prominent spot on Lovejoy's list of concerns. In his newspaper writings, he insisted that holding fellow humans in chains was a moral sin as well as a political one. Lovejoy's columns invoked rape and the ripping apart of families to force his readers to face slavery's atrocities in terms that were raw and draped in horror. He would come to see his weekly newspaper as a tool for mobilizing like-minded people into a wider movement—an act all the more daring because of his precarious location on the lip of the slavery South.

Even though Lovejoy saw slavery as evil, it took him years to abandon a belief that emancipation might happen gradually. Like many well-meaning white Americans of his time, Lovejoy believed that slave owners would do the right thing once they acknowledged that chattel slavery represented a moral transgression. They only had to be enlightened. But the pro-slavery camp did not make that turnabout—it worked instead to concoct an elaborate justification for why slavery was a benefit for all concerned. Most significantly for this story, the forces of Southern slavery sought to muzzle anyone who would criticize the institution—whether they be journalists, abolitionists, or members of Congress. In so doing, slavery's defenders created a de facto censorship regime during the antebellum years unlike any the United States has seen in peacetime. Only after enduring continuing attacks on his newspaper and his family did Lovejoy swap his fruitless, gradualist philosophy for the urgency of abolitionism.

Lovejoy's writings could be over-certain and provocative to a fault. As a preacher, Lovejoy saw himself as a moral custodian pushing his readers to rightness. But he could come off as an uncompromising scold in unnecessary search of a scrap. This didn't endear him to many people who already viewed abolitionism as an existential threat to their social order and perhaps to the Union itself. It is also unnerving to read some of Lovejoy's early columns attacking Roman Catholicism—this while he was living in St. Louis, Missouri, a heavily Catholic city—and it is even more jarring to learn that these notions reflected the accepted thinking of mainstream Protestant leaders of his time. To a modern reader, they are xenophobic and paranoid in the extreme. My examination of that era's highly opinionated newspapers made it clear that, for all of our current discussion about media "echo chambers" and a news landscape splintered by political ideology, hyper-partisanship in the press was hardly an invention of the twenty-first century.

I came to know Lovejoy through years of digging in archives, scouring biographies, poring over family letters, and reading years of his columns in his newspaper, the *Observer*. I tramped through woods in central Maine to find the site of his family's homestead, designated now by a stone marker that is corralled by split rails under big hardwoods. The pondside location where the Lovejoy house once sat is not so different from the pine-thick area where I grew up in western Maine, next to a tumbling brook. It was easy for me to picture the stocky Lovejoy as a young man, diving into that pond but itching to peer beyond his village into a wider world. He dazzled teachers with his intellect all the way through his college graduation, then hiked—literally, walked—to the western frontier to find his place in that world.

As I read the letters Lovejoy exchanged with his parents and siblings, the harsh moral certitude of his family environment came through loudly, as did the exaggerated demands that Lovejoy placed on himself. There were also worrisome episodes of darkness that caused me to wonder how far his family's history of depression extended. Later in his life, Lovejoy's readiness to imagine his own demise in the name of a righteous cause at times hinted at a man bent on martyrdom.

Having spent nearly all of my adult life as a news reporter, I grew to see Lovejoy as an exemplar of bravery, if not of tact. It takes a certain degree of moxie to work as a journalist—in run-of-the-mill ways, like walking up to perfect strangers to ask them for opinions that are none of your business, and in more consequential ones, like deciding whether to creep a block deeper toward the shooting in an active combat zone. Or, closer to home, facing police tear gas and rubber bullets while covering street protests. It is sometimes brave enough simply to decide that a story needs telling—and then to tell it. Understand that courage and recklessness are shades of each other on the color wheel. Finding Lovejoy's proper spot on that spectrum is tricky.

What stands out to me about Lovejoy's brand of courage were the stark choices he faced in exercising it. He was physically isolated, on the frontier in Missouri and Illinois, hundreds of miles from his mother and siblings back in Maine. Especially during his early years, Lovejoy acted largely on his own—without the sponsorship or direction of any organized antislavery movement—when he wrote columns assailing the institution of slavery even while living alongside its practitioners. Many people urged him to stop, then turned to threats and sustained harassment, including multiple attacks on his printing press, when he persisted.

It would have been easier—and quite reasonable—to simply quit. But with the support of his wife and a few committed friends (most of them fellow Presbyterians who had also trooped west from New England or New York), Lovejoy did not relent. Instead, he set the type in his printing press and converted his moral outrage over slavery into a twin crusade: freedom of the press and his right as an American citizen to publish a newspaper and write whatever he chose. He insisted on delivering the Truth—capital *T*—as he saw it, on matters divine and secular. And that included the unconscionable injustice of human slavery. Lovejoy was well aware that using a printing press to protest the enslavement of two million Black souls, even in the ostensibly free state of Illinois, was akin to putting a bull's-eye on his back. He did so anyway.

The story of Lovejoy's struggle seems an apt way to remind ourselves of the sacrifices, many times tucked from view in the folds of our history, that have been made to safeguard liberties we mistakenly believe were conveyed for free. In reality, they were fought over and won, like strategic hilltops on a battlefield, even at the cost of blood. Press freedom is one of those. The First Amendment protections we take for granted did not spring fully formed at the time of the nation's founding. Nor were the Supreme Court's helpful rulings during our most recent century the only bolstering they received. In between, it took insistent journalists like Lovejoy—an obscure editor, working his press by hand, alone—to test the guarantees they were certain the Founders had intended. Lovejoy's fight, and the heartening public response to it, drew us closer to a modern conception of journalism.

Threats against journalists haven't ended, of course. A shotgun-wielding man storms a newspaper office in Maryland and shoots and kills five employees. Despots around the world censor, jail, or murder journalists because the truth represents peril to their grip on power. Terrorists target journalists in the field and in their offices. A vainglorious American president recklessly labels the independent press as an "enemy of the people." Others who feel threatened by the work of legitimate journalists attempt to strike back with made-up claims of untruth—"fake news." Lovejoy's tale and others like it resonate because we still need them. They are all, each in their way, tiny blows for freedom.

FIRST
to
FALL

CHAPTER ONE

WHERE THE EVIL EXISTED

THE NEWS WAS BIG, but Elijah Lovejoy wasn't letting on. As Lovejoy laid out his St. Louis newspaper on a July day in the summer of 1836, he tucked a piece of life-changing news into a small space on page 3. Lovejoy was announcing that he was moving his newspaper, the *Observer*, across the river to Alton, Illinois, and thus leaving town for good. He topped the brief with a spare headline—"THE OBSERVER—REMOVAL"—that gave little hint of the turmoil and threats of violence that had hovered around Lovejoy for months. Nor did the five-paragraph article convey that Lovejoy's shift to Illinois could have been more accurately described as an inglorious shove out the door.

"After much deliberation, and a consultation with a number of our friends, we have decided here after to issue the 'Observer' from Alton, Ill.," Lovejoy wrote. His explanation made only oblique reference to his troubles with local mobs: anonymous threats, break-ins, and acts of vandalism against his newspaper office. "So long as duty seemed to require our remaining here we were determined to remain, at whatever sacrifice of personal comfort, reputation or safety," he continued. But rather than dwell on those safety concerns, which were already known to many in town, Lovejoy presented his shift across the river as a cool-headed decision to go where the business prospects for the *Observer* seemed brighter. "[T]here is no doubt the paper will be better supported there than it now is, or is likely to be, remaining in St. Louis," Lovejoy wrote. "We hope this reason will be perfectly satisfactory to all our good friends in Missouri, who might otherwise think its removal uncalled for." That very issue would be the *Observer*'s last in St. Louis.

The bare-bones report was one of the less-problematic things Lovejoy had written in recent memory. Tensions over his antislavery writings had been creating sparks since the previous year. More recently, Lovejoy had been locked in an on-again, off-again war of words with a St. Louis judge over the horrid public burning of a biracial man. Lovejoy's reaction to the killing had led powerful men in St. Louis to label him an abolitionist, which in those days, in that place, was akin to classifying him as a public enemy. It is quite likely that his detractors would cheer his announcement as a form of surrender. Yet there was another meaning that came through in the notice about his move to Illinois—a tone that sounded more like determination. Lovejoy was going where he hoped Missouri's vigilantes would no longer torment him, that much was true. But he was still going to publish.

Alton was merely twenty-four miles up the river, but its location on the Illinois side of the Mississippi placed it in a free state, where slavery was ostensibly absent and where a newspaper editor troubled by the moral implications of human bondage might be free to comment on it. But Lovejoy would discover soon enough that in border zones such as the one he inhabited, the rules could be blurry. He would learn that a line drawn on a map to distinguish slave state from free state provided limited practical clarity when it came to whether a newspaper could criticize the nation's so-called "peculiar institution."

St. Louis wasn't yet finished with Lovejoy, however. The ink was barely dry on his July 21 farewell when the mob there struck—just hours after the notice appeared. Vandals trashed his St. Louis newspaper office and destroyed his family's belongings, which had been packed in preparation for the cross-river trip to Alton. Lovejoy managed to salvage his hand-operated press from the mess and put it on a ferry to Alton, where it would wait on the dock until his arrival. But his trial was hardly done. By the time Lovejoy arrived in Alton to start his new life, a group of "miscreants," as he called them—possibly the same people who trashed his office in St. Louis—discovered the press on the riverbank spot where it had been delivered on the Illinois side. The group then proceeded to smash the press to pieces there on the bank. In the span of a few days, in other words, Elijah Lovejoy—a thirty-three-year-old minister, editor, now refugee—had been victimized by tormenters on both sides of the Mississippi River, in a slave state and a free one.

* * *

FOLLOWING THE BACK-TO-BACK ATTACKS, Lovejoy was justifiably concerned about the welfare of his young wife, Celia, and their infant son, Edward. The couple was married the previous year in Missouri, where Celia, who was ten years Lovejoy's junior, had grown up as member of a slave-owning family. Now, Lovejoy sent Celia and Edward to her mother's home in St. Charles, Missouri, about thirty miles from St. Louis, while he sought to establish their new home and life.

Lovejoy was arriving in Alton under circumstances that could hardly have been less auspicious. Behind him lay an abandoned life under threat, rather neatly embodied by the ruins of his vandalized St. Louis office. Before him was the already-dented promise of a fresh start, his printing press destroyed before he'd had a chance even to contemplate his first issue of the relocated *Observer*. Anyone in such a position would have a right to be discouraged, but Lovejoy sounded a more matter-of-fact note when he reported the events to his family back in Maine, with the help of an Alton newspaper article. "By the Alton *Telegraph*, which I send you today, you will learn that I have had the honour of being mobbed at last. I have been expecting the catastrophe for some time, and now it has come," he wrote in a July 30 letter to his brother Joseph a week after the twin incidents. The St. Louis attack "was the more mean and dastardly, inasmuch as I had previously determined to remove the office of the *Observer* to this place, and had made all my arrangements accordingly, and had so stated," he continued. "You will also see that on my arrival here, a few miscreants undertook to follow the example of St. Louis, and so demolished what was left of the printing office."

In a sense, Lovejoy had been victimized in Alton by his own strict moral code. The press rescued from his St. Louis office had been shipped by steamboat to the other side of the Mississippi. But contrary to Lovejoy's order, the cargo was landed on the Alton dock on Sunday morning—the one day of the week when the Presbyterian minister refused to conduct business. The awaiting press proved too tempting a target for the five or six men who moved in during the wee hours of darkness the following morning to destroy it. Strict observation of the Sabbath had been a frequent subject of Lovejoy's *Observer*, both in his own columns and the articles he reprinted from other religiously themed newspapers. He was quick to criticize people—mail-wagon drivers and steamboat hands, for example—who labored on what he saw as an inviolable day of rest.

Sabbatarianism at that time was a favored concern of Protestant reformers from the East Coast who took aim at what they viewed as the moral shortcomings of individuals in order to purify overall American society. Observing the Sabbath was such a cause. The end of slavery was another. Lovejoy was active in both. (In his final edition of the St. Louis *Observer*, Lovejoy published the proceedings of a church debate in which he protested against the lucrative practice—overlooked, but common at the time—by which slaveholders hired out slaves on Sundays and collected the wages. Lovejoy labeled the practice "an immorality of the highest degree," noting in pointed fashion that some of his fellow Presbyterians were hiring out their slaves for Sunday work.)

In his letter to Joseph, Lovejoy was quick to try to reassure that he was unbowed by the back-to-back attacks. "Though cast down, I am not destroyed, nor in the least discouraged; and am now busily engaged in endeavouring to make arrangements for starting the *Observer* again. I think I shall succeed," Lovejoy wrote in his sure-handed script. "I do believe the Lord has yet a work for me to do in contending with his enemies, and the enemies of humanity. I have got the harness on and I do not intend to lay it off." The source of Lovejoy's optimism wasn't faith alone. By the time he penned the letter to Joseph, the editor had found possible vindication for his decision to move to Alton—this in the form of potential allies. The day after Lovejoy's press was smashed by the "miscreants" and tossed into the Mississippi, embarrassed Alton leaders stepped forward to offer help to their newest neighbor, as well as to recover the reputation of their booming river town. The rich and well-meaning men of Alton would finance a new press for Lovejoy. But there would be a catch.

Alton's leaders, with high hopes for their up-and-coming community, had no appetite for controversy of the sort that had trailed Lovejoy across the river like a threatening cloud. In St. Louis, he'd been labeled an abolitionist—a term that, even in the North, carried the same worrisome baggage as "fanatic" and "troublemaker." Lovejoy rejected the label, but the town fathers of Alton had no desire for the kind of mob violence that had been bursting forth across many American cities during the previous two years.

Only a few months earlier, in May, a group of men in Alton had burst into the room of a traveling magician named Schweighoffer and, in the midst of his show, destroyed an apparatus with which he had been

entertaining the audience. A local newspaper offered hearty praise when
the ringleader of the vandals was hauled before a jury and fined $100—a
sum that at the time was thought to represent the largest verdict ever
imposed in Madison County. "We congratulate our community that such
a verdict was found against the first symptoms of riot and disorder which
have appeared among us," the Alton *Telegraph* rejoiced in an article that
appeared under the headline "Justice Served in Alton." The newspaper
saw in the community's response to the violence against the magician a
sign that it knew how to nip such trouble in the bud. With a note of satisfaction, the paper declared that the hefty fine "augurs well for a healthy
state of public sentiment."

On the evening after the riverbank mauling of his printing press,
Lovejoy was invited to attend a meeting with some of Alton's most prominent citizens. It was an unofficial gathering but, as with many such
community meetings across America during the antebellum era, one that
could end with decisions. The Altonians wanted to have a conversation
with this fellow who had been all but chased from a neighboring state
and now was the focus of mayhem in their own. They would come to a few
understandings. Understandings such as there wouldn't be much tolerance
for anyone seeking to stir up passions over the issue of slavery. Among
the wary attendees at a newly built Presbyterian church was the future
mayor John M. Krum, an attorney in his mid-twenties who, like many of
Alton's leading lights, had migrated from New York a few years earlier.
Several others who would later prove to be among Lovejoy's staunchest
allies also showed up. There was Amos Roff, the owner of a store that sold
wood stoves, grates, and hardware, and the Reverend Frederick W. Graves,
an Amherst College graduate who was minister at the First Presbyterian
Church in Alton. Both would remain at Lovejoy's side through the months
of trials that lay ahead.

Lovejoy was asked to describe his plans for setting up the *Observer* in
Alton and to make clear to the assembly just how deeply he planned to

delve into the slavery issue. Lovejoy was in a delicate position here: he was in a new town, standing before a church full of residents—many of them strangers to him—who would determine whether his decision to come to Alton had been wise or foolish. They represented a kind of jury, and his answer mattered deeply. Poised before the group, Lovejoy cut a hardy figure: a man of medium height, muscled, with a dark complexion and piercing black eyes.

The editor spoke. His main objective was to edit and publish a religious newspaper, Lovejoy began. He then turned to the issue that was on everyone's mind: slavery. "When I was in St. Louis I felt myself called upon to treat at large upon the subject of slavery, as I was in a state where the evil existed," he explained. Lovejoy said that as a Missouri resident, he had felt a "duty" to inject the topic of slavery into his weekly columns there. But he denied being an abolitionist, and made the point that he had even previously clashed with them from time to time. "I am not, and never was in full fellowship with the abolitionists . . . and am not now considered by them as one of them." Now that he had moved to a "a free state where the evil does not exist," Lovejoy continued, "I feel myself less called upon to discuss the subject than when I was in St. Louis."

The editor's remarks would surely have had a comforting effect on the men inside the church: There was now little reason to expect that Lovejoy's newspaper would become a source of controversy. He had said so himself—slavery might be a hot topic on the far side of the Mississippi, but what need was there to discuss it in Illinois, a free state? Some of those present at the meeting would go even further. They chose to hear—and, later, to portray—Lovejoy's words as a guarantee, a pledge. To their ear, Lovejoy had promised that he would keep his little newspaper free of *all* talk about slavery.

But others who were listening to Lovejoy's presentation, including Roff and Graves, heard no such thing. In fact, as they and others would later recall in a signed declaration, Lovejoy closed his remarks with what ultimately would be preserved as a full-throated defense of his right to publish. "But gentlemen, as long as I am an American citizen, and as long as American blood runs in these veins, I shall hold myself at liberty to speak, to write, and to publish whatever I please on any subject," Lovejoy concluded. Lovejoy would have occasion to repeat similar sentiments many times in print and speeches, but the clashing recollection over the substance of his comments this evening later came to take on outsize significance.

Was Lovejoy telling the truth? Or was he an abolitionist? Did he intend to remain quiet on the sensitive matter of slavery? Or was he fooling himself—and others—by suggesting that he would somehow feel less need to decry an institution he abhorred simply because he had crossed a state line, even one separating North from South? Lovejoy biographers who have parsed his words from the church gathering generally agree that the editor probably made no explicit pledge to remain silent, but may have conveyed a message the crowd was too eager to hear. The historian Merton Dillon, the most rigorous of Lovejoy's earlier biographers, says that Lovejoy's comments were "filled with half-truths and ambiguities," and reflected a considerable lack of self-awareness in failing to realize just how far down the road toward abolitionism he had already traveled. When the Altonians who listened to Lovejoy then voted to approve statements vowing to preserve law and order and to help him replace his ruined press, they clearly were not acting as if they had an abolitionist in their midst—certainly not one who would use a newspaper in Alton as a vehicle to mobilize antislavery opinion. "When the people of Alton later discovered that he continued to oppose slavery," Dillon writes, "their wrath toward him became so much the greater because they believed they had been deceived. Lovejoy, it seemed to them, had abused their hospitality and broken a solemn pledge."

For his part, Lovejoy read the group's declared stand against aboli-tionism as "all for effect." In his July 30 letter to Joseph in Maine, Lovejoy stood by his assurances. "I told them, and told the truth, that I did not come here to establish an Abolition paper, and that in the sense they understood it, I was no Abolitionist, but that I was an uncompromising enemy of slavery, and so expected to live, and so to die," Lovejoy wrote.

In that single sentence, the editor had put his finger on one of the fundamental quandaries dividing antislavery Americans at the time, as organized efforts to bring about the emancipation of the country's more than two million slaves began to sprout in the Northern states. As Lovejoy knew well, it could be problematic in certain places to openly express moral dismay over the enslavement of fellow humans. But it was quite another thing to be identified with abolitionists, whose incipient agitation on the slavery question was often attacked—even in the North—as the work of madmen and insurrectionists.

The abolitionists of whom Lovejoy claimed to want no part were, in fact, men and women very much like himself. In general, they were people of deep faith: Quakers and mainstream Protestants of the Northeast who were drawn to the cause of antislavery out of a sense of moral revulsion. The more far-reaching among them, epitomized by the editor William Lloyd Garrison in Boston, viewed the antislavery cause as part of a larger social-justice struggle that demanded equality for Black people, and that promoted women's rights as well. It was Garrison who had kick-started the newest wave of antislavery activism at the start of the 1830s with his launch of a pugnacious newspaper, the *Liberator*, which served as the clarion for a bold and unapologetic campaign for the immediate emancipation of enslaved people without compensation for their owners.

Garrison's strident energy had won over activist-minded free Black people in the North and rallied to the abolitionist cause thousands of pious, reform-aimed white people in big cities and one-church villages, like the one in Maine where Lovejoy had grown up. Wealthy men such as the well-known Tappan brothers in New York had even lent financial backing. But at the time Lovejoy landed in Alton in 1836, abolitionism remained a fringe crusade—one that to many leery Americans carried the frightening potential to undermine the nation's stability and imperil a slave-dependent cotton economy in the South that also happened to provide handsome profits for the North. Lovejoy wasn't ready to embrace *that* kind of abolitionism, a phenomenon that to him had seemed so confrontational, so extreme. He was keeping his distance—publicly, anyway.

The distinction Lovejoy was making—that is, calling for the eventual emancipation of slaves without embracing "abolitionism"—came down to more than semantics. It reflected an important difference in tone, method, and the urgency with which the project should be undertaken. Lovejoy's own views on these questions had already evolved and would slide to a more militant posture in reaction to mounting pressure against him. Perhaps his disavowal of the "abolitionist" label during the meeting reflected, as Dillon suggests, a certain lack of self-understanding. But in fairness, Lovejoy was himself a moving target, a man undergoing transformation on the question of slavery, with radicalization still ahead. Like his restless new hometown, Lovejoy was a work in progress.

The editor's letter to Joseph pivoted quickly from his travails over the lost press to the more standard fare of family letters known the world over. Lovejoy reported that his health was good. And though Celia had been sick with a fever, she seemed to be on the mend. Their baby, Edward, now four months old, was well. It had been nearly a decade since Lovejoy, the oldest of seven surviving children, left the rest of the family behind in the farm-dotted heart of Maine.

Known to his parents and siblings by his middle name, Parish, Lovejoy had managed over the years to keep up a steady, if not prolific, flow of handwritten correspondence with them. Lovejoy wasn't known to keep a journal, but the years of letters to his family could offer bracingly frank glimpses into his life on the country's western edge. He pulled few punches in assigning his thoughts to paper—whether on religion or his work as a newspaper editor—and on more than one occasion contemplated in writing his own violent death. His closing note this time, however, was a mundane plea for more mail from his family. "Tell sister Sarah I wish she would write to me," Lovejoy implored. "Tell all to write. I am so very busy that I can write no more."

One of Lovejoy's other siblings was already at his side in Alton. John, a younger brother, had arrived on the frontier two years earlier to learn the newspaper business. A few days before Lovejoy sat down to recount to Joseph the recent mob incidents and church meeting, John had already scribbled his own note home, describing the St. Louis attack to their mother, Elizabeth. If his older brother had reacted to the violence with a terse resignation, John sounded horror-struck. In his "Dear Mother" letter, John could barely contain his dismay in describing the attackers. "That they are outrageous, uncivilized, fiendish and dangerous to the preservation of our government is certain. That they are rapidly increasing in the Western country is also true," John Lovejoy wrote, his script looping angrily across the page. "I have become so completely disgusted with the West on account of this."

John, who had not hit his nineteenth birthday, allowed that he was no fan of abolitionists. But, he sneered, these frontier foes of antislavery were "so perfectly ridiculous that it is enough to disgust every person who has the remotest feeling of honor or justice." Before ending, he gave his mother a piece of advice to pass along to everyone back east who already enjoyed a "good business" there: don't be tempted to come west. "Their property is not safe; their lives are not safe; and, in fact, nothing is safe," he wrote. "Stay where you are."

It's unclear whether John's grim counsel stirred any debate within the Lovejoy family back in Maine. Two other siblings—a brother, Owen, and sister, who also was named Elizabeth—were already making plans to journey west to join their brothers in Alton. All three siblings would be present for at least some of the turbulent events soon to face Elijah. The ordeal would change all of the Lovejoys, but perhaps Owen most

dramatically. He would launch himself deeply into the cause of abolitionism and the liberation of Black slaves—and, later, make his own mark
at the elbow of a man who at that moment was a little-known member of the
Illinois legislature, Abraham Lincoln. Like Elijah, Owen would achieve
his fame far from the childhood home in Maine where their values had
been forged.

CHAPTER TWO

A LAND OF STRANGERS

C ENTRAL MAINE WAS A rolling wilderness of forests and teeming
freshwater lakes when hardy souls, armed with axes and a flinty
worldview, arrived in the years after independence to chop clearings
that would become homesteads and, later, the seedbeds of steepled
towns. One of those men was the Lovejoys' paternal grandfather, Francis
Lovejoy, a Massachusetts native who had fought the British during the
battle of White Plains and then settled in New Hampshire after the war.
He married, and in 1790, Francis and his wife made their way north to
an inland section of Maine, where they began to carve the outline of a
family farm from the land flanking a kidney-shaped pond, the biggest
one in the area. The emerging settlement first bore the name of Free-
town Plantation, then incorporated, changed names a couple of times,
and finally became the town of Albion. It was a remote location, and
distant columns of smoke curling through winter's bare trees were the
only signs of other homes. Francis set traps and fished in the pond that
would forever bear the family's name.

His son Daniel was a pious boy, deeply influenced by the religious teachings of his mother, Mary. During an era in New England when the Protestant clergy held esteemed positions of leadership in their communities and indeed across the region, Daniel set his sights on the ministry. He left home at nineteen to begin his studies in Massachusetts at Byfield Academy, and stayed with the family of a well-known clergyman, the Reverend Elijah Parish, who would be the namesake of Daniel's eldest son. Daniel Lovejoy married Elizabeth Pattee and, after his ordination in 1805, combined the life of a Maine farmer with that of a roving Congregational minister, not always with great success. Elijah was born on November 9, 1802, a year and a half into Thomas Jefferson's presidency. At the time, Maine was still part of Massachusetts, and it would remain so until it gained statehood as a free state in 1820 under the famous Missouri Compromise. As chance would have it, Lovejoy would grow up in the free state that anchored one end of that grand political bargain and later shift his life to the other, Missouri, which entered the country as the corresponding slave state.

The seven Lovejoy children—two others did not survive childhood—lived a rather ordinary farm existence: swinging the ax and scythe to clear the land surrounding their house, and then guiding the plow through rocky soil for planting. In summer, the children swam endlessly in Lovejoy Pond, competing to see who could dive to the bottom, twelve to fifteen feet below. Proof of success was a handful of mud or clams. Elijah was strong and athletic, his brothers would recall, and he could impress the crowd by swimming the width of the pond and back—a trip of half a mile or more.

For all the carefree frolicking, the Lovejoy household was soaked through with the rigid imperatives of Puritan devotion. Elizabeth Lovejoy was profoundly reverent. Although she had no formal religious schooling, Elizabeth had grown up surrounded by clergymen who discussed religious issues with her father, and she seemed drawn to the kind of theological and moral questions that would normally fall within the province of trained clerics. Betsey, as she was known, was responsible for her children's religious development and found an eager pupil in her eldest son, who could read passages from the Bible at age four and seemed to have extraordinary powers of recall. In a memoir, two of Elijah's brothers would remember a Sunday school teacher once urging the children to step up their lessons during the coming week. By the time of the next class, Elijah had committed to memory the 119th Psalm—at 176 stanzas, the longest chapter in the Bible—along with a number of hymns to boot.

When it came to earthly issues, Betsey lined up with many New England Protestants in support of the movement to publish and distribute religious tracts around the country. She would eventually find her own way to the cause of antislavery and ultimately adopt the more radical position of the Boston abolitionist William Lloyd Garrison, calling for immediate emancipation—years before Elijah and many others in Maine dared go so far. (Her son Joseph, to whom Elijah would later write from Alton, also eventually migrated to the abolitionists as a distribution agent for the *Liberator*, Garrison's fiery antislavery newspaper.) Still, there was no obvious sign in the children's growing up of any future activist bent. Betsey proved a durable figure in the lives of Elijah and his four brothers and two sisters—a guide and sounding board long into their adult years, even when they were far from home.

Their father was a less steady presence. He never achieved the degree of learnedness to which he had once aspired in his theological studies in Massachusetts with Parish, a prominent figure in Calvinist circles. As a minister, the elder Lovejoy was given short-term assignments that often required him to travel away from home, rather than to oversee a permanent parish in Albion or anywhere else. Among the reasons for Daniel Lovejoy's on-again, off-again work as minister were debilitating waves of depression that had dogged him since adolescence and now rolled over the Lovejoy home like thunderheads. He referred openly to his "mental debility," and friends were familiar with his mood swings.

Although the Lovejoys struggled to get by with modest means, the values of learning and moral education were highly prized in their Albion home. The children of Daniel and Betsey would emerge from these influences religion-minded, highly literate, and attuned to the issues of the day. Elijah, who was subject over the years to his own struggles with melancholy, would follow his father's footsteps into the ministry, as would Joseph and Owen. But of all the children, Elijah was the academic whiz kid. He read Cicero and Virgil and drank in poetry, his brothers claimed, "like water." He plowed through his father's small library of theological works and then attacked the collection in a nearby public library. Even as a teenager, Elijah stood out as a gifted writer, and he sat down to craft long, sometimes overwrought verse in Romantic style. In addition to his schooling at home, Elijah attended local public schools for a few months a year before the family scraped up enough money for him to attend a pair of academies in the area. His success won him a spot, at age twenty, at Waterville College, a Baptist-founded school in the town of Waterville, about twelve miles from the Lovejoy home. (The school would later be renamed Colby College.) To help pay the costs of his education, Lovejoy won financial backing from a generous area pastor, the Reverend Benjamin Tappan, and entered as a sophomore in 1823.

Lovejoy's prior schooling was informal and scattershot, but it seemed to prepare him sufficiently for the rigors of Waterville College. He proved a top student—in fact, he would graduate first in his class—and impressed professors and administrators with his intellectual power. Lovejoy continued working on his writing, especially poetry, whose lines hinted at a brooding sense of alienation. In a poem written while at Waterville, for example, Lovejoy writes, "Thus have I felt—Oh God! why was I born / A wretch all friendless, hopeless, and forlorn."

In letters to his parents, Lovejoy lingered on religious themes and revealed "dreadful moments" of despair that brought to mind his father's troubles. In one such correspondence from Waterville,

Lovejoy discussed the prospect of immortality with such immediacy that it appears he had considered suicide. He said the main lesson of his contemplations was that religion was central to his life and that he was "miserable" without it.

Indeed, as he edged into the world away from the wooded quiet of Albion, Lovejoy did not find it easy to shake the austere strictures of his boyhood home. As a young man, he often seemed to feel out of step—a misfit who could be prudish and disapproving when it came to the conduct of others. Once, as a student at Waterville, Lovejoy traveled to the coastal town of Bath, Maine, for a short vacation at the home of an unidentified "aunt." But he became irritated that he was unable to study because of a boisterous group of eight to ten people who were staying at the same boarding house. In a letter from the place, Lovejoy complained to his mother of the group's "shocking profanity and intemperance" and the "disgusting consequences." The only "positive good" that had come out of the encounter, he reported, was that it had strengthened his ability to withstand such "licentiousness." Lovejoy was not the first young adult to leave home and experience culture shock. But the unbending moral code of Lovejoy's childhood would accompany him far beyond Maine, guiding him to courageous stands of conscience, as well as to trouble.

Lovejoy graduated as Waterville College's valedictorian in September 1826 and did a public reading of one of his poems, an ambitious 113-line work called "Inspirations of the Muse." He settled for the time being on teaching at nearby China Academy, one of the schools he had earlier attended. But it was not long before he grew restless with that and began to consider his next move, perhaps somewhere else. Elijah, whose college career had revealed a first-rate mind, harbored big ambitions, though still undefined. His best prospects probably resided far from the area where he grew up. But where?

* * *

ON OCTOBER 26, 1825, New York governor Dewitt Clinton began an extraordinary weeklong journey aboard a boat called the *Seneca Chief.* Clinton began his trip on Lake Erie and ended it in Albany, 393 miles away. The governor's journey marked the completion of the Erie Canal, a breathtaking triumph of American engineering and a powerful symbol of an ongoing transportation revolution that would play a powerful role in reshaping the new nation through the movement of people and goods. At around the same time, construction was also well underway on a so-called National Road—one that Alton's future boosters hoped would eventually reach their town—that would connect Cumberland, Maryland, with regions to the west. By 1826, it had reached Zanesville, Ohio, and seven years later was extended to Columbus, Ohio. Subsequent extensions through Indiana and Illinois would take the road as far west as its terminus at Vandalia, Illinois, just short of Alton. The road, which was also called the National Pike, would be an early version of the interstate highway system. More important, it served as an artery for carrying waves of migrant families who ventured west to settle the states of Ohio, Indiana, and Illinois. Traveling in the opposite direction were hardened men driving Conestoga wagons brimming with freight.

The two innovations were part of a blizzard of construction—roads, canals, and railroads—that contributed to an air of tremendous flux taking place in American society in the years after 1815. A modernizing economy was altering the way people lived in New England, sending thousands of rural dwellers surging to cities or other places as factories created a market for furniture, housewares, and clothing that had once been produced at home. The youthful country crackled with an optimistic energy and movement. Easterners packed their belongings and set out on unfamiliar roads—in horse-pulled wagons or on foot—to regions that had not even been part of the country when it was born.

The sensation was one of roiling restlessness—propelled, often, by a thirst for quick riches—and it was contagious. Alexis de Tocqueville, the

French political scientist, caught a strong whiff of it when he toured the United States in the early 1830s as one of a slew of European writers and curiosity-seekers who came to see what made this experimental new country tick. Tocqueville took note of an acquisitive people, ever on the hunt for fresh gratification. The American "is so hasty in grasping at all within his reach, that one would suppose he was constantly afraid of not living long enough to enjoy them," Tocqueville wrote in his classic study, *Democracy in America*. "In the United States a man builds a house to spend his latter years in it, and he sells it before the roof is on: he plants a garden and lets it just as trees are coming into bearing; he brings a field into tillage, and leaves other men to gather the crops: he embraces a profession, and gives it up," Tocqueville observed. "[H]e settles in a place, which he soon afterwards leaves, to carry his changeable longings elsewhere."

These altered arrangements shook up the social order, creating new roles in the home as people spilled into an evolving job market as wage earners. The era of the 1820s and 1830s also saw social innovation and experimentation in the beliefs held by Americans on everything from religion to sexual relations. All this churn was deeply unsettling to the fusty men who made up New England's traditional clergy, men like those who had taught Lovejoy at Waterville College and influenced his thinking still. The frontier may have represented America's leading edge to the people who bounced hopefully over rough, log-paved roads from the Northeast and South. But to the fretful keepers of Puritan values, the West was a place lacking in the moral mooring their churches and village parishes had once provided. In their view, the frontier was deeply in need of spiritual tending—possibly even rescue. Protestant leaders on the East Coast were at that moment ginning up a well-financed effort to ship Bibles and religious tracts and to deploy missionaries to sparsely settled corners for exactly that job. Lovejoy would later serve as a foot soldier in that cause.

All of these arguments would have found a receptive audience in Lovejoy as he consulted those around him for advice on his next step.

Although there is no record of the deliberations leading to his decision, Lovejoy came up with a destination. He would go to Illinois. In May 1827, Lovejoy said goodbye to his family through a poem, "The Farewell." He was off, as he put it in verse, "to tread the western vales." Lovejoy's plan was to walk the twelve hundred miles to Illinois from Boston (early Americans did that sort of thing)—meaning that he would tread plenty of the eastern vales, too.

On May 19, Lovejoy caught a schooner from Bath and fought seasickness for three days before passing the islands leading into Boston Harbor, which was crisscrossed by the wake trails of passing frigates and smaller craft on all sides. In the distance poked the spires "and gorgeous temples" of the city itself, Lovejoy wrote in the diary he would keep for the first part of the journey. A week later, Lovejoy began his trip. His entry for the first day, May 29, a Tuesday, is almost comical in its nonchalance toward the scale of the venture he was undertaking: "Left Boston today about 5 P.M. to travel on foot from that place to the state of Illinois." If Lovejoy was worried about the potential difficulties of a cross-country hike—in effect, ignoring the country's thrumming transportation revolution—it did not show yet.

Lovejoy's journal was a small, ruled notebook, bound in specked brown paper. For the next ten days, he would track his daily progress, writing in longhand with a pencil, as he moved slowly through late-spring heat across the full length of Massachusetts. It offers a brief, entertaining account of traveling alone through the Northeast in the 1820s—a chronicle of hiker's fatigue, hunger pangs, loneliness, and occasional brushes with unexpected charity as Lovejoy found himself bereft of food and money. Excerpts from the trip journal, the only one Lovejoy would be known to keep during his lifetime, paint the picture of a wide-eyed young man who sounds like an intrepid voyager one minute and a hapless bumpkin the next.

On May 31, for example, Lovejoy writes that he is "full of aches and pains. Not being accustomed to walking it fatigues me very much. A small piece of bread and cheese was my only breakfast. . . . Doubtless my dear mother is now thinking of me. Ah! if she knew my situation how would her kind heart bleed." Two days later, his entry notes his dire financial condition: "I am now 250 miles from home, in a land of strangers and but 80 cents in my pocket." Penniless, Lovejoy would pawn a watch for $5 to pay for lodging.

At a tavern in western Massachusetts, the young Mainer sounds quite out of his depth to find "3 or 4 buxom wenches traversing the house, bare-footed and bare-legged. Their faces were quite pretty, and by my troth, I had almost determined to tarry the night that I might make their farther acquaintance, but finally thought not best." The next day, on June 6, Lovejoy logs a trying stretch: "Travelled until 3 o'clock P.M. having eaten nothing save a cracker and a small piece of cheese. I then stopped and got a bowl of bread and milk at the house of a poor woman who makes her living making straw bonnets." But Lovejoy's tone brightens a day later, when he scribbles, "Stopped today and bathed in a stream of cool running water. Oh how refreshing!"

Lovejoy's next journal entry comes about seven weeks later, on July 30, from New York City. He reports that he had been in the city for about a month and a half, and "suffered much and seen much." Broke and unable to pay for his further travels, Lovejoy found work peddling newspapers—on foot, of course. He hiked the city "from sun to sun," earning barely enough money to pay for his daily food: breakfast and dinner. Desperate for help, Lovejoy turned finally to the Reverend Jeremiah Chaplin, the president of Waterville College, who sent him enough money to bankroll the next leg of the journey to the West. As he boarded a steamer for a trip up the Hudson River to Albany, Lovejoy worked his pencil across the page in gratitude for Chaplin's assistance. "May the God of the wanderers reward him ten thousand fold," he writes. "Scenery of the Hudson delightful."

It seems likely that he rode by boat on the Erie Canal from Albany to the shores of Lake Erie. By fall, months after his days of nausea aboard the Boston-bound schooner, Lovejoy arrived in central Illinois in a place

called Hillsboro, a pioneer village founded just four years earlier. Lovejoy
found lodging with a former New Englander named John Tillson, but prospects in the tiny settlement appeared bleak for the kind of work that would
sustain a bright college graduate. He began to consider the map again. At a
distance of sixty miles lay the Mississippi River and, just on the other side,
the growing city of St. Louis. It was not long before Lovejoy was lacing his
shoes for the next leg of his journey. In what had already proved an eventful
year, the move to Missouri would mark a significant border-crossing for
Lovejoy. Although there is no sign that it was his intention, he was placing
himself face-to-face with the institution of chattel slavery.

* * *

NOT LONG BEFORE LOVEJOY'S arrival in St. Louis, the local newspaper
carried a captivating tidbit: a steamboat known as the *Liberator* had
traveled up the Mississippi River from New Orleans in a record time—
seven days and seventeen hours, excluding stops. The pace for the journey
of nearly thirteen hundred miles was three times faster than just a decade
before and represented yet another boost to the growing use of steam-
powered vessels that were paddling in and out of St. Louis, loaded with
goods and people. Most river cargo—everything from wood, to produce, to
livestock, to cotton—had moved in multi-ton shipments aboard rectangular
flatboats and longer keelboats. But steam technology was igniting rapid
changes in how Americans were navigating the river highway. Soon these
newer boats, with their big side paddles churning, came through stacked
high with flour, barrels of whiskey, gunpowder, sugar, and bales of cotton.
    If Lovejoy had witnessed one piece of the transportation revolution
when he traveled by boat on the Erie Canal, he was about to see another
in the form of the steamboats thumping along the Mississippi. Despite
the risks of steamboat travel—some vessels snagged on fallen trees and

sank, and others suffered devastating boiler explosions, injuring those on board—traffic increased into the 1830s. More than eight hundred steamboat landings would be logged in St. Louis in 1835, up from 432 just three years earlier.

The river trade was cementing Missouri's ties with cities to the south, such as New Orleans, putting St. Louis at a pivotal spot on the seam between North and South. At the same time, the city had become the gateway to the far West, serving as the trailhead for trading routes to Santa Fe and Mexican traders in the region that later would belong to the American Southwest. These developments combined to turn St. Louis into a place of destiny, a magnet for men from all over the previously set- tled areas of the United States, as well as for immigrants from Europe, especially Irish and Germans. Long an outpost for the French fur trade doing commerce with Native American tribes, St. Louis had grown into a noisy city of five thousand by 1830, and would swell further during the years that Lovejoy lived there.

St. Louis would introduce Lovejoy to a way of life that in some ways was as alien to him as a foreign country. Compared with tiny Albion, the city was cosmopolitan but also rough and unruly, with brothels, taverns, and gambling houses providing amusement for coarse-mannered laborers and rivermen toiling far from the God-fearing towns where they grew up. Police were few, streets were poor, and a lack of proper sanitation resulted in periodic outbreaks of deadly cholera. Unlike in Maine, the people who filled church pews on Sundays were found not at a Congregational parish—there were none—but more likely at a Roman Catholic church, a legacy of the area's roots as a former French colony. (Lovejoy and the Catholic hierarchy would find much to dislike about each other in later years.) And the city's distinctly Southern leanings could be seen in the way it lived and even fought—dueling, the time-honored method of settling disputes in the South, was common enough in St. Louis society that pistol-packing combatants had a favored spot to settle matters, a sandbar called Bloody Island. Those who did battle there included some of the city's leading citizens and politicians.

Lovejoy was greeted in St. Louis with a bout of "ague" that caused his weight to fall and appetite to disappear altogether. But by February 1828, when he wrote to his parents, Lovejoy could claim a full recovery, including refilling his five-foot-nine frame. His weight was up to 180 pounds, though he expressed doubt about whether he could stay healthy in the St. Louis climate. In St. Louis, Lovejoy found natural kinship with fellow transplanted Northerners—a group that he said represented "the most orderly, most intelligent, and most valuable part of the community." He was quick to add, however, that "there are some most lamentable exceptions, and doubtless many a Yankee has fled here, whose vices forbade him an asylum among the descendants of the Puritans."

He launched a private academy that won positive notice in the local press and allowed him to send money to his family back in Maine. But in time, even with his newfound profits, Lovejoy grew antsy, as he had during his teaching stint back home. Despite his mother's growing appeals for Lovejoy to return home—"What special call have you 2000 miles from your parents?" she once wrote—he gazed around St. Louis for opportunities to sate his hunger for greater purpose.

By summer of 1830, he had found it. The owner of a newspaper, the *St. Louis Times*, was in search of a new business partner, and Lovejoy jumped. He sold his school and bought half a stake in the weekly paper. At last, Lovejoy saw himself in a role he had coveted: employing the written word to earn a living, while at the same time influencing community opinion and, perhaps, making a difference. Three years after he had trudged, humiliated and tired, across New York City selling newspapers, Lovejoy, then twenty-seven years old, was co-publisher of his own. True, his credentials were only those of an amateur poet, without so much as an apprenticeship in printing the news. But such considerations mattered little amid the hurly-burly of the 1830s, especially in a borderline frontier town like St. Louis. In the blink of an eye, Lovejoy had joined the ranks of those we call journalists.

* * *

LOVEJOY'S FORAY INTO NEWSPAPERING at the *St. Louis Times* would prove a useful introduction to the workaday rigors of editing and helped hone the jousting skills he would rely on years later when he took over the *Observer*. Although Lovejoy shared interest in the *Times* with co-owner T.J. Miller, he got top billing on the front page: just below the stylized *St. Louis Times* nameplate, bold print announced "By Lovejoy & Miller." The price for a subscription was $3 a year, and no cancellations would be accepted, the editors warned, "unless all arrearages have been paid up." The front page was stacked with an array of advertisements of the era. A clothing store promised pea coats and frocks and capes "at New York prices," while another vendor peddled newly arrived cases of calf boots, brogans, and "Ladies' Leather Bootees and Shoes." Advertisements for saddles, harnesses, and trunks vied for reader attention alongside offers of tin works and fire insurance for steamboats.

Conventional newspapers of the age tended to wear their politics on their sleeve, and the *Times* was no exception. Lovejoy's paper was a strong backer of Henry Clay, the longtime Kentucky politician who, under the National Republican banner, was defeated in the 1824 campaign for president but never gave up his ambitions for the presidency. Lovejoy's *Times* printed texts of Clay speeches on matters such as the controversial tariffs of 1828 and touted his skills as a politician—a task made easier by his disdain for the man Clay would have to topple in the upcoming election in order to reach the White House: Andrew Jackson, the populist former general. Jackson, a slave-owning Tennessean and standard-bearer for the party that would become known as the Democrats, had defeated incumbent John Quincy

Adams in a nasty campaign in 1828. Jackson was Old Hickory, a hero of the War of 1812 and veteran "Indian fighter," who was shadowed by a reputation for a volatile temperament and questionable morals. (Amid the profuse mud-slinging of the 1828 campaign were adultery charges from many years earlier that centered on whether Jackson's wife was yet divorced from a previous husband when she and Jackson settled down together.)

Lovejoy scorned Jackson's personal history and the brand of populist politics that helped carry him to power as states broadened the voting franchise in the 1820s—at least for white men—by removing property requirements. In a letter to his parents soon after Jackson took office in 1829, Lovejoy sneered at the new leader's choices for Cabinet secretaries, saying they were "such as I could have supposed Gen. J. would select." Lovejoy alluded to the Jackson adultery scandal and to the new president's prior penchant for violent confrontations, including a duel that had left his rival dead. "With an adulterer and murderer for our President, and fools and knaves for his advisers, if we survive, than shall I indeed believe that Providence intends to perpetuate our existence," Lovejoy wrote.

Lovejoy viewed his role as editor and writer in terms of morality as much as politics, and he believed that liberty unmoored from the tenets of the Bible would be short-lived. "Say what you please of the religion of the Bible, but without the moral precepts it inculcates, all history and experience teach that neither civil nor intellectual freedom can long exist," Lovejoy would write. "This is a truth that ought always to be kept in mind by those who have any share in directing public opinion."

For the most part, Lovejoy and Miller sought to "direct public opinion" by stocking the pages of the *Times* with the more earthly sparring of partisan politics. They lent prominent space to speeches in Congress by their man Clay and his allies and swatted at pro-Jackson papers, including a favored local target, the *St. Louis Beacon*. Amid the thrusting and parrying of this weekly debate between newspaper rivals, Lovejoy did not shrink from the name-calling that characterized editing of the era. During a months-long exchange of insults with the *Beacon*, a *Times* editorial referred to the editor of the rival paper as an "inflated bladder" of "mephitick gas." The *Beacon* later returned fire by labeling Lovejoy an "animal." Such harshly personal jibes were employed mostly in good sport—partisans expected fierce fare in their favored papers.

For all the noisy jabbing that played out on the pages of the newspapers, there was one matter about which Lovejoy's *St. Louis Times* made little fuss: slavery. The topic that would later set Lovejoy on a collision course with the community around him seemed not to occupy his thoughts at all at the outset of the 1830s. There was no real abolitionist movement to speak of yet—that was only beginning to flicker to life on the East Coast. For now, slavery and its foes appeared to be of no concern to the St. Louis editor. In fact, like many newspapers in Missouri and other slave states, Lovejoy's *Times* served to promote the trade in slaves by advertising auctions or serving as a go-between in posted notices that offered slaves without naming the seller. "FOR SALE—a first rate NEGRO MAN, about 22 years of age. Apply at this office," read one such notice in the *Times* in 1831. Similar advertisements appeared in the *Beacon* and *Missouri Republican*.

Lovejoy did not own slaves, but he employed at least one man who had been hired out by the enslaver—a common practice in Missouri, where slaves were in effect leased to work aboard steamboats or in factories, mines, or farms. In Lovejoy's case, the young man hired out to work at his newspaper office—helping other workers, working the press—would later successfully flee his bondage and gain national fame as the author of a slavery memoir and as an abolitionist lecturer. The fugitive slave was William Wells Brown, who would remember Lovejoy as "a very good man, and decidedly the best master that I had ever had." Brown wrote, "I am chiefly indebted to him, and to my employment in the printing office, for what little learning I obtained while in slavery." If Brown, in turn, left an imprint on Lovejoy, the editor did not mention it.

CHAPTER THREE

BRETHREN

THE DOCKSIDE DESTRUCTION OF Lovejoy's press in the predawn darkness was a bracing blow in Alton, where such overt hostility clashed with the town's attempt to cast itself as a place open to all comers, including from the North. Even if suspicion for the act quickly fell on outsiders from St. Louis, Lovejoy's rough introduction to Alton made clear three obvious needs. He needed a safe place to settle his family and to work. He needed a new press. And he needed friends. As fortune would have it, Lovejoy was able to tap into a ready-made network of fellow transplants from the Northeast who shared in his Presbyterian faith, or at least held some of the same beliefs about the moral well-being of their community on matters such as drink and honoring the Sabbath. Some of these people were connected by marriage, others by business ties. They made up a small but eclectic crew: hardy pioneers who years earlier braved the icy trek from New England and New York, war veterans, a few fellow preachers, some storekeepers. During the course of coming months, they would help bankroll Lovejoy's revived newspaper, attend his sermons, read his articles, and stand beside him when others in Alton began to line up against him. They would be Lovejoy's only real source of security in the absence of local police, and the most stalwart defenders of his right to publish.

Lovejoy was fortunate that two of the men who came to his defense happened to own the biggest business in Alton—and, in fact, in all of Illinois. Winthrop S. Gilman and Captain Benjamin Godfrey were partners in a commercial empire that included a cargo shipment and storage business that moved freight up and down the river, growing into one of the largest of its kind in the West. They also built the Alton branch of the State Bank of Illinois and belonged to a group that held the controlling share of its stocks. This stake in the bank allowed them to lend widely to other Alton businesses amid the town's running quest to become a regional commercial powerhouse, and to capture the lion's share of lead mining in nearby Galena, Illinois, at a time when speculation was running sky-high. Godfrey was also a top investor and president of a company seeking to build a railroad between Alton and Springfield. Anyone who walked along Alton's waterfront in late 1836 would have gotten a fair sense of the pair's local prominence in the form of the stone warehouse of Godfrey, Gilman & Co., which loomed over the river's edge next to the walled state penitentiary.

The two men were not only wealthy—they were also generous philanthropists for a variety of causes. Godfrey had paid more than $4,000 to build a stone Presbyterian church on a lot in lower Alton overlooking the Mississippi, a house of worship also used by Episcopal and Baptist congregations. In addition, Godfrey envisioned and eventually built a school to educate young women, Monticello Female Seminary, on a 269-acre site not far from where he lived north of Alton. For his part, Gilman, tall and gentlemanly, was known to donate a tenth of his income to benevolent works, a share that reached as high as twenty-five percent as his business fortunes soared.

Godfrey and Gilman were early members of Alton's nascent Presbyterian congregation and strict in their personal behavior. They refused to work on Sundays, for example, and Gilman was chairman of a local committee promoting temperance in Madison County. In the months before Lovejoy's arrival, Gilman spoke excitedly about the group's recent launch of a newspaper devoted to the cause, the *Temperance Herald*, and about his hopes to attend a national convention on the issue in New York. "Temperance goes well—we put a copy of our paper into every House in town & they will do the same at many places," Gilman wrote in May to his wife, Abia, who was then in New York. "I feel very desirous that our Temperance paper would circulate extensively & in order to this, want that it should show talent in its columns."

Gilman, born in Ohio but raised and educated in Philadelphia's top schools, had started his working life at age fifteen as a clerk in a New York shipping business. By eighteen, he had won his employer's trust sufficiently to be sent to Cincinnati and New Orleans to oversee aspects of the trade. Gilman traveled the West for three years before finally settling in Alton in 1829—so far ahead of its eventual boom that, Gilman would recall, he "found but one house occupied."

Among the first people Gilman got to know was Thomas Lippincott, who had arrived with his wife and infant daughter in St. Louis in 1818, after an arduous wintertime journey by horse and wagon from New York. Lippincott met Colonel Rufus Easton—the architect of Alton-to-be—and formed a business partnership. (It was Lippincott's hand that drew the plat map laying out Easton's vision for Alton.) That partnership would send Lippincott, working as a storekeeper, across the river into Illinois, then less than a decade old. Lippincott and his family endured the rigors of life in the town of Milton, a place of stagnant water and frequent malaria outbreaks. So foul was the odor of a mill pond that Lippincott frequently passed that he had to hold his nose when he crossed. His wife, Patty, would die, sick with fever, after delivering a child in Milton. A second wife would die of malaria there just a year later, after five months of marriage.

Although born to Quaker parents in New Jersey, Lippincott would become a stalwart of the Presbyterian church in Alton, where he resurrected a Presbyterian congregation. He began preaching in 1831, following his ordination a few years earlier. Lippincott's daughter Abia, still in her teens, would catch the eye of the young Winthrop Gilman. The couple married in 1834. Lippincott, who wore swept-back hair and a thick collar of a beard beneath his chin, carried one other distinction: he was, at the time, the closest thing that Alton had to an antislavery activist. Lippincott had been politically active from the early 1820s, having been elected secretary of the state senate. In 1824, Illinois voters were asked to weigh in on a measure passed by both houses of the state legislature to hold a convention to consider formally legalizing slavery.

Illinois was, on paper, a free state when it was admitted to the Union in 1818. But its founders employed grandfather clauses and a provision allowing "voluntary" indentured servitude to maintain a de facto slavery regime in which Black people continued to be sold or hired out and passed along by will as property, no different from cattle or horses. At the time Illinois leaders had applied for statehood, the territory held twelve hundred slaves and indentured Black people. Free Black people were barred from the state unless they could provide documents, signed by a judge or court clerk and stamped, attesting that they were not held as slaves elsewhere. Kidnappers in Illinois profited by selling captured Black people "down the river" to Southern slave states at a price of $100 per person by the time of statehood. Illinois may have been listed as a free state, but as Lovejoy would later learn, its ties to slavery remained strong, especially in the southern half, where Alton sat.

As an opponent of slavery, Lippincott opposed the pro-slavery convention and took up the fight in the Edwardsville *Spectator*, which assumed a strong stance against the convention. In the end, state voters turned down the proposal by a narrow margin of about seventeen hundred votes—a sign of the state's sharply divided sentiments—and Illinois remained a free state, at least officially. Lippincott later edited two short-lived monthly newspapers in Alton—one that focused on agricultural, mechanical, and commercial issues and another that hewed to religion. He would also eventually lend his pen to Lovejoy's relocated *Observer*.

By far the most mysterious of Lovejoy's benefactors in Alton was Gilman's partner, Benjamin Godfrey. A former sea captain who was known even to his friends as Captain Godfrey, he arrived in Alton in 1832 in search of a new life after an itinerant career as a seaman and businessman that bore the elements of a heart-pounding adventure tale but also darker evidence of involvement in the seagoing slave trade. Born in 1794 in the coastal town of Chatham, Massachusetts, Godfrey was introduced to the seafaring life as a child and later served on a gunboat during the War of 1812. After the war, Godfrey took command of the *Emilie*, based in Baltimore, for seven years, traversing the Atlantic to Europe, the Mediterranean, and the West Indies. Godfrey sailed to New Orleans, navigated the waters off the coast of Texas, and, according to accounts of his friends at the time, nearly drowned in a shipwreck at a passage called Brazos Santiago, off what is now Padre Island in the Gulf of Mexico. Godfrey lost everything in the wreck "and sat down upon the beach there and wept over all lost," a close friend, Theron Baldwin, would recount in a memorial testimony many years later.

Godfrey moved his base to Matamoros, Mexico, and engaged in an unspecified trading business for six years. He achieved enough success there to pay back his creditors and still have $100,000 left in his pocket by the time he moved with his family back to New Orleans in 1830. It was there that he met Gilman, who had traveled from Alton as part of his budding business moving freight between the two cities. Gilman persuaded Godfrey to move to Alton, and he did so in 1832. By the time Godfrey arrived, he had experienced an epiphany, Baldwin would later relate. Godfrey had been reading a religious text by the Christian thinker Emanuel Swedenborg when he was bowled over by a question: "For what shall it profit a man if he shall gain the whole world and lose his soul?" As Baldwin told the story, "this struck him with such force, that he rose from his berth and solemnly recorded a resolution to procure a bible and read it." Baldwin notes that Godfrey knew he had much for which to make amends, "that he had become openly profane and wicked, and, previous to his spiritual change, had not been in a christian church for twenty years. But now all his views were revolutionized, the whole current of his feeling changed, and entirely new purposes animated his soul." By this account, then, Godfrey recognized his spiritual shortcomings and resolved to fix them through good works. A competing account, unearthed from a newspaper article and described by Judy Hoffman, an Alton-area historian, holds that Godfrey's moral turnabout followed a near-fatal illness in New Orleans, suggesting that his transformation may have stemmed from a hastily arranged deal with God while he stared at oblivion.

But questions over Godfrey's regrets do not end there. Hoffman, who wrote a book about the town bearing Godfrey's name, points to overwhelming evidence that he was involved in the seaborne transportation of slaves from Baltimore and Norfolk, Virginia, to New Orleans. That Southern port city was the busiest destination for a domestic trade that forcibly shipped one million Black people from states in the upper South to the Deep South between 1808, when the United States prohibited the importation of slaves, and the Civil War. My own review of port records from that time confirms Godfrey's role. On at least twelve occasions, a Godfrey-skippered vessel—the brigantine *Emilie* and a second brig, the *Intelligence*—is shown arriving in New Orleans with slaves aboard, according to U.S. Customs records collected at the port. The manifests, many of which have been transcribed and made available online, list the names, sex, ages, height, and skin tones of slaves for each arriving ship. The ships with Godfrey listed as captain carried at least 314 named slaves, including children and infants, from 1819 to 1822. Many more such records for later years remain to be transcribed.

Godfrey never spoke of this chapter of his life—publicly, anyway—and was decidedly cryptic when discussing the years before his arrival in Alton. When his pastor once asked about Godfrey's early life, the businessman answered only that "it would make a novel." As Hoffman notes, "Whatever occurred between the time Godfrey left Mexico in 1830 and the time he arrived in Illinois in 1832—whether it was a religious conversion, a near death experience, a bargain with God, or something yet to be revealed—Benjamin Godfrey was a changed man. . . . The 'wicked and profane' Godfrey became generous and genial."

Lovejoy's small circle of reliable backers would also include Enoch Long, a fellow Presbyterian who was among the early wave of Easterners to make their way to Alton. Long's was the kind of story that could only have been written in the early 1800s: the son of a Revolutionary War veteran who was raised in the wilds of New Hampshire before deciding to head west—yes, on foot—at precisely the moment that a new war was breaking out in 1812. Long, then in his early twenties, ran smack into the zone of hostilities in upstate New York and joined the U.S. forces near Fort Niagara in 1813. He became a sergeant and was made regimental fife major until the unit was disbanded when fighting subsided in the area.

Long returned home to New Hampshire, married, and set out alone again in 1819, aiming for St. Louis. He arrived first in Alton and stayed for a short time. In order to reach the St. Louis side, Long would need to cross the Mississippi. He answered the problem by gathering driftwood into a pile and fashioning the pieces into a raft using tools from a sawmill that was under construction there. By the time he reached St. Louis, his sagging craft was barely visible above the water—a group of soldiers on the riverbank stood by, "startled at the strange appearance of a man apparently riding on nothing." Long sprang onshore, holding his bundle of belongings in his hand, and let the jury-rigged vessel float off. But he later decided to return to Alton and settle there.

In the ensuing years, Long, with a ruddy face topped by dark brown hair, was an avatar of industry. He was a cooper, grocer, justice of the peace, cooper again, miner, storekeeper and, much later, railroad contractor. Tocqueville could have been describing Long when he wrote about Americans of the era jumping from one job to the next, driven by their sense of opportunity. When it came time to bring his family west, Long rode a horse for a month and a half to get to New Hampshire, then bought a second horse, covered a wagon, and hit the road again with his wife, daughter, and sister-in-law, making use of an early stretch of the National Road. He was ingenious and dauntless. To avoid impassably muddy roads, Long bought a flat boat, loaded the wagon on the roof, and floated, with the horses and his family, down the Monongahela and Ohio rivers until the land path was clear—at which point he sold the boat and the party of travelers clambered back aboard the wagon for the rest of the journey to Alton. The state of New Hampshire issued Long a passport for the trip, requesting that all "foreign States, Potentates and Powers . . . do permit him to pass safely and freely." The passport described Long, then twenty-eight years old, as five foot ten, with dark brown hair and "dark or florid complexion." It also declared his moral character as "fair and his standing in society reputable."

In Alton, Long quickly established himself as a pillar of civic and religious life. He was appointed to a public office as a justice of the peace for Madison County. (In a telling indication of the temper of the times, the official notification of Long's appointment carried a declaration that he "has not been engaged in a duel, by sending or accepting a challenge to fight a duel, or by fighting a duel . . . and that he will not be engaged, in any manner, in a duel during his continuance in office.")

Long was not a man of the cloth in the manner of Thomas Lippincott, but nonetheless was a central player in the formation and running of the local Presbyterian church in Alton. He was one of the founding members of the first congregation, and later offered his home as a site of worship when it was reestablished in 1831, with Lippincott as the pastor. Long was involved in forming the local temperance society. He served as church deacon. One of his earliest projects in Alton was to establish its first Sunday school, having attended the first such institution in New Hampshire as a youth. Long gathered spelling books for the younger children and copies of the New Testament for those old enough to read, and held contests to see who could memorize the most verses. (The doors of his grocery store were open to those who wanted to practice between Sunday sessions.) Wherever souls were in need of tending in Alton, it seemed, Long was at the ready. "Mr. Long's influence was always on the side of morality and religion," one of his students would later write.

The group that would make up Lovejoy's safety net in Alton was at first glance a motley jumble: an antislavery preacher, a pious grocer, and a pair of business tycoons (one a temperance activist, the other a reformed slave trader), plus a handful of others, including Roff and Graves. But the collection wasn't as random as it appeared—Lovejoy's supporters were joined by strands of shared faith, geographical origins, and even family relationships. In his first letter to his mother after the Alton church meeting at which he was questioned about his slavery views, Lovejoy referred to the men as "brethren," in the way he tended to speak of fellow churchmen. That part was true, of course—religion offered an important tie among them. But they also proved like-minded on matters of individual liberty and the right of expression, which would keep them close at Lovejoy's side when he needed not just friends but protectors.

CHAPTER FOUR

THE ONLY WEAPON

THE GATHERING AT THE Alton church after Lovejoy's unhappy arrival managed to produce one tangible gain for the editor: money. Gilman and Godfrey agreed to kick in some funds, supplemented by a loan from the local branch of the state bank that they controlled. Lovejoy would be able to start his newspaper from scratch once he had bought a new hand-operated press (the cost for launching a frontier newspaper in the 1830s was between $1,500 and $1,700). Popular hand-operated printing presses during Lovejoy's time consisted of a waist-high worktable attached on one end to a heavy, cast-iron frame, set upright on legs, that served as anchor for the platen—a thick metal plate that was lowered by lever to press the paper against the type. Such presses, which could be operated by one person, were relatively compact, occupying scarcely more space than a child's bed, but heavy because of their metal parts. The type of press that Lovejoy favored was built in Cincinnati, a trip of nearly four hundred miles by steamboat that made use of the Mississippi and Ohio rivers. Fortified by the moral and financial support he received from the Altonians, Lovejoy wasted no time in setting out.

It was a miserable trip. The emotional strains of the previous weeks—the twin mob attacks on his property, the rigors of relocation under duress—had left him fatigued and feverish. "By the time I reached Cincinnati," Lovejoy wrote, "I was fit only for the bed." He pressed on, nonetheless, and finished his purchase of the new press. On the way home, he could proceed no more and took to a sickbed in Louisville at the home of a Connecticut transplant named Reverend Banks, "with a bilious fever deeply hold of me." A doctor's care got Lovejoy up and back on the road home in a week's time. Once back on the Mississippi, he saw Celia and young Edward in St. Charles, where the two had taken shelter at the home of her mother. But the press of business called in Alton, the home base of the new *Observer* and of the family's new life. Lovejoy's final early-morning ride there by horse was raw and chilly, and within a few days of harried activity, he was sent to the bed again with fever. "Thus you can see, my dear mother, that my path through this life is not a flowery one," he wrote.

Lovejoy's frustration came through in his written words. Why at such a moment—when his services were so much in need, and "angry, and wicked men" sought to torment him—should Lovejoy be struck ill and useless? He missed Celia, who was safely ensconced on the far side of the river, but worried about the toll of the recent months' events on her health, which tended to be fragile (and was poor again now). The couple had been married for just eighteen months and already had endured enough controversy to last most couples a lifetime. The ugly cascade of events that had driven Lovejoy from St. Louis remained a raw wound, and he questioned what impact further trouble might have on Celia's delicate state. Only weeks earlier, he had gone to bed wondering if assassins would find him during the night. Lovejoy was now well aware that his determination "to 'fight valiantly' for the truth" put at risk not only his life and reputation, but Celia's as well. "My wife is a perfect heroine," Lovejoy told his mother in a letter dated August 31, 1836, a month after his arrival in Alton. "She has seen me shunned, hated, reviled . . . and she has only clung to me the more closely, and more devotedly. When I told her that the mob had destroyed a considerable part of our furniture along with their other depredations, 'No matter,' said she, 'what have they destroyed since they have not hurt you.' Such is woman! And such is the woman whom God has given me."

Lovejoy had been thirty-two and Celia Ann French not yet twenty-two when the couple wed in March 1835. Celia was "tall, well-shaped, of a light, fair complexion, dark flaxen hair, large blue eyes. . . . In short she is very beautiful," her smitten new husband wrote in a letter soon after their marriage. Of perhaps greater importance, given the travails the couple would face, Celia was also intelligent and built of strong character. "She is also sweet-tempered, obliging, kind-hearted, industrious and, good-humored and possessed alike of a sound judgment and correct taste," Lovejoy wrote. The couple's son, Edward Payson, was born a year later. By now, Lovejoy's giddy delight after the couple's marriage had given way to a more complicated set of emotions, as he surveyed the threats and horrific images of the previous year. Suddenly, Lovejoy told his mother, he felt as never before "the wisdom of Paul's advice not to marry." He felt bereft without his wife and son, yet racked with dread over what he still might end up putting them through.

As he laid bare these feelings, Lovejoy was providing clues about his own plans in Alton, and they didn't appear to include shutting up. The men at the church meeting who thought they heard Lovejoy promise silence on the subject of slavery might have been disturbed to read the letter he was now scribbling. Lovejoy seemed to have decided that the new incarnation of the *Observer* would pick up where the last one had left off. He noted that he had made some good friends in Alton but worried about the spiritual health of so many other people around him, chasing profits at a time of rampant speculation in town. (He declared them to be excessively "worldly minded.") On slavery, Lovejoy's pen carried passion as it moved across the page. "The cry of the oppressed," he wrote, "has entered not only into my eyes, but into my soul, so that while I live I cannot hold my peace." He warned Betsey Lovejoy of possible dark days ahead for his project, elaborating in a way that could not have sounded comforting to a fretful parent on the other side of the country. "I may not live to see its success," Lovejoy wrote. "I may even die."

The first issue of the Alton *Observer*, he noted, would come out the following week. Lovejoy hoped that his brother Joseph, a minister in Maine, would enlist clergymen in Maine to support his paper. One such pastor from the coastal town of Brunswick had already given Lovejoy great credit by saying that he was doing more to end slavery "than any other man in the United States." Lovejoy likely recognized that as overstatement, but "if half that be true, surely my paper ought to be supported."

* * *

IN FLEEING TO ALTON, Lovejoy was staking his fortunes on a fast-developing river town determined to eclipse St. Louis as a commercial hub on the Mississippi. Such ambitions likely seemed presumptuous to the larger and more established neighbor in Missouri. Alton was an upstart, a pretender, when compared with St. Louis, now an important terminus for lucrative river commerce with Southern cities like Memphis and New Orleans. Alton sat perched on a bend in the Mississippi, edged by dramatic, one-hundred-foot limestone bluffs. Alton's location placed it a few miles above the point where the Missouri River poured into the Mississippi, swelling a meandering, shallow band into a majestic river highway that was capable of handling the steamboats and other craft that had turned St. Louis into the dominant crossroads of the American West. With the river at its front door, plus sturdy stands of timber and limestone and lead deposits to be mined all around, the area that would become the town of Alton appeared to many frontier types as the sort of place that might one day serve as an important trading center in its own right, with links to the northern backcountry and the East Coast, as well as to the Southern states.

Alton had been a mere sketch of pencil lines on a plot map less than two decades before Lovejoy's arrival. It had been the brainchild of Easton, a wealthy St. Louis lawyer and former delegate to Congress from the Missouri territory. In 1818, Easton laid out his vision on a plat of fifty-five tidy, numbered blocks and named it for his first-born son, Alton, with several streets named after family members: George, Alby, Langdon (plus one for the entire family, Easton). The developer hired out the construction of four log houses, and the building of Alton was underway.

Alton remained sparsely settled until 1830, but quickly became a magnet for men of enterprise and pioneers of more humble means. This was the American frontier, and those drawn to Alton saw among its virtues cheap land and the chance to get in on the promise of a town that its boosters pitched as poised for great prosperity. Local histories describe a "tide of immigration" from other parts of the United States that included a significant number of businessmen, many of whom brought their wealth with them. The Alton-area historian Judy Hoffman notes that around fifty businessmen moved into Alton between 1829 and 1832—many from New York or the New England states.

Many of these residents would settle in Upper Alton, a more bucolic precinct two and a half miles from the busy waterfront area. Few such "Yankees," a term used to denote anyone from east of the Allegheny Mountains, had found their way to southern Illinois prior to 1817; most of those who came were "vendors of wooden clocks and tin ware," according to one history of Madison County, of which Alton was part. "Strong sectional prejudices existed, especially toward the Yankee . . . but among intelligent classes, the emigrant from the East soon came to be appreciated at his real worth, and recognized as among the most valuable citizens of the county," according to the 1882 account titled "History of Madison County, Illinois." Alton's "rapid growth and business prosperity were almost entirely due to Eastern men."

But Madison County had long drawn even more of its newcomers from states in the South, lending it a pro-Southern bent when it came to questions of cultural identity or regional affinity—questions such as slavery. Southerners on the frontier frequently bristled at the moralizing that seemed ever to issue from these Eastern transplants, with their parson-like scolding on everything from tippling to opening for business on Sunday. At the same time, many newcomers from the Northeast saw themselves as playing a civilizing role on the rough-and-tumble frontier. Along with their business wiles and carpet bags, they brought a pious worldview, forged in the stern tradition of Calvinism, to a chaotic part of the country that many of them saw as deeply in need of its lessons.

Thomas Ford, who would serve as governor of Illinois during the 1840s and later write a two-volume history of the state, noted that the two sides harbored thoroughly unflattering views of each other. "The people of the south entertained a most despicable opinion of their northern neighbors. . . . They formed the opinion that a genuine Yankee was a close, miserable, dishonest, selfish getter of money, void of generosity, hospitality, or any of the kindlier feelings of human nature," Ford wrote. "The northern man believed the southerner to be a long, lank, lazy and ignorant animal, but little in advance of the savage state; one who was content to squat in a log-cabin with a large family of ill-fed and ill-clothed, idle, ignorant children."

The result of this animus in Alton was a potentially combustible mix of clashing social values within a town that was itself situated along the fault line separating North from South, astride tectonic forces of politics, economics, and morality pressing from both sides. "Perhaps no area in antebellum America experienced more cultural and social extremes than the confluence region in downstate Illinois," Hoffman writes. "Northerners, southerners, blacks and whites all gathered in the region."

As the 1830s unfolded, the riverfront area called Lower Alton would emerge as the town's commercial center, a bustling flurry of haphazard growth: shops, hotels, and taverns erected along muddy, half-paved streets and overwhelmed drainage ditches. By the time Lovejoy arrived in 1836, newcomers had boosted the town's population to twenty-five hundred or so—roughly double the number from just a few years earlier. Workmen came across the river from St. Louis to frame houses or stack bricks to create retail shops. In some of Alton's earliest workshops, coopers turned wooden slats into barrels, while steam-powered saw blades churned logs into lumber. Demand for land, once cheap, pushed prices steadily upward, especially in the main commerce zone along the river, where the cost of land parcels rose from $20 to $300–400 per foot or more, and house lots farther away went for $50 to $100 a foot. Some of the biggest wholesalers were taking in half a million dollars a year. Propelled by actual growth and the giddy energy of speculators, Alton gave the air of a place in too much of a hurry to finish nailing all its newly hewn boards into place before moving on to the next project.

The Reverend John Mason Peck, a Baptist minister, noted that Alton's strategic location—eighteen miles downriver from the mouth of the Illinois River and just a stone's throw above the confluence of the Missouri and Mississippi—placed it "at the point where the commerce and business of the widespread regions of the north east, north, and north west must arrive." In a gazetteer of Illinois published in 1834, two years before Lovejoy's arrival, Peck nodded to Alton's soaring vision of its future self, the sort of boosterism that in modern times might be found on the pages of a glossy real-estate brochure or investment prospectus.

Peck wasn't buying all of the hype, however. "Lower Alton has its disadvantages," he cautioned. "These, in impartial justice, I have no wish to conceal." Peck went on to itemize Alton's shortcomings, starting with the "uneven, abrupt, and hilly surface of a portion of the town site" and moving on to "the confined and low situation of another portion, which will prevent the circulation of a pure and healthy atmosphere." He then turned to the river itself, seeing as a flaw its "extensive and low bottom on the opposite side of the Mississippi" and then threw in the fact that there was a "powerful rival in trade and commerce to be found in St. Louis." Peck said Alton's drawbacks could impair the extensive growth it was hoping for "and make it quite problematical whether it will ever become the great commercial emporium of the upper valley of the Mississippi."

Peck's concerns over Alton's long-term prospects were valid, and a note of skepticism was warranted in the face of so much ambition. However, the reverend in 1834 could not have foreseen the nature of the blow that would help demolish Alton's aspirations—a trauma that lay three years in the future. When Alton's civic collapse came, it would have less to do with its sharp topography or competition with St. Louis traders than with something more elemental: the practical meaning of freedom, and the extent to which the town would protect a man intent on testing it.

* * *

THE INAUGURAL ISSUE OF the weekly Alton *Observer* came out on September 8, a Thursday. Like its now-obliterated predecessor in St. Louis, the *Observer* would be primarily a religious newspaper, featuring news and columns designed to appeal to Presbyterians and other readers concerned with sometimes arcane spiritual matters, but also with more quotidian issues, such as the support of church missions abroad or the need for prayer. The revived *Observer* wasn't unknown in Alton, of course, since Lovejoy's St. Louis–based forerunner had also circulated among the faithful in the border area of southern Illinois. But in his September 8 issue, Lovejoy included a prospectus and opening column to introduce readers to the weekly publication, which he noted had been expanded in size a bit—it was printed on what he called a "large Double Medium sheet"—and now ranked among the largest-format newspapers in the country. The *Observer*, he noted, would be "devoted to Religious, Literary, Agricultural and Miscellaneous Information and Discussions"—a kitchen-sink description that gave Lovejoy free rein to address just about any topic in the four-page weekly. He promised more column inches for secular news and "general intelligence" and two or three columns of agricultural news on the last page for farmers.

The cost was $3 a year, a not insubstantial amount in 1836—the equivalent of $82 in 2020 prices. Lovejoy alluded to his recent troubles and pointed out that supporters in Alton had stepped forward to get the *Observer* running again. But the paper would need at least two thousand subscribers—twice the number of his previous readership—in order to meet its estimated weekly operating costs of about $75, or $4,000 a year. To that end, Lovejoy appealed to readers to pay on time while he stepped up the hunt for new readers. "Nothing short of two thousand paying customers will place the Observer on a firm basis, and enable it to go on unembarrassed," the editor wrote.

Having taken care of the fine print, Lovejoy turned now to the large-font questions that had caused him so much difficulty in St. Louis. To wit, his introductory article served to explain his flight from that city and to get in the last word in his verbal tussles with old foes, including the judge he blamed for much of his year's plight. Lovejoy's language here was moderate and grounded in conventional moral considerations, but it bluntly established his stand on slavery. Lovejoy wrote that he had been targeted for his belief "that the system of American negro-Slavery is an awful evil and sin . . . that no man has a right to traffic in his fellow-man . . . and that it is the duty of us all to unite our hearty and zealous efforts to effect the speedy and entire emancipation of that portion of our fellow-men in bondage amongst us." He was not disavowing those beliefs now.

Lovejoy recognized that it was risky to sink money into a venture that would require drastic expansion in order to break even. But he said there was more at work than dollars and cents: he was banking on the public to support the *Observer* as way to stand up for free expression itself. "We consider the existence of this paper as identified, in a great measure, with the maintenance of principles which ought to be dearer to every American patriot and Christian, than even life itself," Lovejoy wrote. "For what is there desirable in life, to one deprived of his civil and religious liberty? [O]f the right to entertain and freely express his opinions?" Lovejoy invoked the Inquisition and wondered if such a regime was to be imposed on the "prairies of the West" in defense of another type of repression. "Are the American people, with the Declaration of Independence in their hands, prepared to engage in a general crusade in favour of the perpetual Slavery of a portion of the human family?" he asked.

And here Lovejoy set out the guideposts that would govern his approach to editing the *Observer*, leaving little room for misinterpretation. Lovejoy vowed as his "settled purpose" never to give in to mob violence that was aimed at squelching "the rights of conscience, the freedom of opinion and of the press." He promised to avoid "harsh denunciation" and said he had no intention of disrupting Alton life: "[W]e would provoke no violence from any portion of the community; the only weapon we would use is the TRUTH, the only sentiment we would appeal to, the moral sense of the community." He wanted the town to know he wasn't looking for trouble.

But there could be no mistaking Lovejoy's bottom line, which was delivered in the next twenty-three words and could be read as both a credo and warning. "If we cannot be permitted to do this, except at the risk of property, reputation, and life," Lovejoy wrote gravely, "we must even take the risk." Anyone looking for a pledge from Lovejoy as he reestablished his newspaper in Illinois could find one spelled out here in the black and white of his inaugural column. Lovejoy didn't plan to go out of his way to rankle, but he was abdicating none of the rights he believed belonged to him as an editor. And that meant discussing slavery if he so chose. The Alton *Observer* was born, and with its opening breath let the world know it would be no pushover.

CHAPTER FIVE

NOTHING BUT A NEWSPAPER

N EWSPAPERS OF THE 1830S were a distant, though recognizable, ancestor of the print medium we would come to know as a professional newsgathering operation. They had played a key role during the colonial period and war against England as a force for rallying pro-independence sentiment, with printers such as Samuel Adams employing the columns of their news sheets to excoriate the British (often with exaggeration) and to stoke the fires of rebellion. By the time of the country's birth, the hook was set—Americans were a nation of committed newspaper consumers.

A high rate of literacy, especially in New England, and the movement of people from farms to towns and cities helped spur Americans' thirst for news during the following decades. They read together in the home. They pooled money with neighbors for subscriptions and passed the papers back and forth. They retired—the men, at least—to the tavern, which stocked newspapers, and thus doubled as watering hole and reading room. In churches, ministers read the news to their seated parishioners. Even as early as 1822, historian Daniel Walker Howe notes, the United States led the world in the number of newspaper readers, regardless of population.

Newspapers were such a prominent feature of American life that foreigners from Europe who visited the young republic saw in it a phenomenon unlike anything back in the Old World. "The influence and circulation of newspapers is great beyond anything ever known in Europe. In truth, nine-tenths of the population read nothing else," wrote Scottish writer Thomas Hamilton, who arrived in 1830. "Every village, nay, almost every hamlet, has its press." Unlike books, Hamilton reported in a two-volume travelogue called *Men and Manners in America*, "newspapers penetrate to every crevice of the Union. There is no settlement so remote as to be cut off from this channel of intercourse with their fellow-men." Tocqueville, the French writer who was traveling the United States at around the same time, saw American newspapers as both silent counselor and social glue. "Nothing but a newspaper can drop the same thought into a thousand minds at the same moment," he wrote. "A newspaper is an adviser who does not require to be sought, but who comes of his own accord, and talks to you briefly every day of the common weal, without distracting you from your private affairs." Tocqueville added that "if there were no newspapers, there would be no common activity."

Despite the noble-sounding talk about the ideals of democracy, American newspapering by 1830 also was a rough-edged trade, often practiced by not-very-educated men and frequently in the service of narrow political ends. Scholars politely refer to the phase of American journalism as the era of the "party press," when most newspapers had a strongly partisan bent or were sponsored financially by one political party or the other and treated as its mouthpiece. Newspaper editors also worked as commercial printers—among the potential spoils of a party's electoral victory were its governmental printing contracts. The parties of the post-independence era had by the 1820s broken apart and morphed into two new groupings, the Democrats of Andrew Jackson and the National Republicans, later known as Whigs, who were affiliated most prominently with Lovejoy's man, Henry Clay. Both parties employed networks of newspapers and editors as part of their nationwide machinery. (Jackson-aligned papers played a big role in getting him elected president in 1828, and two of the editors involved—Amos Kendall and Duff Green—would join the Jackson administration as advisers in his "kitchen cabinet." Jackson, a keen practitioner of patronage, later named Kendall to the powerful position of postmaster general.)

Hamilton, the Scottish writer, was unimpressed with the practitioners of this style of partisan journalism. "The conductors of these journals are generally shrewd but uneducated men, extravagant in praise or censure, clear in their judgment of everything connected with their own interests, and exceedingly indifferent to all matters which have no discernible relation to their own pockets or privileges," he sniffed. Tocqueville was even more blunt: "The journalists of the United States are usually placed in a very humble position, with a scanty education and a vulgar turn of mind."

An opinion-oriented press required editors with, well, opinions—not to mention the writing chops that would be sufficient to engage in what Tocqueville said was their core job: "an open and coarse appeal to the passions of the populace." In real life, this translated into a form of journalism that was often harsh, disparaging, and startlingly personal. Editors of the era debated each other—and the politicians they backed—through the pages of their papers, hurling insults and threats from one week's edition to the next, often laced with healthy dollops of outright falsehood. Amid such intense partisanship, big-city editors faced off against each other in fistfights in the 1830s. James Watson Webb of the New York *Courier and Enquirer* fought two rival editors and attacked a third—three times—on the streets of New York. In the country's opening decades, several disputes arising from the news pages ended up in duels. Journalism could be a sharp-elbowed affair that often seemed more combat than craft.

The number of newspapers soared during the antebellum period, from about two hundred in 1800 to twelve hundred by the mid-1830s. (That number would rise further to more than sixteen hundred by 1840.) Much of that growth stemmed from the nation's expansion in the frontier West. Newspapers were fast to sprout, but not always profitable. Many were forced to swallow unpaid debt in order to avoid cutting off coveted subscribers, who were sometimes unable to keep up with subscription prices that amounted to $2 to $3 a year. The historian Thomas C. Leonard notes that during the period before the Civil War, many newspapers swapped their publications for products as a way to make ends meet. "Country newspapers announced they would settle bills for crops. Newspaper offices took in flax and wool, cheeses and feathers. Journalists came to accept cattle, hides, beeswax, and rags in payment for the news," Leonard writes. "Of all American vices, non-payment of subscriptions was among the most egalitarian." Over the years, Lovejoy would become all too familiar with the financial challenges of keeping a newspaper afloat on the frontier.

Like Lovejoy's *Observer*, nearly all of the newspapers during this era were issued on a weekly basis—daily newspapers were mostly found in big cities, such as New York, that could provide the volume of advertising needed to sustain them. The paper on which newspapers were printed was still made from rags during the 1830s—years before the advances in technology that would allow cheaper wood pulp to be used. And newspapers in this period were big—conventional broadsheet pages measured eighteen inches wide by about twenty-four inches long, requiring readers to spread their arms wide when reading an open paper or learn to fold creatively. (In later years, some papers swelled to dimensions of nearly twenty-four inches wide by twenty-eight inches long.) The papers weren't thick, though; many contained just four pages.

The work of an editor often seemed to require the skills of a clever stock clerk—figuring out how to jam as many items as possible into a limited amount of space. Photographs were still years away from hitting newspaper pages, and illustrations were used almost exclusively for display advertising, meaning that the news pages usually resembled a broad carpet of gray: five or six tightly packed columns of often minuscule type, interrupted by the (only slightly) larger type of headlines. Hair-thin lines acted to separate one article from the next, so it could be quite hard to know where one article ended and another began. Sturdy readers who picked up a newspaper in the early 1800s were on their own to navigate a dizzying mishmash: advertisements, minutes of local meetings, complete texts of windy congressional speeches, hometown editorial columns, and assorted news items, the majority of which came from abroad or other parts of the United States (and usually days or even weeks old).

Newspapers favored foreign and national news and offered scant news about the communities where they resided. Editors packed their pages without apparent regard for layout considerations based on newsworthiness, a concept that had not yet been developed in American journalism. Rather, much of the material that Americans read was in uncooked form, arranged verbatim from other publications onto the editor's own press alongside whatever other items good fortune had swept to his shores. Newspapers of the early 1800s resembled inside-out versions of their modern-day descendants, stuffing the biggest news into their inside pages. The precious real estate of the front page was reserved for display ads for everything from hats to hardware, plus small notices for professional services—lawyers, shipping brokers, auctioneers—that many years later would be called classifieds.

One reason for the abundance of news from afar was the practice by newspapers of swapping editions with other papers, even those in distant locations in other states. Editors would mail a copy of their paper to their faraway counterparts, who would collect the bundles from U.S. mail coaches and then reprint selected articles in their own papers, usually by attributing the original source of the news items. Editors thus won in two ways: they got notice for their work in other parts of the country, while at the same time gaining a potent and cost-effective tool for gathering news. The exchanges were, in effect, an early (and slower) version of the news collective that would become known as the wire service. Newspaper exchanges played a huge role in fomenting national conversation on seemingly parochial issues—a flood in Virginia could get play in Missouri, for example—and therefore serve part of the broader, unifying function that foreign observers noticed when they looked at American journalism at the time. As Thomas Hamilton put it, the reach of newspapers ensured that "the most remote invader of distant wilds is kept alive in his solitude to the common ties of brotherhood and country."

If newspapers of the era succeeded in turning Americans into news junkies, they owed a large measure of thanks to a surprising sponsor: the federal government. Or, more specifically, the U.S. Post Office. An uncelebrated act of Congress—the Post Office Act of 1792—helped bring about a stunning transformation in how Americans communicated by launching a vast expansion in the postal system and providing a cheap way for mountains of newspapers to crisscross the nation in the age before the telegraph. Although the creation of a postal system might seem inevitable in a new country, it took Congress several years after passage of the Constitution to lay out a vision of what would be the biggest function of the central government. Until then, exchange newspapers were admitted at no cost into the mail stream at the discretion of riders carrying the mail. But in passing the Post Office Act, Congress sided with those who argued that allowing newspapers into the mail on a selective basis created an opening for the federal government to favor one publication—and its political stances—over another. The answer was to allow all newspapers to be sent through the mail, at a nominal cost of a penny for distances under one hundred miles.

The effect of the postal law was to promote a communications revolution that was on par with the dramatic advances surrounding transportation through road and canal building and the steamboat. Historian Richard R.

John, who has written about the transformative role played by the postal system in U.S. society, said the number of newspapers sent by mail sky-rocketed from 1.9 million a year in 1800 to 16 million by 1830—though still just a fraction of all the newspapers published around the country. By 1832, John writes, the towering heaps of newspapers, in sacks weighing up to two hundred pounds each, accounted for 95 percent of all the weight carried by postal carriers. "By underwriting the low-cost transmission of newspapers throughout the United States, the central government estab-lished a national market for information 60 years before a comparable national market would emerge for goods," John writes.

The federal government, through its postal law, helped make the lowly newspaper editor a force to be reckoned with—and one highly depen-dent on the regular arrival of the mail sack. (Editors complained bitterly in print when delays in delivery left them bereft of news to publish.) By making it possible for news and essays from one part of the country to appear in another, the mail system served as a binding agent for a nation spreading far beyond its original contours along the Atlantic coast. But the conversation wasn't always welcome. Later in the 1830s, the Post Office's crucial role in the flow of fact and opinion would place it in the middle of a debate over censorship, when antislavery activists sought to promote their viewpoint in the South.

* * *

ALL THOSE BRUISING EDITORIALS and partisan harangues couldn't have run unless editors were free to publish—or believed that they were. Indeed, editors of the 1830s enjoyed a remarkable level of freedom to print what they chose. Most editors, Lovejoy included, took it as an article of faith that their liberty to publish was inherent in their rights as Ameri-cans, as human beings granted life by their Creator. Their understanding

of press liberty derived as much from an ideal of freedom as from any law
or Constitutional provision.

At the time Lovejoy was running a newspaper, there still had been no
federal court rulings to help define the extent of press freedom under the
U.S. Constitution, such as those that would aid journalists of a later epoch.
Modern-day Americans know that freedom of the press is enshrined in the
First Amendment, along with the freedoms of speech, religion, assembly,
and petition. But in Lovejoy's age, those federal guarantees were of limited
consequence on the ground, where press freedom depended to a much
greater degree on protections that the individual states had written into
their own constitutions, along with laws regarding libel. The balance would
not tip in favor of federally guaranteed rights until after the Civil War.

Unlike an earlier generation of editors, who during the John Adams
administration faced politically motivated prosecutions under an egre-
gious measure known as the Alien and Sedition Acts of 1798, Lovejoy
and his colleagues had little to fear from government sanction. That
earlier law targeted foes of Adams's Federalist government by punishing
speech and writings deemed "false, scandalous and malicious" if they
attacked the U.S. government, Congress, or president. The law, which
was almost surely unconstitutional, was mainly used to charge Adams's
political foes—that is, the Democratic-Republican supporters of Thomas
Jefferson. It was allowed to lapse after Jefferson's election as president
in 1800, ending an early and short-lived attempt at federal censorship of
the press. The individual states, however, would enjoy almost complete
formal jurisdiction over the extent of press rights until the 1868 ratification of the Fourteenth Amendment, which applied the Bill of Rights'
protections across the states. It is fair to say that, during Lovejoy's time,
press freedom still lay in a gray area between Constitutional promise and
bankable protection. Perhaps the best way to describe the climate for
journalists at the time would be "free, but . . ." Although editors were
able to publish their newspaper without prior censorship or fear of

criminal charges, they did so with an understanding that they would be held responsible for perceived abuses of that liberty, however that might be defined in the communities where they worked.

It is easy to see how this could be fraught with risk. Americans saw newspapers as an essential aspect of life, and readers appeared to tolerate differing viewpoints. But editors were alone to negotiate an uncharted legal landscape and made decisions about what to publish based on their faith in the nation's founding principles—that liberty meant liberty. In a sense, it was up to them to make clear what America meant by a free press. Those who chose to take on slavery were attacking a structure through which a number of fundamental forces coursed: economy, morality, racial identity, culture, and sectional political clout. It was one thing for an outspoken editor to sound off on a tariff proposal, but a far riskier matter to take aim at what amounted to the American order itself.

CHAPTER SIX

TO THE WEST

A S LOVEJOY SET INTO place the foundation blocks of his new life in Alton, the stormy turbulence of summer eased by fall into an almost placid normalcy. He and Celia settled into a house—a two-story clapboard structure with a chimney—on Cherry Street, just two blocks from the waterfront. Nearby was his printing office, a sloping, low-slung building situated in the shadows of taller neighbors in the heart of the business district of Lower Alton. Just up the street, which ran parallel to the river and was now crowded with commercial enterprises, squatted the state prison and the Godfrey, Gilman & Co. warehouse. By late 1836, the image of a full-grown Alton was coming into view, filling the ambitious outlines that its boosters had sketched years earlier. And as he settled in, Lovejoy and his newspaper promoted a nearly breathless view of the place—he ran no fewer than three articles by the end of the year depicting Alton as a city on the move, one that was living up to its hype.

"It is well known that we have always been among the sceptical as it regards the growth of Alton. But we confess the last few weeks have very much shaken, if not entirely carried away, our doubts. The amount of business transacted here is truly astonishing," he wrote in a column in November, two months after the *Observer*'s launch. Steamboats crowded the river's edge and the landing "was literally covered with merchandise of every kind." Equally remarkable was the flow of newcomers: "The boats come crowded with emigrants, and the two towns of Upper Alton and Lower Alton are literally full to overflowing with new comers." The influx had sparked an explosion of house building, and rents were "most astonishingly high," he wrote: "Stores on Second Street rent from $600 to $1500 per annum, and dwelling houses, with three or four rooms, from $250 to $350 per annum, and none to be had even at that price."

What's more, Lovejoy noted, Alton boasted three churches—Presbyterian, Methodist, and Reformed Methodist—and a Baptist church was under construction. Lovejoy wrote that residents had a choice of three weekly newspapers besides his *Observer*—a pair of "political" newspapers, the *Spectator* and *Telegraph*, and another religious paper, the *Western Pioneer*, a Baptist publication. Of the four, Lovejoy's *Observer* enjoyed the highest circulation: around thirteen to fourteen hundred. Lovejoy nodded with approval at signs of Alton's moral uprightness as well. He noted with satisfaction that there were depositories of the American Bible Society and the American Tract Society, as well as the American Sunday School Union. The cause of temperance was also well represented in Alton—it served as the executive headquarters of the Illinois State Temperance Society, the group for which Lovejoy's friend Winthrop Gilman was directing the publication of the weekly *Temperance Herald*. "These things certainly indicate Alton to be a place of some importance," Lovejoy said.

He took an equally upbeat tone in a similar column the following month. It is easy to envision Lovejoy strolling through the town, amid the clatter of horse-drawn wagons and shouts of dock workers, to tally evidence of its restlessness: twenty wholesale stores ("one of which . . . imports directly from Europe"), thirty-two retail shops, eight lawyers, seven physicians, and eight clergymen serving eight different denominations. Wages for bricklayers and stone masons (at $2.50 to $3 a day) and laborers ($1.50) were far higher than the 40¢ workers could earn back East, he wrote. "Here they may soon realize a little fortune," Lovejoy said. He ticked the number of hotels—four—and boarding houses—nine—and took pleasure in noting that Alton even had a lyceum for holding lectures, a venue at which Lovejoy would later promote an ill-starred slavery debate. For now, Lovejoy sounded enchanted by his new town, and impressed by the odds it had already beaten. "Scarcely a town site could have been selected on the Mississippi more unpromising in its appearance; and yet in five years, probably, it will attract the admiration of every beholder," he wrote.

Lovejoy seemed to have backed off his earlier concern about Alton being too "worldly minded" and sounded convinced that the "foundations of its prosperity are based on the broad basis of public morals and christian benevolence." The town was getting rich quick, perhaps, but Lovejoy was giving it the benefit of the doubt. He pointed with pride, for example, to the civic role that Godfrey was playing by investing $10,000 of his own money to found the seminary for young women, and underscored the businessman's moral rectitude by describing how Godfrey once had forced a steamboat carrying a delivery for him to wait at the dock overnight to avoid violating the Sabbath. Lovejoy was clearly pleased by the presence of so many other residents from New York and New England, and declared them to represent a majority of the town's transplanted residents— a statistically questionable assertion that may have betrayed how much time he spent in their company. (The gritty section of Lower Alton was made up predominately of Southerners, while the more well-to-do Upper Alton was the preserve of residents who hailed from the Northeast.) In any case, it was the solid morals of Alton that "will give it a fame as abiding as the hills of granite that environ it," Lovejoy concluded, "while without them, its glory will be as short-lived as the fading flower."

* * *

LOVEJOY COULD ALSO FIND reasons to imagine that the *Observer* would find its footing in this new setting. He was slowly finding new customers and was able to report to his readers in October that 140 new subscribers had signed up. On top of that, editors of religious newspapers back East were publishing articles celebrating the revival of the relocated *Observer* as evidence that Lovejoy, and the wider fight against slavery, had survived the recent attempts to smother speech. He excerpted their heartening words in the *Observer*. "Brother L. will now have more encouragement and less to fear than ever," announced one Boston-based antislavery newspaper. "The tide of liberty is rising," declared another sympathetic paper in Pittsburgh.

Perhaps even more significant for the *Observer*'s prospects, Lovejoy won formal pledges of financial support from a group of Presbyterian church members who had attended a meeting of its Illinois synod. The group agreed that the *Observer* ought to be sustained and pledged to keep it afloat for at least two years, offering Lovejoy a measure of breathing room as he sought to get the paper off the ground. A resolution signed by the supporters asked other men of means to join the sponsorship drive. The list of signers included the reliable Gilman, as well as a number of merchants of lesser wealth, such as Enoch Long and Royal Weller, another Alton businessman.

The list of backers was topped by the Reverend Gideon Blackburn, a revivalist minister from nearby Macoupin County who was known to oppose slavery. Blackburn was something of an éminence grise within the frontier Presbyterian community and was linked with abolitionists like the Reverend David Nelson, who had won a reputation for barn-burner revival meetings that ended with dozens of rapt attendees noisily proclaiming their religious conversion. Blackburn and Nelson represented strands in a small but closely connected network of religious men in the region who opposed slavery with varying degrees of fervor. In a sense,

Lovejoy had already begun knitting his own life into that same network, for it was Nelson who had converted him four years earlier in St. Louis, setting Lovejoy on the religious path that he now walked as a minister and editor.

Nelson was a former physician from Tennessee who had freed his slaves after hearing a speech by the roving abolitionist activist Theodore Dwight Weld. Nelson stood over six feet tall, with a thicket of brown hair and an often unkempt appearance—he was said to wear ragged, soiled clothes and mismatched shoes—that belied his taste for the likes of Shakespeare and Milton. Lovejoy heard Nelson preach in St. Louis in early 1832, a time when revivals—some in churches, others in open fields or clearings in the woods—were sweeping like a wildfire across parts of the South, the Northeast, and the frontier West. One area of upstate New York where fervor proved particularly strong was so frequent a site of revivals that it became known as the "burned-over district."

Lovejoy had still been an editor at the *St. Louis Times*, publishing fawning articles about Henry Clay and disparaging Andrew Jackson, when he began to attend Nelson's revival meetings at the First Presbyterian Church in St. Louis. He looked on enviously as other attendees experienced that, in his words, the "power of God to salvation is manifested, so that the blindest must see and the hardest feel." But for him, nothing happened. Lovejoy grew frustrated and discouraged. In a letter to Daniel and Betsey Lovejoy in January 1832, he reported that the hopes he had once held for that same elation of conversion had evaporated, leaving him "a more hardened sinner than ever." He sounded near desperation as he urged his parents to pray and to forgive him for being "vile, sinful and disobedient as I have been." Lovejoy voiced consternation that his sins—he did not specify them—had become "infinitely more numerous and aggravated."

Then, barely a month later, everything changed. He wrote home to proclaim that his long-awaited spiritual breakthrough had arrived at last, during a Nelson revival with thirty-five other people. But that wasn't all.

Lovejoy decided that he would abandon his post at the *Times* and push off in an entirely new direction: the ministry. And he would do so immediately. A little over four weeks later, in March 1832, Lovejoy arrived at Princeton Theological Seminary in New Jersey. On the same day, he was admitted for studies to prepare for a role in the clergy. America's evangelical army had its latest recruit.

Princeton Seminary was a Presbyterian-led bastion of orthodox Calvinism and a site of establishment dogma when it came to social issues of the day, such as slavery, and it would help etch the contours of Lovejoy's early thinking on such matters. The seminary's founders and its handful of professors had nearly all at times voiced impassioned criticisms of slavery as a moral wrong. But several had employed slave labor themselves. Most of these men held the patronizing belief that Black people, once freed from the debilitating state of slavery, would never thrive in a state of freedom alongside distrustful, racist white people. The answer was to remove freed Black people by ship to Africa, where they could prosper and, as an added benefit, might help spread the word of Christian faith to a continent of the unconverted—a win-win, in the eyes of these clerics.

Lovejoy saw his training at Princeton as his entrance to the ministry, the start of a fresh personal and professional path that would be devoted, as he put it, to "work in the vineyard of the Lord." He appeared to see himself as just another seminarian preparing to be a preacher. It was not hard to envision in Lovejoy's future the comfortable life of a New England pastor—respected, tending to the spiritual well-being of his neighbors, close to his family in Maine. With a Princeton Seminary pedigree, excellent connections, and the same sharp mind that had excited teachers since childhood, Lovejoy seemed a likely candidate for an influential Eastern pulpit someday. Instead, he would wind up on the frontier once again, attempting to save souls, yes, but with a newspaper.

* * *

LOVEJOY'S CONVERSION EXPERIENCE THRUST him solidly into the country's larger evangelical movement, in which the future *Observer* would act as a trumpet of religious values. Revivals such as the ones that he attended in St. Louis were an outward sign of a burst of almost frenzied religious energy known as the Second Great Awakening during the early decades of the 1800s. Just as revolutions in the young nation's economy and transportation were transforming the way Americans lived, old religious principles—at least among Protestants—were also coming under challenge by the same forces of innovation, optimism, and movement that were upending other conventions.

The notion that a person's salvation was foreordained—a central tenet of the Calvinists who had served as the dour custodians of American piety—was crumbling before a thrilling new belief: that everyone had a personal responsibility for determining the eventual fate of his or her own soul. Evangelical preachers fanned out in every direction, offering varying flavors of revivalism, from a buttoned-down, bookish version promoted to Congregationalists and Presbyterians in New England to a more theatrical brand, often associated with Methodists and Baptists, in the South and frontier West. By the thousands, Americans flocked to churches and wooded camps for days-long revivals that often reduced crowds to heaving, moaning masses, overcome by the fiery exhortations of the traveling preachers and the ecstatic sensation of release through mass conversion. The revivals proved a potent recruiting tool—membership in Protestant denominations soared during the antebellum period.

Evangelicals of various stripes agreed that the same goodness that could serve to help along a person's salvation could be harnessed to pave the way for the millennialist promise of a Kingdom of God. Evangelicals believed the United States bore a special role in God's plan for this glorious future, and offered society a road map for morally righteous actions to prepare for it. Evangelicals such as Charles Grandison Finney and the Yale-trained Lyman Beecher took aim at a roster of national sins: drinking,

dueling, violating the Sabbath, slavery. This explosion of reform spirit in
the 1830s inspired newly awakened men and women to throw themselves
into a range of efforts, from peace to prison reform. This process created,
as James Brewer Stewart has written, the notion of activism as a profession
for young people—many of them aspiring ministers—who lectured and
served as agents for reform groups, all supported by benevolent organizations. They also edited newspapers, as Lovejoy would with the *Observer*.

Religious newspapers were a fairly prominent part of the American
media scene in the early 1800s, and represented an important piece of a
multipronged industry of religious publishing that would be characterized
as a forerunner of the mass media in the United States. As Americans scurried into the vastness of their new nation, the religious men back East who
worried after those souls came up with strategies to ensure that they did not
outrun the teachings of mainstream Protestantism. Church leaders hired
traveling missionaries to preach in underrepresented areas of the rapidly
growing West, where the guardians of New England Calvinism feared an
erosion in belief, not to mention competition from Roman Catholicism and
nontraditional faiths, such as Universalists.

But even amid the surge of revivalist gatherings—which, of course,
required a crowd's physical presence—there was no better tool for
widespread proselytizing than the printing press. A crucial aspect of the
shoring-up strategy was to print and distribute Bibles and religious tracts
across the United States, both to win converts and promote the spirit of
evangelical reform. The most prominent organizations behind such
publishing drives were the American Bible Society, formed in 1816, and
the American Tract Society, founded nine years later. (A related group, the
American Sunday School Union, worked to establish Sunday schools and
stock libraries—an effort that drew the participation of Enoch Long
and other Lovejoy associates in Alton.)

The various projects were bankrolled by evangelical benefactors such
as the New York businessmen Arthur and Lewis Tappan, who were prime

movers of a "benevolent empire" that included crusades for temperance and a separate petition drive to close post offices on Sunday. Arthur Tappan, a silk merchant, helped form the tract society in 1825. The volunteer groups made use of technological advances in printing, such as steam-powered presses, to quickly produce and disseminate mass quantities of Bibles and tracts, which used an accessible, entertaining style to reach a far-flung population through teachings cranked out with machine-like uniformity and economy.

The goal of the publishing groups—audacious, to be sure—was to put religious materials into the hands of every single American family. They fell far short of that, but handed out one million Bibles and fifteen million religious tracts between 1829 and 1833, according to the scholar David Paul Nord. The New York–based religious societies also seeded the countryside with thousands of local, largely independent affiliates to raise money and pass out materials. Lovejoy and friends such as Long, Lippincott, Gilman, and Graves would be active members of these groups in Illinois. By 1837, for example, the American Tract Society would claim three thousand auxiliaries.

Religiously themed newspapers were part of this unprecedented, spreading media ecosphere. Some papers, such as Lovejoy's Presbyterian-affiliated *Observer*, targeted a particular denomination, while others were written for general audiences. But editors swapped papers with each other through the mail in the same way editors of mainstream publications did, allowing them to debate with each other on narrow questions of religion as well as on broader topics, such as slavery. To refer to newspapers of that era as strictly "religious" is also something of a misnomer because it suggests a distinction between news and religion that wasn't observed as keenly as in modern times. In colonial America, for example, religious themes and events were a dominant source of what appeared in early newspapers, which typically printed news of sermons and baptisms and even biblical verses in their columns, writes the media historian David

Copeland. In deeply pious, colonial society, the religious content served to keep people in line as much as to inform by shaming anyone seen as guilty of such transgressions as "a breech [sic] of the Sabbath, prostitution, sodomy and adultery," Copeland writes. In such a way, religious beliefs became a form of local news.

* * *

THE OPPORTUNITY FOR LOVEJOY to combine his religious training and newspaper background had come not long after he finished his theology studies at Princeton in 1833. Back in St. Louis, a group of Presbyterians urged Lovejoy to return to the frontier with a plan to start a religious newspaper after seminary. Lovejoy, with his previous experience at the *St. Louis Times* and now the status of a minister, was just the man for the job of editor. He wrote to tell his mother and ailing father, and offered to go back home to New England if they felt strongly enough that he should. But his sights were set on a return to the West, which Protestant leaders such as Lyman Beecher saw as the locus of an epic battle for the soul of the country and, indeed, for the future of free civilization. Lovejoy the revivalist saw a chance to join the struggle as an evangelist spreading the message of every person's role in vanquishing sin. Even his father's death that same year did not slow his plans. Lovejoy had heard the call of duty and had not a minute to lose. "They are impatiently calling me to the West," he wrote from New York to his brother Owen. "And to the West I must go."

By autumn of 1833, Lovejoy was back in St. Louis to start the weekly St. Louis *Observer*, using $1,200 in seed money invested by his Presbyterian friends there—a group that included Hamilton R. Gamble, a future Missouri governor—to buy a new press, type, and other supplies. It would focus on religious matters, though Lovejoy was granted full control over what to print. He could keep yearly profits up to $500—any sum above that would go to the owners. Lovejoy was a different man on his return to St. Louis, a man of God, and this paper would be distinct from his earlier venture at the *Times*, with its pro-Whig bent and fists ever raised for a scrap. The way Lovejoy saw things, the Christian church—and by this he meant the church of orthodox Protestantism—was on the march toward a grander fight. The St. Louis *Observer* would be among the ranks.

Writing in the paper's first issue in November 1833, he promised that "peace will be its aim, as far as that is consistent with the defence of the Truth." But Lovejoy warned at the time that his *Observer* "will never shrink from the post of duty; nor fear to speak out lest some over sensitive ears should be pained. Opinions honestly entertained will be fearlessly declared."

Three years would pass before Lovejoy would shift his newspaper to Alton, but his approach to running a newspaper there would be no different.

CHAPTER SEVEN

THE ASHES OF McINTOSH

O N DECEMBER 15, 1836, Lovejoy squeezed a ghastly news item inside his Alton *Observer*. It was a reprint of an article from the *Missouri Republican* about an enslaved man named William, who had been seized by a mob from the Hot Springs, Arkansas, sheriff's office after his arrest on suspicion of killing his enslaver. The article, with the headline titled "Horrible!," recounted how the men had tied William to a tree and built a fire underneath him, burning him alive in "slow and lingering torture." The article condemned the action as "disgraceful and barbarous," and it called upon authorities to bring to justice those who took part. Lovejoy shared in the outrage expressed by the St. Louis–based paper, but his nose detected something else in the paper's outpouring of dismay. He smelled hypocrisy. As Lovejoy knew well, the *Republican* and everyone else in St. Louis needed to look no farther than their own backyard if they wanted an example of breathtaking cruelty. Only months earlier, a lynch mob in St. Louis had carried out a similar act of gruesome violence—involving a victim named Francis McIntosh—and set off a chain of events that resonated still.

To Lovejoy's thinking, it was the ugly fallout from the McIntosh episode, more than anything, that in the end had forced him to flee Missouri. Months after the fact, he still harbored bitter memories of what had happened when he chose to speak out about the killing. In an acidly worded paragraph introducing the short *Republican* article, Lovejoy said that the Arkansas vigilantes had acted on "a lesson taught them from St. Louis." Lovejoy said the St. Louis mob members should not be relieved of "their awful guilt, until they have repented before God and man." But Lovejoy knew that they roamed free, and he blamed the judge who allowed them to do so. Lovejoy said he had no intention of "raking up the ashes of McIntosh." But it was clear that, at least in his mind, they remained unburied.

Francis McIntosh was a free biracial man working as a cook aboard the steamship *Flora* when the boat docked in St. Louis on April 28, 1836. After McIntosh disembarked, a brawl broke out between two steamboat workers. When a pair of sheriff's officers showed up to arrest the men, McIntosh was captured for interfering with their work and allowing the combatants to flee. The officers escorted McIntosh to a judge and gained a warrant to jail him. On the way to the lockup, McIntosh broke free and unsheathed a long knife that he apparently had kept hidden on his body. McIntosh jabbed with the blade and wounded one of the officers, a constable named William Mull. The constable's partner, deputy sheriff George Hammond, grabbed at McIntosh, but the cook lunged again with the knife, slicing into Hammond's neck and severing a carotid artery. Hammond's lifeless body lay on the ground as McIntosh fled. But the crowd, summoned by the surviving constable, recaptured the suspect not far away and hustled him into jail. After this point, versions differ on certain details, but not on the central reality: McIntosh would be burned alive.

Lovejoy, who at the time was still running the St. Louis *Observer*, did not witness the incident. But by drawing on other reports, he would craft an account that was urgent and affecting, and run it under the headline "Awful Murder and Savage Barbarity." (He called his account "a tale of depravity and woe.") In Lovejoy's telling, townspeople, enraged by the killing of a peace officer, descended on the jail where McIntosh had been taken. The sheriff, a man named Brotherton, made only half-hearted attempts to stop the mob, and a separate citizen appealed vainly for the mob to stop. Instead, the crowd set to work demolishing the jail doors with an eerie intent. "All was still," Lovejoy wrote. "Men spoke to each other in whispers, but it was a whisper which made the blood curdle to hear it, and indicated the awful energy of purpose, with which they were bent sacrificing the life of their intended victim."

The mob succeeded in breaking in and soon was dragging McIntosh by the arms, legs, and hair. It appears likely that the mob took McIntosh to the outskirts of town. There, he was tied to a locust tree, facing the crowd, according to Lovejoy. Scrap wood and shavings were placed at his feet and a fire kindled. As the flames grew, McIntosh, who until then had not spoken, began to cry out, begging for someone to shoot him. He sang a hymn and tried to pray. "Shoot me. Shoot me," he called, "though the fire had obliterated the features of humanity," Lovejoy wrote. Death came after an interval of about twenty minutes. Afterward, once the crowd had dispersed, "a rabble of boys who had attended to witness the horrible rites, commenced amusing themselves by throwing stones at the black and disfigured corpse, as it stood chained to the tree," Lovejoy wrote. "The object was to see who should first succeed in breaking the skull!"

Lovejoy's account of the McIntosh slaying roughly matched other versions, including those of the *Missouri Republican* and of a St. Louis physician who witnessed some of the events and recorded them in a diary. Both of those described a slow death before a large crowd. In its report two days later, the *Republican* called the lynching a "revolting spectacle" but appeared more interested in tamping the obvious public relations damage from such a horrific event in its hometown. The newspaper sought to paint the crowd, which it said numbered "several thousand," as having acted in an orderly fashion. "There was no tumult, no disturbance of any kind; but the crowd retired quietly to their several homes," it said. The *Republican* seemed intent on depicting McIntosh in an unfavorable light, calling him a "most desperate villain" and declaring as fact that he had been guilty of two previous stabbings, including one that had left a man dead in New Orleans months earlier.

The *Republican* lamented that such a deed had taken place in St. Louis, but said the same circumstances would likely have produced a similar mob action in any other American community. The best thing the city could do now was forget the whole thing. "Let the veil of oblivion be drawn over the fatal affair!" it urged. (The paper's concern for possible public relations damage was reflected in an item suggesting that abolitionists from back East intended to collect McIntosh's bones for use in their campaign against slavery.) The *Republican*'s desire to let the episode fade from public view almost certainly reflected the thinking of St. Louis's establishment, and other newspapers joined in attacking accounts of the affair by out-of-town outlets. A critical account in the Alton *Telegraph* (which employed Lovejoy's brother John) drew sharp condemnation from the St. Louis press, with one local paper saying that it represented a failed attempt to tar all of the city's residents.

But if civic leaders in St. Louis hoped to dismiss the McIntosh murder as an unfortunate incident and be done with it, Lovejoy had other ideas. To him, the killing was horrifying sign of a bigger problem, and he wasn't inclined to let St. Louis off the hook so easily. His graphic account in the *Observer* days after the lynching thrummed with a moral indignation. In lacerating language, he cited a flurry of vigilante actions that had recently taken place across the South, and for good measure he threw in mention of prior mob actions in St. Louis. Those included the sacking of brothels several years before and of a gambling house the previous winter. Although it is unlikely that Lovejoy the minister would have mourned the loss of such dens of vice, Lovejoy the editor sought to sound an alarm over the impulses that moved his fellow citizens to take the law into their own hands. McIntosh may have been a "hardened wretch certainly, and one that deserved to die," Lovejoy allowed. "But not *thus* to die."

"Is it not time to stop?" Lovejoy asked. "We must stand by the constitution and laws, or all is gone!" At noon on the day after the murder, Lovejoy walked over to the site to survey the sickening scene that remained. He stood before the blackened corpse, still bound to the tree and, he wrote, "prayed that we might not live." As Lovejoy gazed upon the aftermath of the mob's violent spasms, he could be forgiven if he caught a nightmarish glimpse of himself at the receiving end of the crowd's wrath.

* * *

DURING HIS THREE YEARS in St. Louis as a minister and an editor, Lovejoy had generated a good deal of suspicion and hostility over his writings, which displayed an increasing militancy on the issue of slavery. (His frequent barbs against Catholics were also alienating a hefty share of city residents.) At first, Lovejoy tiptoed gently into the slavery issue. His Princeton training had left him a committed gradualist, convinced that it was up to slave owners to choose the time and method for stepping onto the righteous path of emancipation. It was his job as a minister and an editor to preach, write, and publish in order to help them come to this righteous conclusion.

The Princeton approach to ending slavery was called "colonization," which captured the imagination of many respected white church figures and political leaders across the country during the 1820s and early 1830s, when its luster then dimmed. The strategy was rooted in a racist view that held Black people as inferior and unsuited for free life in the United States on an equal basis with white people, and it came to be seen by many elites as a favored alternative to freeing slaves into white-dominated society, where trouble would surely ensue. Princeton Seminary leaders played prominent roles in the American Colonization Society after the organization was established in 1816 by some of the country's most famous figures, including Henry Clay and Francis Scott Key, a lawyer who had written "The Star-Spangled Banner." (In fact, Lovejoy's favorite theology professor proudly claimed that the idea of deporting Black people to Africa was first broached at Princeton by Presbyterian minister Dr. Robert Finley.) Not surprisingly, then, the scheme to remove untold thousands of Black people to Liberia—a colony on Africa's western coast that had been established by the colonization society—became the favored approach of the Presbyterian Church with which the seminary was associated.

By the time Lovejoy left Princeton Seminary, his views on slavery hewed closely to the teachings he received there. He saw slavery as a moral wrong, an "evil." But, importantly, he had not yet decided it amounted to a "sin." At this time, Lovejoy thought slavery should be eradicated in a gradual manner, and he followed the lead of church fathers in energetically backing colonization as the best solution to the young country's racial conundrum. He believed that slaves had a fundamental right to receive Christian instruction: It was the responsibility of slave owners to nurture the souls of those they held in bondage. His approach was cautious, accommodationist—not unlike that of the Presbyterian Church itself, which fifteen years earlier had dared to forcefully denounce slavery as "utterly inconsistent with the law of God" but then pushed the matter to the back burner to avoid sectional strife within the church. (When the issue of slavery came before the church again later, Lovejoy would take a more outspoken role.)

Like his elders at Princeton, Lovejoy viewed abolitionists such as the firebrand Garrison in Boston as dangerous radicals whose proposed cure—immediate, as opposed to gradual, emancipation—was worse than the disease. When he was still a divinity student, Lovejoy took a scolding tone in a letter home in which he expressed dismay that his mother had adopted the urgent antislavery positions of Garrison, whose *Liberator* newspaper then circulated in Maine, with the help of Lovejoy's brother Joseph. In the letter, Lovejoy called Garrison an "incendiary fanatic" and "not only crazy, but wicked." Lovejoy noted that, like him, Garrison had previously lived in a slave state (Maryland) "and does therefore know that he libels the character of such states. Neither the condition of the slaves nor of their masters is such as he represents it to be." Lovejoy accused Garrison of misrepresenting the writings of the colonization camp, saying they had been purposely "garbled and falsified."

Lovejoy concluded by saying that he was not surprised that the Boston abolitionist's positions had captivated "silly women and boys," but felt only "regret and mortification that my Mother should be among their number." Lovejoy may have had second thoughts about his chastising tone before putting the letter into the mail, however. The section about Garrison was crossed out with a large "X," and Lovejoy wrote in the words "Stop here" in the tiny space at the end of the preceding page, along with a cramped sign-off, "Your son, E.P. Lovejoy." (Although the passage beneath the "X" remained fully legible, Betsey Lovejoy did not mention her son's scolding in any subsequent letters that I have reviewed.) In the ensuing years, Lovejoy struggled to find a sweet spot, a stance that could somehow accommodate his moral outrage over slavery with the notion that such a wrong might somehow be eradicated through half measures.

Lovejoy wrote his first pieces on slavery in the St. Louis *Observer* in 1834, months after his return to the frontier. His early forays appeared eager to find this agreeable middle ground. In a column simply titled "Slavery," in June 1834, Lovejoy labeled slavery as "a curse, politically and morally," but noted that the subject was "exceedingly delicate," and that "there is real difficulty" in identifying what should be one's "duty" in addressing it. In the piece, Lovejoy struck a nonconfrontational tone toward the Southern slave owner, noting that it was quite understandable that such a person should grow upset at being denounced as a "heartless man-stealer" and "a monster in human shape, a tyrant who delights in the pangs inflicted upon his fellow-man." He cautioned against the angry rhetoric that was issuing from the growing number of gatherings of abolitionists back East, and instead urged "cool and temperate argument, supported by facts" to prevent the two sides from sinking into irreconcilable antagonism. "No one will be persuaded by naked denunciation or misrepresentations," Lovejoy warned.

Nonetheless, Lovejoy acknowledged that the abolitionists had performed some good by getting Americans to think harder about slavery and by looking with a critical eye at the workings of the American Colonization Society, of which he remained a supporter. And he did not rule out a change of heart toward a more forceful abolitionist approach at some later date. Lovejoy was keeping his options open. "We do not promise by any means, that we shall not become an Abolitionist, strictly, at some future day . . . but arguments of sufficient weight must be laid before us," he wrote.

Ten months later, Lovejoy tackled the slavery topic again, now sounding more urgent about the need for a solution, though still resistant to the call by abolitionists to free the nation's 2.5 million enslaved people without conditions. In an April 16, 1835, article, Lovejoy addressed a separate piece in the same issue of the *Observer* that was signed "N" and written by David Nelson, the revivalist preacher who had converted him. Lovejoy argued that it was the Christian duty of slaveholders to introduce a "thorough change" in their treatment of slaves when it came to providing religious instruction. But, he said, "we do not believe that this change ought to be immediate and unconditional emancipation. We are entirely convinced that such a course would be cruel to the slave himself, and injurious to the community at large." This pithily captured the race-based position of the colonizationists: immediate freedom would damn slaves to a society that held them as inferior and in which they were unprepared to survive as productive citizens. Plenty of abolitionists, such as Garrison, also had once embraced colonization, but they and a number of prominent free Black leaders had increasingly rejected that position in favor of one with racial equality as its goal.

Although Lovejoy remained in the gradualist camp, he was passionate about the need for slaveholders to provide religious teaching to their bondmen, to accept that slaves, too, had "immortal souls." On this, he counted himself among the immediate abolitionists. Lovejoy also found his footing in denouncing the cruel excesses of human bondage. In that April 16 column, he invoked "the groans and sighs, and tears, and blood of the poor slave," and laid them in contrast with slave drivers "who go up and down our own streets, lifting their heads and moving among us unashamed and unrebuked." Why was the slave driver not "driven from the face of day, and made to hide himself in some dark corner"? Lovejoy asked. "Why? Simply because public sentiment has never been aroused to think on the subject." Lovejoy was suggesting that the answer to the slavery conundrum was in somehow moving public sentiment against its practice. He continued in this vein. "If the laws protect the miscreant who coins his wealth out of the heart's blood of his fellow creatures," the editor wrote, "he can at least be crushed beneath the odium of public opinion."

One element in such a persuasion campaign—at least in Missouri, where some antislavery residents were pushing vainly for a convention to consider amending the state constitution to ban slavery—was to demonstrate slavery's toll on the economy, Lovejoy asserted. Echoing an argument frequently made by antislavery activists about slave states in general, he asserted that slavery was holding back Missouri's development, and that ending it would "soon place her in the front rank along with the most favoured of her sister states."

Lovejoy returned to the same economic point a month later, when he described a boat journey on the Mississippi that took him within view of the Illinois side. Someone on board said, "That is a land of liberty!"

Such an observation was evidence, Lovejoy said, that "the atmosphere of slavery is an unnatural one for Americans to live in. The institution is repugnant to the very first principles of liberty." Lovejoy said he did not begrudge Illinois's emerging prosperity, but why didn't Missouri share in that progress? "Alas! The single word SLAVERY, tells us why," he wrote. Slavery was impeding Missouri's developments in "art, science, and the habits of social life, which mark a rapidly advancing community," Lovejoy said, "but they can never be ours." In his mind, slavery represented both a moral offense and a millstone. He pointed to the way Britain had passed legislation two years earlier to emancipate slaves in its West Indies colonies as proof that "gradual abolition is safe, practicable and expedient."

But by year's end, Lovejoy was attracting the kind of attention that could spell trouble in slavery country. Although he continued to espouse a cautious approach to emancipation, Lovejoy's growing outspokenness had become a source of worry to fellow St. Louis residents, many of whom probably cared little whether his brand of antislavery was of a gradualist or immediatist stripe. It all amounted to troublemaking. The *Observer* now regularly carried items about slavery, many of them from the exchange papers that came in sacks of mail from the East Coast, where the growing abolitionist movement was now making liberal use of the printing press to spread its calls for emancipation.

Meanwhile, Lovejoy's own writings also reflected the change that was taking place in his thinking. Slavery continued to rise on his roster of moral affronts, alongside drinking and violating the Sabbath. His circle of acquaintances included some others in Missouri who had vigorously taken up the cause of antislavery, including Nelson, the eccentric revivalist preacher. Lovejoy, in his role as a Presbyterian minister, was also now pushing the church itself to throw its weight behind ending slavery, a politically risky move for a skittish institution that had long sought to avoid possible rifts.

His efforts attracted the support of like-minded churchmen, including one who would become a critical ally later: Edward Beecher, son of the

Protestant leader Lyman Beecher. The younger Beecher had, like Lovejoy, moved to the frontier to educate and "evangelize" the West—in Beecher's case as president of a newly founded Illinois College across the river in Jacksonville, Illinois. Lovejoy discussed his antislavery viewpoints with Beecher and other faculty during a visit to the college, and Beecher was clearly moved by Lovejoy's attempts to get the church in Missouri to adopt antislavery resolutions. (In the meantime, in Beecher's Illinois, the body representing the state's presbyteries sought to toe a middle ground by condemning slavery as a "great evil," but also denouncing abolitionists for "unjustifiable" methods.) Beecher told Lovejoy that if even religious men still weren't persuaded to take a strong stand against slavery, "it is time that someone teach them."

Perhaps more disturbing to many residents of St. Louis were items in the *Observer* that now appeared to veer dangerously close to abolitionism. On October 1, 1835, Lovejoy published in full the declaration of principles of the American Anti-Slavery Society, the New York–based abolitionist group that had been founded two years earlier by an amalgam of activists, including militants such as Garrison and avatars of the benevolent empire led by Arthur and Lewis Tappan, along with justice-minded Quaker reformers and others. When the founding convention was held in Philadelphia in December 1833, more than two dozen students from Lovejoy's alma mater, Waterville College, sent letters backing the society's goal of freeing slaves without sending them out of the country. The abolitionist group was deeply influenced by Christian revivalist thinking and had targeted slavery as a sin demanding to be attacked without delay.

* * *

IT BEARS REMEMBERING THAT human bondage, so often treated as a distasteful given, was actually a source of considerable moral anguish in early America, where the first shipload of captured Black Africans landed in the Jamestown colony in Virginia in 1619. During the colonial era, certain Quakers, such as the educator Anthony Benezet, and other religious-minded critics wielded moral and philosophical objections against slavery as an offense to God and to the Enlightenment ideals of equality and liberty that provided the intellectual scaffolding for the call for independence. The nation's founders wrestled with how to deal with the country's seven hundred thousand enslaved people, but in the end they wrote a Constitution that essentially gave its blessing without ever mentioning slaves or slavery (indeed, the country's architects lent the South outsize political power through the three-fifths provision, rendering the institution of slavery even more difficult to dislodge at some future date).

Antislavery agitation went largely dormant during the first three decades of the 1800s, after most Northern states ended slavery. During this period, the bulk of the activity aimed at urging emancipation took place in the states of the upper South, such as Virginia, Kentucky, and Tennessee. The colonization movement was a balm for some consciences, but its supporters' most evident result may have been in promoting, even in the North, the notion of Black people's racial inferiority. This belief would help relegate abolitionists to a radical fringe.

In the states farther to the south, where the profitability of the cotton economy had exploded since the invention of the cotton gin, slavery's grip would grow tighter and the region's efforts to protect it more determined by 1830, aided by an alliance with Northern business and political interests. Then, in 1831, the same year that Garrison helped ignite the abolitionist movement when he began publishing the *Liberator*, the slave revolt in Southampton County, Virginia, led by Nat Turner, sent a terrifying chill throughout the slavery states. The message was clear: any challenge to slavery represented an existential threat.

This revived antislavery movement of the 1830s, drawing on the moral ardor of the Garrisonians and business wiles of the Tappans, assigned itself the task of agitating the issue of slavery through the printing and dissemination of more than one million antislavery pamphlets and illustrated journals, circulation of antislavery petitions, and deployment of a small army of traveling lecturers, such as Theodore Dwight Weld, one of the greatest of the movement's foot soldiers. Many of the antislavery society's efforts were aimed at changing public opinion, including that of enslavers, through a strategy of social rebuke that its adherents called "moral suasion."

Sectional lines hardened. Garrison's attacks on the colonization society as "pernicious, cruel and delusive," plus the growing hostility toward colonization on the part of free Black people in the North, eroded the gradualist's strategy's appeal as a feel-good middle path for dismantling slavery. Meantime, antislavery sentiment in the South, which once had been quite freely expressed, was now almost never uttered in public. Even in the North, abolitionists were typically viewed as wild-eyed radicals intent on destroying the Union and frequently were hounded by mobs or greeted with hurled rocks and eggs as they attempted to hold meetings. Although abolitionism remained a marginal movement, hundreds of sympathetic groups sprang up in cities and small towns across the North. By 1838 more than 250,000 Americans would join the American Anti-Slavery Society.

Not everyone in the organization was cut from the same cloth as Garrison, whose outspoken approach had defined abolitionism since he launched the *Liberator* and rankled people like Lovejoy with his famous takedown of colonization. (As recently as late 1834, Lovejoy told his brother Joseph that his disdain for Garrison was so thorough that "I seldom permit myself to write the name.... How can you hold communion with such a foul-mouthed fellow?") By late 1835, the society also had taken on the reputation of a dangerous interloper as a result of its campaign to use the U.S. mail to send tens of thousands of pamphlets and journals to clergymen, politicians, and editors—even, remarkably, those in slave states. In addition to the mail campaign, the group was cranking up renewed efforts in the North to mobilize activists—including women, who threw themselves into American politics for the first time—to circulate petitions in their hometowns calling upon Congress to end slavery in the District of Columbia. Both of those drives generated widespread fury across the South, and its political leaders sought ways to smother what they depicted as attempts by outsiders to stir slaves to violent insurrection, such as the Turner Revolt in Southampton.

Lovejoy was not a member of the antislavery society, but by printing its principles in the *Observer*, he was, in effect, airing its propaganda behind enemy lines—in a slave state. What's more, Lovejoy declared in an introductory note, he found little with which to disagree in the group's declaration, which called upon Congress to abolish slavery in the nation's capital, even though it conceded that the authority to ban slavery in the states rested solely with them. The declaration characterized slavery as "sinful," saying it was the duty of enslavers to immediately emancipate their slaves—a course it called "wise and safe." The document was hardly incendiary. Lovejoy said he took issue only with the provision calling upon slaveholders to immediately free their slaves. He wrote that he would reword it to say that emancipation should be *"immediately commenced, and carried on to its completion as fast as the welfare of the whole* community would admit." In other words, freeing of the slaves could begin now, but unfold over time according to a still-undefined timetable—a position that, in fact, echoed the approach of many abolitionists, who held varying definitions of the word "immediate."

Lovejoy was careful to point out, however, that he found the antislavery society's methods overly confrontational. He said its language was often too "harsh, denunciatory" to change minds. Instead, he recommended, antislavery activists should "say, in the language of kindness to the slaveholder, 'Come now and let us reason together.'" The fruits of such an approach, Lovejoy concluded, would be the "gradual but sure" removal of slavery from the entire nation. The editor believed that a peaceful path to end slavery was possible if only the two sides could be brought to see the attendant moral issues through the same lens.

Other suspicions about Lovejoy's abolitionist leanings were already swirling in Missouri. A month before he published the antislavery society's principles, Lovejoy had caused a stir after shipping a box of Bibles to Jefferson City in his role as a distribution agent of the American Bible Society. When the box was opened, it was discovered that stuffed around the Bibles were various newspapers that had apparently served as packing material. One of those papers was the *Emancipator*, the house organ of the American Anti-Slavery Society. Was Lovejoy smuggling abolitionist literature under the guise of passing out Bibles? A religious friend in Jefferson City wrote to Lovejoy to describe the tense atmosphere there and warned him that the Bible and tract societies must keep their work in the slave state strictly apart from that of abolitionists or risk having their agents tossed out of town. "There was a spark which could be blown up to a blast with little encouragement," the friend wrote, urging Lovejoy to act "with great caution."

Lovejoy denied having knowingly shipped the *Emancipator*, saying he had never sent it, or any other abolitionist publication, to anyone in Missouri. The editor then pivoted swiftly from denial to defiance. Lovejoy said that although he did not send the offending newspaper, "I claim the right to send ten thousand of them if I choose, to as many of my fellow-citizens. Whether I will exercise that right or not is for *me*, and not for the *mob*, to decide."

Murmured concerns about Lovejoy and his position on slavery grew more audible, particularly after the October 1 publication of the anti-slavery society's declaration of principles. Even the editor's financial backers feared a backlash that could jeopardize the safety of the *Observer*. In a telling indication of this fraught atmosphere, a group of nine of Lovejoy's friends and supporters—including William Potts, the clergyman who once urged him to become a minister and who had presided at the Lovejoys' marriage—pressed him to drop any discussion of slavery in the newspaper. "The public mind is greatly excited. . . . Indeed, we have reason to believe that violence is even now meditated against the 'Observer Office,'" the group warned in a letter to Lovejoy four days after he published the antislavery document. The prudent course now, the group counseled, was to ignore his own impulses and "pass over in silence everything connected with the subject of Slavery."

The owners took matters into their own hands. At the time, Lovejoy was away attending a Presbyterian gathering, and in his absence they placed a notice in the *Observer* announcing "an entire suspension of all controversy upon the exciting subject of Slavery. . . . [N]othing upon the subject will appear in its columns, during the absence of the Editor." Two weeks later, on October 22, with Lovejoy at a separate meeting of the Missouri synod in the town of Marion, the *Observer*'s proprietors published a new notice in the face of rumors that "certain evil disposed persons" planned a violent attack against the newspaper. The owners declared their opposition to "the mad schemes of the Abolitionists" and pleaded with community members to rule out an assault on the paper. "We call upon all prudent men to pause and reflect upon the probable consequences of such a step—there is nothing to justify it," they wrote, suggesting the use of force to resist any attack.

In Marion, where Lovejoy's spiritual guide David Nelson now presided over a college that was developing a reputation as a den of pro-abolition teachers, the editor ran into a different form of resistance. A few weeks earlier, he had persuaded representatives of Presbyterian congregations near St. Louis to back a series of resolutions in opposition to slavery—a well-timed show of church support for Lovejoy at a time when critics were circling. But the reception to Lovejoy's resolutions at the statewide gathering in Marion was decidedly less friendly. This time, conservatives were swayed by a church elder from St. Louis who argued that the Missouri church should denounce any form of abolitionism, "or the Presbyterian

Church would be destroyed in Missouri," Lovejoy would later report. Although most of the ministers backed Lovejoy's antislavery resolutions, he lost the vote of lay elders and the measures went down in defeat. The Missouri church could not be expected to back him if Lovejoy insisted on striking at slavery.

As Lovejoy prepared to return home after the synod gathering, word arrived from St. Louis of a terrible commotion: Two white men from Illinois allegedly had ushered a group of slaves from St. Louis to safety across the Mississippi River, but were seized and taken to Missouri. There, a group of sixty townspeople took turns whipping the men until they confessed—up to two hundred lashes in total—after voting against hanging them. The men, named Fuller and Bridges, were returned to the Illinois side alive, but the incident served to heighten fears among slaveholders that the real aim of abolitionists was to stir slaves to insurrection. The *Missouri Republican* decried the "reckless and wicked interference" of abolitionists, saying they "must be met, *promptly*, *efficiently*, and *decisively*." The newspaper went on: "The time has arrived when the citizens of St. Louis must not only speak, but *act*."

The whipping episode reminded everyone with a fearsome clarity that a so-called new code of vigilante justice would mete out swift punishment against anyone who dared act on antislavery impulses. A month earlier, Lovejoy had learned of an aborted plot by two men to tar and feather him as he returned from a revival meeting in the town of Potosi. But the would-be attackers gave up and went home after lying in wait for half a day, Lovejoy learned. Besides that, someone had printed and circulated a handbill calling for a mob to tear down the *Observer*'s office.

Now, Lovejoy was setting out for home by horse under conditions that appeared even more explosive. He learned that "the whole city was in commotion," as colleagues in Marion warned him against returning to St. Louis. In a sign of how gravely they viewed the prevailing conditions, one of the friends rode alongside for seventy miles, urging Lovejoy to avoid the city. Lovejoy turned the matter over in his mind. He worried that Celia, whose health was ever in a delicate state, would be undone if serious harm came to him. Even as he rode away from Marion, Celia lay ailing at the home of her mother in St. Charles. Lovejoy was also falling ill. In his weakened state, he proceeded to St. Charles to be with his wife and recuperate. St. Louis, and whatever troubles were convulsing it, could wait.

* * *

WHEN LOVEJOY RETURNED TO St. Louis a few days later, he found the city in "a state of dreadful alarm and excitement." He was dismayed to learn that during his weeks-long absence, the *Observer* had, in his words, been "muzzled" by his erstwhile backers, including his old friend, Reverend Potts. Meanwhile, a rival newspaper had tagged Lovejoy as an abolitionist, and the church elder who had spoken out against Lovejoy's antislavery proposals at the synod meeting in Marion was now accusing him of acting against the will of the Presbyterian church. Lovejoy was also now learning of the earlier stirrings against the *Observer*. And if all that weren't enough, men were approaching him on the street to warn that he wasn't safe, even during the day.

Isolated, Lovejoy faced mounting calls from the city's political elite to go silent on the slavery issue. On October 24, some of St. Louis's leading lights, including former mayor William Carr Lane, called an unofficial public meeting to stanch the building tensions. Although Lovejoy wasn't identified, he was unquestionably the main target. The gathering agreed on a number of resolutions, including one that portrayed abolitionism as a threat to the Union and another accusing abolitionists of promoting "amalgamation," or racial mixing, as a "preposterous" and "repugnant doctrine" whose practice would toss America back into the Dark Ages. The assembly recognized a constitutional right to free speech, but said that freedom did not extend to criticisms of slavery—spoken or in the press—because such attacks in a slave state were "seditious, and calculated to incite insurrection & anarchy." And, in a final flourish aimed at blunting moral objections to human bondage, the group turned to the Bible to argue that the ancient prophets owned slaves, and thus had given it sanction. "[W]e consider Slavery as it now exists in the United States, as sanctioned by the sacred Scriptures," the group agreed.

Lovejoy was hemmed in by forces on many sides: pro-slavery politicians, certain St. Louis newspapers, the ruffians he called "hurrah boys," conservative Protestant churchmen, and the city's Catholic hierarchy, with which he was now engaged in a pretty constant war of words. His friends thought he should stay away—only Celia had endorsed his return to St. Louis. ("She said go, if you think duty calls you," Lovejoy would recall.) Lovejoy's next move was perhaps the riskiest response he could have chosen: he raised his pen and went to battle. In the November 5 issue of the *Observer*, Lovejoy offered up a long, manifesto-like public letter that blended an impassioned defense of his right to speak with a thunderous attack on slavery. The piece, titled "To My Fellow Citizens," surged with angry energy and represented a remarkable declaration of the path Lovejoy now intended to follow—a course from which it would be difficult to turn back.

Lovejoy began gently. "It is not my design or wish to offend anyone," he wrote, "but simply to maintain my rights as a republican citizen, freeborn, of these United States, and to defend, fearlessly, the cause of TRUTH AND RIGHTEOUSNESS." He lashed out at the actions of mobs, saying he likely would have been whipped, or tarred and feathered, if he had been in Jefferson City when copies of the *Emancipator* were pulled from the crate of Bibles. "I am not aware that any law of my country forbids my sending what documents I please to a friend or citizen," he wrote.

Lovejoy turned to the resolutions of the October 24 citizen meeting. He denied any attempt to sway slaves into action, saying he recognized that he had the right to communicate with their slaveholders alone. But he then invoked the U.S. and Missouri state constitutions to defend his right to write about any subject he chose. "Here, then, I find my warrant for using, as Paul did, all freedom of speech," Lovejoy said. He laid out the slippery-slope argument: attempts to gag the press on one topic would lead inexorably to limitations on other writing that might be deemed unpopular. "If you give ground a single inch, there is no stopping place," Lovejoy warned. "I deem it, therefore, my duty to take my stand upon the Constitution. . . .We have slaves, it is true, but *I* am not one."

When he turned his attention to slavery, Lovejoy dispensed with the usual generalities concerning the South's "peculiar institution" and instead sought to make real the outrages perpetrated in the cold facts of buying, selling, and lording over other human beings. He was giving no quarter to those looking to the Bible to justify their support for slavery. "I have not words to express my utter abhorrence of such a sentiment. My soul detests it, my heart sickens over it," he wrote. Slavery, he wrote, was "a system which tolerates the existence of a class of men whose professed business is to go about from house to house, tearing husband and wife, parent and child asunder, chaining their victims together, and then driving them with a whip, like so many mules, to a distant market, then to be disposed of to the highest bidder."

He conjured more grim images, alluding darkly to sexual violence—the "nameless pollutions, the unspeakable abominations"—that would trail these slaves to their miserable cabins. Such horrors could *not* have been sanctioned by God, Lovejoy insisted. These were remarkable words to publish from within a city that itself served as a shipment point for shackled slaves destined "down the river" to the Deep South. Unlike Garrison, firing indignant broadsides from his Boston print shop for an audience of Black readers and like-minded white people in the North, Lovejoy sat firmly within slavery country, jabbing provocatively at the consciences of his own neighbors. "I have appeared openly among you, in your streets and market-places, and now I openly and publicly throw myself into your hands," Lovejoy wrote. "I can die at my post, but I cannot desert it." He closed his column with a rather unusual appeal to his foes: if you must do harm, please spare the newspaper office, whose owners and young printers would end up unfairly punished. "If the popular vengeance needs a victim, I offer myself a willing sacrifice," Lovejoy offered. "To any assault that may be made upon me, I declare it my purpose to make no resistance."

But if he awaited a retaliatory blow, Lovejoy found quite a different response to his emotional column. He sensed a shift in opinion in his favor during the weeks that followed, and sounded almost surprised when he wrote to his mother later that month. "I am not yet *hung up*," Lovejoy wrote, with jarring bluntness. "Neither have I been tarred and feathered, nor yet whipped, nor indeed, in any way molested bodily. . . . We are getting quiet again. The *Lynchites* are getting ashamed of their doings."

The *Observer*'s owners decided to dump Lovejoy now that his column had made it clear that he planned to continue writing about slavery. The proprietors asked him to step down, and Lovejoy acceded. ("I gave up, and thought my work done in St. Louis," he recalled.) But an unexpected turn would help keep him in charge. The newspaper's financing arrangement had left a $500 mortgage in the hands of a lender named Moore, who surprised everyone when he chose to keep the paper rather than sell the note at auction—and then asked Lovejoy to return to the editor's chair. It was a stunning twist, one that would continue to lend Lovejoy a platform and keep the controversy burning in St. Louis. "It was as if life from the dead, as light out of thickest darkness," Lovejoy wrote.

To his delight, Lovejoy found that his bold words in the *Observer* had struck a chord among some members of the community, and even drew in some new subscribers. Still, the paper's finances remained a daily challenge, and his commission as a roving preacher for the American Home Missionary Society came to just $200 yearly. "My trials here are exceedingly great . . . I have much to endure, in a thousand ways," he would write. The most promising source of new support most likely lay across the river in Illinois, where Lovejoy had already found a reservoir of antislavery opinion among people such as Beecher and his colleagues at Illinois College. Beecher, impressed by Lovejoy's attempts to get the Presbyterians to speak out against slavery, pledged $20 for the newspaper and said his faculty would likely raise another $100 to $200. (Lovejoy's efforts to win condemnation of slavery had a big impact on Beecher, who would later pinpoint 1835 as the moment when he adopted a view of immediate emancipation as "philosophical and safe," after deciding that gradualism was "fallacious.")

Because of the ongoing upheaval, Lovejoy very nearly left for Alton in late 1835—more than six months before he would make the move for good. Moore, the *Observer*'s new owner, directed Lovejoy to relocate the *Observer* to Alton for safety reasons, but then changed his mind almost immediately after Lovejoy had crossed the river to meet with fellow church members there. The editor returned home to several months of what might best be described as a cold peace in St. Louis: Lovejoy kept bringing up slavery in his paper, while detractors continued to grumble in public about his stances. But the violence that had seemed inevitable in autumn didn't occur.

Amid this frosty calm, Lovejoy seemed unsure exactly how to define himself on the question of slavery. No longer was he advocating the colonization strategy of his Princeton past. In the face of the violent threats against him, it was becoming harder to envision, as he once had, that it would be possible to calmly persuade enslavers to free their bondmen. He was not certain these people could, or would, be swayed. But he continued to steer clear of a more far-reaching form of abolitionism—one with equal rights as its goal—that was being promoted by Garrison and now followed by Lovejoy's mother, Betsey, and brother Joseph. "I am not an abolitionist—at least not such a one as you are," Lovejoy affirmed in a letter to Joseph shortly before the November 5 publication of his "To My Fellow Citizens" appeal. Yet the brutality of the slavery regime was also taking a toll. Lovejoy was horrified over a pair of publicized cases in St. Louis in which white residents had severely whipped their female slaves, one of them to death. He found bitter irony in the fact that neither abuser had been punished, while he—a mere scribbler—had to fear retribution for daring to call slavery a moral wrong.

The campaign to silence him was having an effect—but not the one Lovejoy's critics intended. Instead of bringing him to heel, the editor's opponents seemed to be driving him deeper into the arms of antislavery. By January 1836, two months after his letter to Joseph, Lovejoy privately admitted to a fellow Presbyterian minister, the Reverend Edwin F. Hatfield, that his views on slavery had "changed materially." Hatfield, who had once lived in St. Louis but moved to New York, was "an abolitionist of the first water," Lovejoy wrote approvingly. "Well so am I." He took pains to note a distinction between their views, however. "You have lived in a slave state and you know that practical emancipation cannot be effected in a minute," Lovejoy cautioned.

But then he said something that seemed to put him squarely in the abolitionist camp: Lovejoy declared slavery a "sin." This was no accident. Fired by evangelicalism, abolition activists such as Weld had chosen to characterize the continuation of the slavery system as a "sin," rather than as some abstract "curse" or "evil" that had been left behind by the British. The purpose here was to prod Americans into individual action. Any sin, after all, demanded to be addressed immediately, directly, by every moral person. (Some labeled this approach as "gradual emancipation, immediately begun.") Lovejoy's use of the term—even in a private correspondence with a friend—suggested that he shared this urgency. But he acknowledged such work would take time. His solution: "begin the work of abolition immediately, and to carry it out in good faith." His timetable? "As fast as it can be done."

CHAPTER EIGHT

A JUDGE
NAMED LAWLESS

THE MOB'S KILLING OF the boatman McIntosh in the spring of 1836 had created a public relations mess for St. Louis, as word spread far beyond Missouri through the exchanges of newspapers, not least Lovejoy's *Observer*. The slaying also became exhibit A in Lovejoy's now-regular denunciations of mob violence, but it presented a tricky legal problem. McIntosh was dead, so there was no way to prosecute him for the stabbing death of a sheriff's officer and wounding of the second. But who would be punished for killing McIntosh? With so many people involved in the sudden eruption of crowd violence, where did legal responsibility rest for this monstrous lynching by bonfire? And at a time when crowd violence was flaring across the country—quite often aimed against the abolitionists—how would the city's justice system deal with its own mob atrocity? These questions fell to a St. Louis judge named, incongruously enough, Lawless.

Luke E. Lawless was an immigrant from Ireland, a former colonel in Napoleon's army and a tart-tongued jurist with a knack for landing in controversy. Lawless, then fifty-five, was no stranger to combat. He carried scars from the battlefield incurred in the fight against England and walked with a limp from an injury sustained in a duel in France. (It would not be the last time Lawless took part in a duel: in 1817, he served as a second to future U.S. senator Thomas Hart Benton of Missouri in not one but two duels against rival Charles Lucas. The do-over confrontation, on Bloody Island, would leave Lucas dead.)

Lawless was granted citizenship in 1822 and sworn in as a lawyer in federal court in St. Louis by U.S. judge James H. Peck, handling speculators' claims to the former Spanish land grant in the upper Mississippi Valley. Lawless and Peck faced off as foes in a major legal battle in 1826 after Lawless took to the newspaper to criticize a Peck ruling on land titles. In return, Peck ruled Lawless guilty of contempt of court, briefly jailed him, and then suspended the lawyer from practicing for eighteen months. At this point, Lawless looked for help from the U.S. Congress by requesting that Peck be impeached. It took Lawless four years of pressure to get the House of Representatives to impeach Peck, but the federal judge was finally acquitted in a publicized Senate trial. Lawless won a partial victory, however: Congress quickly passed a law barring judges from using contempt charges to punish conduct that took place outside the courtroom.

In early 1835, Lawless was named by Missouri governor Daniel Dunklin to serve as a circuit judge—a roving position that required him to travel on horseback to hear cases around the St. Louis region. The slender Lawless was known as a gifted linguist—besides English, he was said to be fluent in French, German, and Spanish. On the bench, he won a reputation for a military bearing, keen logic, and a biting verbal style. "Irony, sarcasm, and wit were his weapons, and he used them with an unsparing hand," recalled one chronicler. But by late 1835, the *Missouri Republican* was declaring him "most unfit" for the bench after a dispute over Lawless's conduct in handling a dueling case.

Lawless was the judge in charge when the St. Louis grand jury convened on May 16, 1836—a little over two weeks after the murder—to investigate and consider possible criminal charges in the McIntosh matter. Lawless began the session by running through his analysis of the various legal issues, saying that to simply toss the matter into the laps of jurors would look "timid and cautious" and "unworthy of a judge." On the question of McIntosh's role, he said, there was little to ponder. Although there was no doubt that the boatman had stabbed the two officers, his subsequent death had rendered moot any prosecution. "The murderer is no more—his ashes have been scattered to the winds," the judge noted.

But it was a more ticklish matter to determine how to handle McIntosh's death—"the destruction of the wretched murderer"—at the hands of the mob. Lawless cited the Constitution's guarantee of a fair trial and prohibition of cruel and unusual punishment, noting that McIntosh had been dragged, without a trial, from a jail where he had been placed by authority of a magistrate's warrant. Then, Lawless pointed out, McIntosh was chained to a tree and burned alive. Lawless condemned the action, saying there could be no justification for anyone to strip McIntosh of his right to be heard on the question of his guilt or mental condition. "I should be unworthy of the place I occupy did I not raise my voice from the bench of justice in solemn protest against such a proceeding," he told the jurors. "If the Constitution and the law come to be disregarded by the multitude, there can be no longer any safety for life or property." So far, Lawless sounded no less disturbed by the mob's action than Lovejoy had been in condemning "mobism" in his *Observer* column.

But what to do about those guilty of having taken part in the killing? Lawless conceded that he had been unable to find guidance in case law—based on his research, no similar matter had come before a court. In the absence of legal precedent, the judge had come to his own conclusion on how to chart the grand jury's course. The question, Lawless said, boiled down to this: was the killing of McIntosh "the act of the 'few' or the act

of the 'many'"? If the act was of a few identifiable persons, he said, the
answer would be to indict them. But Lawless maintained that it would
be a different matter if the killing were instead the act of the many, "of
congregated thousands, seized upon and impelled by that mysterious,
metaphysical and almost electrical phrenzy, which, in all ages and nations,
had hurried on the infuriated multitude to deeds of death and destruction." Under those circumstances, the case was beyond the jurisdiction
of the grand jury—and, indeed, Lawless declared, "beyond the reach of
human law."

The judge wondered aloud how criminal suspects would be identified
from among a multitude and how a crowd of "two or three thousand" could be
tried in a manner that bore any resemblance to fair. A despot could
punish a symbolic number from among the crowd as a warning to all, but
this was not possible in America, he said. Lawless pointed to the recent
mob torching of a Catholic convent in Charlestown, Massachusetts, as an
example of violence fueled by bigotry that produced few criminal indictments and just a single conviction. (Interestingly, Lawless used "mob"
in describing the Charlestown case, but not when he spoke about the
McIntosh killing.) By contrast, he argued, the St. Louis "multitude" had
acted not out of bigotry or hatred, but under the effects of a "generous
excitement" touched off by witnessing an officer of the law, a fellow resident, slain before them. "Is it not something to be allowed for human
sympathies in those appalling circumstances?" Lawless asked.

It was clear he was moving toward clearing the crowd of responsibility,
but he had another point to make first—and this one implicated Lovejoy.
To punish McIntosh's killers would distract from what the man had done,
and from "similar atrocities" committed in Missouri and other states by
"individuals of negro blood against their white brethren," Lawless argued.
And those who were guilty of igniting such violent impulses in McIntosh
and other Black people were none other than the abolitionists, offered
Lawless, himself a slave owner. His evidence against the abolitionists? As

the chained McIntosh burned, Lawless said, he let loose "rabid denunciations of the white man" and "professions of hostility to the whole white
race"—an outpouring of sentiment that could only have been inspired by
abolitionists. (Lawless's detailed account of what McIntosh said as he died
has led some historians to suggest that he may have been present at the
lynching.) To Lawless's way of thinking, the murder of Deputy Hammond
was, "morally speaking, only the blind instrument in the hands of the
abolitionist fanatics." It was the abolitionists who were at fault for inciting
McIntosh to his initial burst of violence.

Lawless then held up a copy of the *Observer* that contained Lovejoy's
account of the murder as well as a pair of antislavery sermons that had
been written by New England preachers. Lawless read aloud from the
offending passages: "Slavery is a sin and ought to be abandoned. . . .The
slave-holder would suppress discussion, because discussion would blast
his iniquitous system of oppression." Such language served to encourage
slaves to violence, the judge asserted, and Missouri lay vulnerable: "The
negroes are numerous—they are quartered on our farms, in our families."
They would need only to make alliance with hostile native tribes to present
a serious threat, he warned.

Lawless turned now to the culpability of the press, which he viewed as
a spear pointed at the heart of civil order. "I can see no reason why the
Press should be made a means of wide-spread mischief," Lawless said. "It
seems to me absurd to contend that the law should not protect society from
abuses of the Press, as it may from the abuse of any other means which
perverse or misguided men can wield for the purpose of harm either to the
individual or to the mass." Lawless, a Catholic, then took aim at Protestants like Lovejoy who employed religious arguments to criticize slavery.
He said such people were in the grip of a "religious hallucination" that
had caused them to believe they were "special agents" of God. "Are we to
be the victims of those sanctimonious madmen?" Lawless asked, in conclusion. In a few nimble hops of logic, Lawless had forded the challenging

waters of the legal questions that lay before the grand jury. His conclusion seemed clear: if anyone deserved blame for the mob's heinous impulses, it was not the frenzied mob, but rather Lovejoy and his publishing ilk.

The grand jury issued no indictments in the lynching of McIntosh.

* * *

LAWLESS'S DISQUISITION REPRESENTED ONE man's thinking, but it offered a revealing window into the justifications for a national wave of crowd violence that had spiked at alarming levels during the previous year. The tumultuous Jacksonian era, with its exaltation of popular will and the disruptions of urban growth and immigration, saw extrajudicial violence surge as never before, particularly during the years from 1833 to 1837. The historian David Grimsted counted 147 riots in 1835 alone, a year he calls "the crest of rioting in the United States." Mobbing, as it was called, was not merely a regional phenomenon, or one limited to cities, but rather "a feature of American life," writes the scholar Leonard L. Richards. The 1830s that Lovejoy inhabited was a rough decade, indeed.

The aims of such mobs were widely varied—squads of vigilantes hit everything from gambling and prostitution houses to mixed-race schools and the Catholic convent cited by Lawless. But the attacks were often—at times, mostly—aimed against antislavery activists. Anti-abolitionist riots and vigilante attacks were especially intense in Northern cities, where mobs burst into churches and meeting halls in order to disrupt organizational meetings and lectures. Racism often provided the fuel.

The Tappan brothers, for example, had the dubious honor of being set upon multiple times. They were chased by a hostile crowd in 1833 as they tried to hold a meeting in New York City to organize the American Anti-Slavery Society. Months later, in 1834, the philanthropists, who were white, were targeted again during a week of violence cheered on by the city's anti-abolitionist press. Editors such as James Watson Webb had stoked public fears that the abolitionists were promoting racial mixing. Amid the turmoil came rumors that the crowd planned to tar and feather Lewis Tappan, forcing him to flee his home in lower Manhattan. The attackers sacked Tappan's home, tossing his belongings into the street, and set it on fire. Marauders also attacked the homes of a dozen Black families. A separate mob moved against the store of Tappan's brother, Arthur, but was interrupted by members of the city militia and the mayor. Tappan ally Elizur Wright took to barricading his door "with bars and planks an inch thick" after so-called vigilance committees in the South offered rewards for the capture of well-known abolitionists in the North. (A Louisiana group offered $50,000 for anyone who brought in Arthur Tappan, dead or alive.)

A year later, in October 1835, a Boston mob, enraged that the British abolitionist George Thompson planned to speak at an antislavery meeting there, forced William Lloyd Garrison into hiding, then captured the editor and paraded him in the streets, a rope looped around him. Aggressors grabbed at Garrison, tearing his clothes, and shouted for him to be hanged in Boston Common. He was rescued from the mob's grasp by city constables, led by Mayor Theodore Lyman. That same day, a group of about eighty leading citizens—bankers, lawyers, and businessman—stormed into a Presbyterian church in Utica, New York, to disrupt a meeting of the New York Anti-Slavery Society. It was but one of a number of cases in which violent anti-abolitionist actions were orchestrated by a local elite—so-called gentlemen of property and standing. In addition to facing rioters and angry mobs, abolitionist lecturers such as Theodore Weld regularly were assaulted by rocks and eggs. There were dozens of such incidents across the North, where abolitionism continued to be viewed by most as a threat to the Union and its advocates as reckless incendiaries.

The mobbing phenomenon was seldom deadly in the North, though Southern mobs, which set upon Black people as alleged insurrectionists or simply to intimidate, were known to resort to mutilation and torture that far more frequently resulted in death. The cruelties were often baroque in their excess: slaves were whipped, hanged, tied in a swamp to be bitten to death by mosquitoes, baked in an oven, mauled by dogs, decapitated—their heads plunked on poles to send a terrifying message to others. Abolitionists took their lives in their hands when they ventured south, where mobs often held a semi-official status as local "vigilance committees" made up of leading citizens. Amos Dresser, a follower of Weld, was subjected to whipping in Nashville in August 1835, after antislavery newspapers and other materials were discovered in his carriage when he took it to be repaired. Dresser later recounted his "trial" by a vigilance committee and punishment by flogging: twenty lashes on his bare back. He was ringed by members of the vigilance committee and stripped of his clothing.

"I knelt to receive the punishment, which was inflicted by Mr. Braughton, the city officer, with a heavy cowskin. When the infliction ceased, an involuntary feeling of thanksgiving to God for the fortitude with which I had been enabled to endure it arose in my soul, to which I aloud began to give utterance. The death-like silence that prevailed for a moment was suddenly broken with loud exclamations, 'G—d d—n him, stop his praying.'"

* * *

HISTORIANS HAVE POINTED TO a variety of reasons for the remarkable rise of violent mobs—a phenomenon referred to at the time as "mobocracy" or "mobism." Ordinary politics were rough and often physical, and partisan newspapers helped whip up sectarian passions. Many American cities at the time lacked adequate, or any, police, which left citizens to take the law into their hands to enforce majority opinion. In addition, Americans drank copious quantities of liquor in the early 1800s—an average American over fifteen years old downed about seven gallons of alcoholic beverages a year, or triple today's rate for adults—and overindulgence sometimes served as an accelerant. Mobs, notably in Northern cities, could be spurred into violent action over fears of "amalgamation."

The most obvious reason for attacks on abolitionists is that the activists were seen by many as extremists intent on destroying the Union, or at least hurting business ties with the South. It was up to the rest of society—businessmen, anti-abolitionist newspapers, laborers—to bring them to heel. James Gordon Bennett, the virulently anti-abolitionist editor of the popular New York *Herald*, put it this way: "The abolitionists, a few thousand crazy-headed blockheads, have actually frightened fifteen million people out of their senses. So terribly scared are these fifteen million that the ordinary operation of laws against these evil-doers are thrown aside as too slow." In many instances, especially in acts against abolitionists, the "gentlemen of property and standing" saw themselves as enforcers of the majority's will during a time of flux—this during an era when Americans placed a high premium on making sure that newcomers and other members of a community conformed with the accepted way of life. Anyone who sought to disrupt that order became a threat to be eradicated, violently, if necessary. In this sense, leaders did not view their actions as unlawful: in some cases, they saw the use of violence against antislavery activists as a form of nuisance abatement to maintain the community's living standards, an idea that they held was solidly grounded in American legal principle.

* * *

LOVEJOY, CELIA, AND THEIR newborn son, Edward, had traveled to Pittsburgh to attend the 1836 Presbyterian general assembly when Lawless led the St. Louis grand jury through his reasoning that no one was legally to blame for the McIntosh murder because of the mob's "electric" frenzy. So the editor was gone when, soon after the judge's presentation, vandals broke into the *Observer*'s office, damaged the premises, and stole a batch of eight or nine "composing sticks." (Composing sticks were small metal trays used by printers of the time to arrange letters, one at a time, into lines of type that were then assembled into a full page for printing. To complete the process, the printer would apply ink and feed a sheet of paper, then pull hard on a lever to lower a heavy platen, which pressed the blank page against the inky letters to create the impression.) The following week, intruders again broke into the *Observer*, destroying enough type to force Lovejoy's stand-ins to use a smaller paper size. If Lawless had hoped to redirect ill will in the direction of the paper, someone seemed to be listening. The mobs were having their way.

Meanwhile, at the Pittsburgh gathering, Lovejoy had seen firsthand the philosophical fault line that was beginning to split his church over the slavery issue. The Presbyterian assembly had received numerous memorials and petitions urging the church to adopt an antislavery position but set aside the entire matter without discussion. That move prompted Lovejoy and nearly thirty other members to sign a letter protesting the body's handling of the issue. Upon arriving home to St. Louis in July after the long absence, Lovejoy announced that he was back "with health even better than when he left . . . and renewed purpose." Yet, besides the attacks on the *Observer* office, there had been other ominous signs that the climate in Missouri was growing more hostile. In May, Lovejoy's friend and spiritual guide David Nelson had been chased from the state for his antislavery views after a mob came after him while at a camp revival. To escape his pursuers, Nelson hid for days in the bushes and crept at night until he was escorted to safety by a pair of church members who smuggled him by dugout canoe to the Illinois side of the Mississippi River.

By the end of the month, Lovejoy would abandon Missouri, too. The thought of moving had been on his mind as local resentment grew and the possibility beckoned of better business prospects on the Illinois side. Lovejoy had yet to address Lawless's provocative comments to the grand jury of late May, but he had plenty to say. His published response to Lawless would serve as a coda to his life as an editor in St. Louis. In a single column, he managed to capture all the reasons—his determination to print freely, his loathing of mobs, his hostility toward foreign-born Catholics—that explained why his continued stay was almost surely untenable.

The column came out on July 21, two months after Lawless's speech to the grand jury and nearly three since the McIntosh killing itself. But the passage of time had done nothing to diminish Lovejoy's disgust over the entire chain of events, or over what he called the judge's "monstrous doctrines." He flung exclamation points across the page by the angry handful, as if dismay could somehow be conveyed through typographical excess. (When he cited Lawless's "electric-frenzy" passage asserting that the mob was too big to face criminal liability, Lovejoy finished the judge's sentence with no fewer than twelve exclamation points: "it is beyond the reach of human law!!!!!!!!!!!!") As he wrote, the editor knew something that his readers did not: this would be the *Observer*'s last edition in St. Louis. This was the same issue of the paper that contained his "removal" article announcing the shift to the Illinois side. Whatever bridges Lovejoy burned in St. Louis now would probably be of little use, anyway.

Lovejoy mocked Lawless's reasoning, saying that it implied that a crowd was legally permitted to commit a crime for which one or two perpetrators would be punishable. Lovejoy didn't stop at the legal rationale, though. Lawless, he argued, was hopelessly incapable of understanding U.S. legal principles because he was "a foreigner—a naturalized one it is true, but still to intents and purposes a foreigner." The judge was born and educated amid the turmoil of Ireland, Lovejoy wrote, and later had spent a formative period in the French army—poor preparation for comprehending the democratic principles of American constitutional law. "[H]is notions of practical justice, at once so novel to Americans, so absurd and so wicked, will have little influence with our sound hearted, home educated republicans" he argued. Here, Lovejoy introduced his companion criticism: Lawless's Catholic faith. "Judge Lawless is a Papist," Lovejoy wrote, "and in his

Charge we see the cloven foot of Jesuitism, peeping out from under the
veil of almost every paragraph. . . . Popery in its very essential principles
is incompatible with regulated, civil or religious liberty."

Anyone who had grown used to reading Lovejoy's commentary could
have anticipated his attack on Lawless's religion. Ever since Lovejoy
had begun publishing his newspaper nearly three years earlier, he had
regularly salted its pages with his own anti-Catholic screeds, along with
excerpted articles from other Protestant publications portraying "Popery"
or "Romanism" as a superstition-laded bastardization of true Christianity,
not to mention a potential threat to the ideals of American democracy. A
series of columns in the *Observer* called "Letters from Rome" took issue
with various aspects of Catholic belief and practice, from miracles and
vestments to the canonization of saints and the number of religious orders.
Lovejoy took aim at the idea of an infallible Church, "the doctrine of
passive obedience," and mocked as rank foolishness that anyone would
believe in transubstantiation—the belief that the bread and wine of the
Eucharist are converted into Christ's body and blood. ("He might as well
believe that fire is cold and ice is hot, or that a thing is and is not at the
same time," he once scoffed in a column.) Lovejoy enthusiastically joined
a chorus of Protestants in promoting an anti-Catholic trope widely circulated at the time: that convents were dens of licentiousness in which lustful
priests preyed upon young nuns for their carnal delights. "The Nunnery
has generally been neither more nor less than a seraglio for the friars of
the monestary," Lovejoy wrote.

Coupled with Lovejoy's deep suspicion of Catholicism was a corresponding concern over the supposed threat to the United States represented by foreign influences, most notably the pope and his Catholic
allies in Europe. Lovejoy pointed to countries such as Ireland to warn
of the turmoil that likely awaited the United States if Catholicism made
deeper inroads. The Mississippi Valley was a special focus of this worry,
amid expanding immigration and the overall westward flow of people. In

voicing harshly nativist views toward Catholics, Lovejoy was echoing the antagonistic line espoused by mainstream Protestant elders, who saw in Catholicism a conspiracy by hostile religious and antidemocratic forces to vanquish the young American nation.

It would be difficult to overstate the breadth of anti-Catholic sentiment that coursed through the country during the 1820s and 1830s, fanned by people such as Lyman Beecher and Samuel F. B. Morse, the inventor of the telegraph. The number of Catholics had risen markedly during the first decades of the century, almost entirely through immigration. Although the United States counted just seventy-five thousand Roman Catholics in 1810, the figure would reach one million by the end of the 1830s. To the guardians of American Protestantism, this swelling presence represented an existential threat to both Christianity and republicanism, and they sought to marshal their foot soldiers—organizations such as the American Bible Society—into a force that would meet the enemy where danger was greatest, in the West. Beecher's widely read book *A Plea for the West*, published in 1835, was a fevered call to arms against this dangerous European plot. Lovejoy saw the *Observer* as part of this holy army.

American readers seemed eager to gobble up such fare. Anti-Catholic newspapers had circulated for years in cities on the East Coast, and one of the best-selling books before the Civil War was the purported memoir in 1836 of a young nun forced into service as a sex slave for priests in a Montreal convent—a salacious and preposterous tale called *Awful Disclosures of Maria Monk*. In the end, the story proved to be a fraud promoted by anti-Catholics. (Lovejoy gave the book's publication limited ink in the *Observer*, but used the story as a way to cast suspicion on convent life in general.)

As one might expect, Lovejoy's frequent written assaults on Catholicism—he claimed to harbor no ill will toward individual Catholics, whom he saw as simply misguided—turned many people in St. Louis against him. The fast-growing city had been majority Catholic since the French settled it,

and by 1830, three thousand of its five thousand inhabitants were Catholic. Bishop Joseph Rosati supervised a fast expansion of churches and
schools and built a cathedral during Lovejoy's time in St. Louis. When
the cathedral was consecrated in October 1834, with celebratory cannon
blasts and a military-style parade featuring fifes and drums, Lovejoy's
response was to publish a scornful column by a writer with the pen name
"Waldo," a frequent contributor of anti-Catholic diatribes. In the piece,
Waldo derided the cathedral as ostentatious (and funded with foreign
money) and the consecration ceremony as a noisy violation of the Sabbath.

In response to the *Observer*'s regular denunciations, the St. Louis diocese
counterattacked through its own newspaper, the *Shepherd of the Valley*, by
fact-checking Lovejoy's descriptions of church rituals and blasting him as
a "forger and slanderer" and his hostile words as "sickly bile." The result
was a bitter newspaper war—Presbyterian versus Catholic—that may have
boosted sales but ultimately produced no clear winner, theologically
speaking. It also proved the wisdom of the old saw about picking a fight
with someone who buys ink by the barrel. By antagonizing the St. Louis
Catholic community and its primary mouthpiece, Lovejoy was poking a
bear, with no obvious means of escape. In a sense, the editor was employing
the *Observer* to do battle with overlapping foes: the city's majority Catholics
and its determined defenders of slavery. When the mobs threatened him
in late 1835, he assumed they were targeting him for his attacks on
Catholicism, not slavery. (It is impossible to confirm his hunch, since in all
likelihood the motivation was a combination of both.)

To Lovejoy, the two fights were closely related: Catholicism was hostile
to the notion of liberty, and its leaders served as apologists for a slavery
system he was coming increasingly to detest. "Popery and Freedom,
whether civil or religious, are incompatible with each other—they cannot
co-exist," Lovejoy had written in August 1835, nearly a full year earlier.
In truth, the Roman Catholic hierarchy seemed untroubled by slavery—it
had never denounced the institution, and seemed generally to accept its

standing as legal in the United States. Church thinkers viewed abolitionists as extremists and rejected the idea of slavery as a sin—placing them
squarely at odds with Protestant reformers who aimed to cleanse the nation
of human bondage.

This all made Lovejoy's response to the slave-owning Catholic judge
from Ireland a rather tidy assignment: Luke Lawless's foreign roots and
Catholic faith blinded him to the cause of liberty that was represented not
only by the slave but by the newspaper publisher as well. Lovejoy believed
that press freedom was endangered by the same flawed doctrine that had
permitted McIntosh's killers to walk free simply because they were many
people involved, not few. It was rule by mob. In his response to Lawless's
ruling, Lovejoy was practically issuing a dare to the mobs to come get him.
"[B]etter, far better, that the office of the 'Observer' should be scattered in
fragments to the four winds of heaven; yea, better that editor, printer, and
publishers, should be chained to the same tree as McIntosh, and share
his fate, than that the doctrines promulgated by Judge Lawless from the
bench should become prevalent in this community," Lovejoy wrote.

That very night, a crowd of men went through the streets of St. Louis,
beating drums and calling for recruits. When the mob had swelled to 150
to 200 men, they made their way to the *Observer* office. A smaller group
among them broke open the door and set to work trying to obliterate the
infernal newspaper. The vandals tossed type into the street and hurled
work stands, a sign, and other contents into the river, or smashed them on
the street outside. John Lovejoy's trunk, with his clothes and $4 in cash,
was heaved into the water. The attackers also tried to destroy the heavy
iron press, but in their haste failed. Even still, the loss was substantial:
about $700, which is roughly equivalent to almost $21,000 today. *Observer*
subscribers would read the details of the attack in a special edition of the
paper that arrived a few weeks later. Lovejoy printed it from Alton.

He was gone, of course, and he wasn't coming back.

CHAPTER NINE

MR. BIRNEY
FREES HIS SLAVES

L OVEJOY SAT DOWN IN St. Louis one day in early 1835 and tried to imagine the ideal antislavery advocate for a state such as Missouri. At that moment, white Missourians were contemplating a convention to consider amending their state constitution to bar slavery and emancipate the forty thousand Black people or more held in bondage. As Lovejoy mulled the idea of a perfect antislavery spokesman, he was quite aware of the rhetorical shortcomings of a person such as himself—a transplant from a free state in the North, with little direct experience in a slavery environment beyond what he'd witnessed while living in St. Louis. Instead, he envisioned someone with a nearly opposite profile, a son of the slavery South who could speak plainly to the denizens of a slave state in the language they would understand, from an experience they could relate to, and thus perhaps turn their minds. "We do not want a man from the northern or middle states; we want one who has himself been educated in the midst of Slavery, who has always lived in contact with it, who knows, experimentally, all its evils, and all its difficulties," Lovejoy wrote. "To such a man a golden opportunity of doing good is offered."

In fact, such a man did exist, and he was preparing his own daring leap into the fight against slavery at the moment Lovejoy was writing those words. The man's name was James G. Birney, and he embodied a number of the traits that Lovejoy thought would be exemplary for a slavery fighter. Birney, a trained lawyer, had been raised in Kentucky, the son of an aristocratic, slave-owning family who kept slaves himself as an Alabama plantation owner. He was a true white native of the slavery South—not someone, as Lovejoy had put it, with thoughts on slavery that floated somewhere in "the region of abstract speculation." It's not clear whether Lovejoy yet knew Birney when he sought to conjure an ideal activist, though the two would eventually become acquainted. But for the next two years, the pair would share much in common, as Birney's own attempts to employ a newspaper in the crusade against slavery thrust him into conflict with community leaders and angry mobs in Cincinnati—which, like Alton, was a Northern river city on the edge of the South's slavery regime.

During the same months that Lovejoy was being threatened and eventually chased from St. Louis for his writing in 1836, Birney would watch his own printing press destroyed by men trying to get him to stop publishing abolitionist columns. The Kentuckian, like Lovejoy, had once believed strongly in colonization, but Birney grew to see it as a fraud that provided political cover for white pro-slavery interests while doing little to improve the lives of the people they held in bondage. And like his counterpart from Maine, Birney was a Presbyterian who had concluded after a spiritual awakening that slavery was a moral wrong that needed to be eradicated for the benefit of a Christian nation. Although the two antislavery editors lived somewhat parallel story lines for a time—in different states and nearly four hundred miles apart—the endings would take dramatically different forms.

James Gillespie Birney was born February 4, 1792, in Danville, Kentucky—coincidentally, the hometown of Lovejoy's spiritual mentor David Nelson. Birney's father had immigrated from Ireland as a teenager and turned himself into one of the state's wealthiest businessmen as a merchant, banker, and planter. Birney's mother, the daughter of an Irish political exile, died when the boy was three years old, and he was raised by his father and an aunt on that side. Birney grew up privileged on an estate called Woodlawn, where his father, James Sr., relied upon the labors of twenty-odd slaves and enjoyed political connections that included the Kentucky workhorse Henry Clay.

Although a slaveholder, James Sr. favored emancipation if Kentucky were ever to make itself a free state, and he was part of the political campaign to accomplish that end. The elder Birney and his father-in-law backed a drive at the time of Kentucky's statehood in 1792 to write a constitution that would outlaw slavery there. In doing so, they lined up behind their Danville pastor the Reverend David Rice, a well-known abolitionist who had been selected as a delegate to the constitution-writing convention. But the effort to bring Kentucky into the Union as a free state failed, as did a similar push seven years later. Although attempts to abolish slavery in Kentucky never died completely, they did not regain the traction they had enjoyed during the 1790s, when Birney was a child. (His own plans to promote the antislavery cause in Kentucky years later would be short-lived.) At home, young Birney juggled mixed messages about slavery. His father reportedly advocated humane treatment of slaves but was waiting for a political solution, such as making Kentucky a free state, before emancipating his own. Meanwhile, the aunt who raised Birney refused for religious reasons to own slaves herself and insisted on paying for work done by her brother's slaves, according to an account of Birney's life by his son, William. So although Birney did not grow up an abolitionist, he was surrounded by people willing to act on their convictions that slavery was wrong.

Birney, an athletic youth fond of riding, shooting, and swimming, was sixteen when he entered the College of New Jersey, which would become Princeton University. There, he rubbed elbows with young men from the North and South who would later gain prominence in law and politics. The Princeton ties paid off: After graduation, Birney went off to study law under Alexander J. Dallas, the father of a roommate who was an eminent lawyer and the U.S. attorney in Philadelphia. Young Birney was no struggling law student—he lived a dandy's existence in Philadelphia, propped up by family largesse that included the use of a pair of thoroughbred horses from home and a fancy carriage.

He returned to Kentucky as a freshly minted lawyer, got married, and threw himself into the life of influence for which he had been bred—the dapper Birney was elected to the Kentucky legislature in 1816. In an early sign of his independence from pro-slavery forces, Birney used his vote in the legislature to oppose a measure asking the state's governor to open talks with Ohio and Indiana to pass laws aimed at promoting the capture and return of fugitive slaves. "Shall the State of Kentucky do what no gentleman would—turn slave-catcher?" he asked. The measure lost, but Birney faced no backlash in his home county. His vote was one piece of evidence that, at least in the years before the boom of cotton and the growth of a slave-based economy in the South, it was still possible to criticize slavery without facing punishment. By the 1830s, that would change.

Birney's stay in Kentucky was brief, however. A fellow lawmaker persuaded Birney to accompany him on a trip to check out Alabama, which had emerged as a magnet for Kentuckians—a Southern version of the frontier, where land was still cheap and business opportunities wide open to the bold. Birney went and soon was making plans to move his wife and infant son to a plantation outside Huntsville for his new life as a gentleman planter. He would take three slaves, domestic servants who had been given to him by his father and grandfathers. In Alabama, Birney soon concluded that cotton growing required more hands, so he bought more slaves, enough to bring the number to about thirty. He later would receive five more slaves from his father. (Births would bring the total number of Birney's slaves to forty-three.) Looking back years later, Birney recalled that his views on slavery during his years in Alabama "did not materially differ from those which prevailed among the generality of planters."

Birney was fond of spending and gambling (he liked betting on horses), but proved not to be very adept as a cotton grower. He fell into debt and sold his land and slaves in 1823, keeping a couple and their three children as house servants when he moved to Huntsville to take up the full-time practice of law. Although he was a Henry Clay man—a political misfit in a region that heavily favored Andrew Jackson of Tennessee—Birney managed eventually to be elected as mayor of Huntsville, a rollicking town with a reputation for its frequent brawls and shootings.

But it was Birney's spiritual conversion and connection with the Presbyterian church in 1826 that set him on the path to antislavery activism and, eventually, to politics on the national level. His conversion came amid the same rising wave of revivals that would sweep up Lovejoy in St. Louis six years later, and it inspired Birney to embrace some of the same causes of moral reform. Once a tippler, Birney enthusiastically took up the cause of temperance, and as mayor even pushed through a city ordinance barring the sale of liquor to be consumed on site. He joined local branches of the American Tract Society and American Bible Society, twin pillars of the Tappan brothers' benevolent empire, and of the American Sunday School Union. Birney had joined the evangelical army taking aim at the nation's moral failings, and it was not long before his religious awakening would stir him to ponder slavery's oppression and his own responsibility in relieving the misery of the nearly two million then-enslaved people.

Not surprisingly, Birney was drawn to the work of the decade-old American Colonization Society, whose biggest names included Clay, the fellow Kentuckian, and respected figures from other states, such as Key and Daniel Webster. The ACS had the trappings of philanthropy and a national reach, and it appeared to promise a sweeping solution to "the slavery problem"—the removal of freed Black people to Africa, far from American communities where they might prove a troubling presence—on terms that were designed not to unsettle slaveowners. The colonization society was to be the go-slow alternative to an unsavory choice between a perpetual, expanding slavery and unregulated emancipation, though few white people in the South were advocating that extreme of a move. South-erners dominated leadership of the group, allowing enslavers to present themselves as willing to stem the spread of slavery. Colonization allowed Northerners to feel that they were part of an effort at moral uplift without broaching the nearly unthinkable notion of racial equality. For his part, Birney donated money to the group and helped organize a branch in the Huntsville area. As his involvement in the slavery issue deepened, pushed along by discussions with the visiting Theodore Dwight Weld during a lecture stop in Huntsville, Birney took a paid job in 1832 as the ACS agent for Alabama, Mississippi, Tennessee, Louisiana, and the Arkansas territory. Birney's assignment: to raise money and pitch the virtues of colonization in a cotton-growing region that was increasingly dependent on slave labor and deeply wary of any schemes that carried the risk of slave rebellion. He saw in the project undeniable benefits for free Black people and the South in general, if its white residents could only hear the word. "I believed there was in the project so much of a vivifying spirit, that to ensure its success it was only necessary for the people of the South *once* to become interested," Birney later recalled. The advantages of the colonization approach "could be so clearly and powerfully exhibited that there would be none to gainsay or resist."

Birney traveled and wrote on the colonization program, but discovered before long that colonization was not the easy sell he had imagined. He wrote a series of more than a dozen articles in the Hunstville *Democrat* that disturbed many Alabamans by advocating even a gradual form of eman-cipation. "And they were written by a Southerner! A man of standing!"

Birney's son William would exclaim. In the face of objections, Birney stopped submitting the articles for publication and began to consider whether the colonization drive should first be focused on the slave states to the north—Maryland, Virginia, and his home state of Kentucky.

Birney would soon discover another obstacle to marketing colonization as a way of ending slavery: free Black people proved unwilling to sign up to be placed on a ship to Africa, a land few of them were old enough ever to have seen. He proposed to his own slaves that he would emancipate them and include them with other freed slaves on a planned colonization society expedition from New Orleans to the destination in Liberia. "[B]ut they all refused absolutely, being much frightened at the proposition," William Birney recounted. Northern Black people had been fiercely attacking the colonization approach for years and instead were calling for slaves' emancipation and increased opportunities in school and employment. They were roundly rejecting mass deportation to Africa.

By June 1832, Garrison in Boston had published a seventy-six-page book that attacked the case for colonization with his usual fierce, prosecutorial rigor, using scores of quotations by ACS backers to argue that it served mainly as a shield for slavery interests. By the time the book had made its way widely among white people in the North who opposed slavery, it effectively killed colonization as a viable strategy for ending slavery. For different reasons, Birney was concluding that his own colonization work faced poor prospects in the Deep South. In New Orleans, he had spoken before a church and placed notices in the city's newspapers offering free passage to Liberia, but was dismayed to encounter "a thorough indifference." With the Africa-bound ship *Ajax* standing by to receive passengers, "only one free colored person came to converse with me on the subject. He was irresolute at the first interview, and never sought another," Birney recounted.

Birney's tally of the number of slaves and free Black people who had actually been transported by ship showed dismal results: twenty-three Africa-bound expeditions had carried away only 2,061 people, including just 631 slaves. (Over four decades of trying, the ACS would manage to remove fewer than fifteen thousand Black people from U.S. soil.) "However much soever they may be cherished by the sincere advocate of human liberty, in common with the slaveholder," Birney would conclude, the principles of colonization "have in them nothing attractive to that particular class of people for whose benefit the whole plan was set on foot." In other words, there was no market in the Deep South for what Birney was peddling. In late 1833, he made a decision: he would shift his colonization work to his home state of Kentucky, which as a border state presumably would be more amenable to his message. It already had dozens of local colonization societies and, along the way, had been home to various emancipation-minded newspapers.

But Birney's own belief in gradual emancipation was weakening the deeper he plunged into abolitionist thought. He read a wide range of antislavery writings by the likes of John Greenleaf Whittier and the activist Elizur Wright, and subscribed to newspapers such as the *Emancipator*, the journal of the American Anti-Slavery Society launched by Arthur Tappan in early 1833. Birney also began to delve into the history of slavery in the West Indies and United States, and pored over the parliamentary debate in Britain that had preceded the 1833 vote to emancipate slaves in its Caribbean colonies.

Perhaps the biggest blow to Birney's slipping faith in colonization, though, came as the result of a remarkable early case of what subsequent generations of Americans would call student activism. This episode took place on the campus of Lane Theological Seminary outside Cincinnati, a school established by the Tappan brothers to serve as a training ground for evangelical preachers preparing to proselytize the West. The school's president was none other than the seasoned churchman Lyman Beecher. Among the students—many of whom were men already in their late twenties and thirties—was the tireless Theodore Dwight Weld, the Birney friend who was by now an experienced antislavery lecturer.

Over the course of eighteen evenings in early 1834, Weld led seminary students through a series of emotionally wrenching discussions on the subjects of slavery and colonization—discussions that initially had been encouraged by Beecher. The so-called Lane Debates centered on two questions: whether slavery should be abolished immediately, and whether colonization merited the support of the Christian community as a way to end forced servitude in America. Over the course of weeks, the students, including some from slave-owning families in the South and one former slave, discussed the cruelties of human bondage and the slave trade, the intrinsic rights of Black people as human beings, and the moral burden the students themselves faced to confront oppression. (One would report that "the facts developed in the debate have almost curdled my blood. . . . Facts are the great instruments of conviction on this question.")

The "debates," which amounted to more of an extended revival than a real clash of opinions, ended with student votes embracing immediate emancipation as the proper response to the sin of slavery and a rejection of colonization's morally nebulous gradualism. To this end, Weld and his fellow students formed an antislavery society. But they went a big step further than that. In an attempt to promote equal rights, the group committed itself to work to improve the lives of Cincinnati's free Black residents by directly offering school classes and religious teaching in the neighborhood known as Little Africa. This was a bold—some thought reckless—initiative in a Southern-leaning city. Only five years earlier, Cincinnati had erupted in racial violence sparked by rampaging mobs of white people who had grown alarmed after watching the population of free Black people swell to about 10 percent from about 4 percent a decade before. The riots ignited after city leaders announced a drive to enforce Cincinnati's twenty-year-old so-called Black Laws that sought to keep Black people out by requiring new arrivals to post a $500 bond guaranteeing their good behavior. Rioters burned houses and furniture and stole property in the largely Black Bucktown section, prompting many of the traumatized residents to flee the city. Many left for good: within five years of the rioting, Cincinnati's Black population had plummeted to 740 from about 2,300 in 1829.

The program of grassroots uplift put Weld and the other students into close association with the city's Black people—including overnight stays in their homes—and produced horrified reactions from white people in Cincinnati and from Lane's trustees, who urged the students to desist or risk expulsion. Weld would later note that his time at Lane was spent almost solely among Cincinnati's Black residents: "If I ate in the City it was at *their* tables. If I slept in the City it was at *their* homes. If I attended parties, it was *theirs—weddings—theirs—Funerals—theirs—Religious meetings—theirs*—Sabbath schools—theirs—Bible classes—theirs. During the eighteen months that I spent at Lane Seminary, I *did not attend Dr. Beecher's church once*."

Beecher was on a fundraising trip back East when his campus erupted in turmoil. The faculty pressed students to cease their mixing with local Black people, and the school's trustees ultimately ordered a halt to their antislavery work and threatened to expel the students. In addition, the trustees imposed a curb on possible topics of further discussion—setting up a standoff between the students and Lane's faculty and overseers. Beecher found himself trapped in an unhappy spot between the opposing forces, and he ultimately signed on to the trustees' resolution.

The so-called Lane rebels, Weld included, were outraged by what they saw as an assault on their freedom of expression, and withdrew en masse from the seminary to seek a new place to study. (Most would eventually land at Oberlin College, where the Tappans agreed to finance a new center of evangelical study under the direction of the revivalist Charles Grandison Finney.) Weld took a job as an agent of the American Anti-Slavery Society and later would call upon many of his fellow Lane rebels to create a corps of abolitionist lecturers to travel through Northern states and preach the message of immediate emancipation. In doing so, they became, in the words of the scholar Gilbert H. Barnes, "evangelists of abolitionism." They were truly early civil rights workers.

Birney was keenly aware of the Lane controversy. From his perch in Danville, Kentucky, he read in abolitionist newspapers accounts of the lengthy debates and their audacious decisions. In spring, as the tensions mounted over the students' startling activism, Birney made the 120-mile trip across the Ohio River to meet with Weld and the other rebels. The effect of Birney's visit to Lane was powerfully clarifying to a man already in the throes of reexamining his convictions. Gradual emancipation increasingly looked to Birney like a failed way to "lay hold of men's consciousness," as he would put it later. And colonization, rather than a strategy for firing interest in emancipation, had done the opposite: "Colonization has done more to rock the conscience of the Slaveholder into slumber, and to make this slumber soft and peaceful, than all the other causes united."

Birney's visit with the Lane rebels, then, was not so much a conversion in his beliefs as it was the final collapse of an idea on its last legs—a gust felling a tottering, lifeless tree. Birney—a son of the South, a man bred to privilege amid the slavery system and who still owned a handful of slaves—was ready to declare it: he was an abolitionist, at a time when Lovejoy was still steering a decidedly gradualist course. Birney returned to Kentucky to finish what he had begun. On June 2, he summoned his family and six slaves—the family of five, plus a biracial girl of about six years old who was unrelated to him—and distributed to each a piece of paper. The document, signed and witnessed by his two teen sons, was a deed of emancipation that declared, in part, that slavery was "inconsistent with the Great Truth that all men are created equal, upon which as I conceive our Republican institutions are founded—as well as with the great rule of benevolence delivered to us by the Savior Himself that in all things whatsoever ye would that men would do unto you do ye even so to them." Birney's former slaves were now free, but they would remain with him as paid employees during the months that he would stay in Kentucky. (To

Michael, the father in the family, Birney paid back wages for years of work, plus annual interest—funds that Michael used to set up a livery stable.)

Having freed his slaves, Birney turned next to the community of colonization supporters with whom he had worked and to the world beyond Kentucky. The following month, in July 1834, he crafted an impassioned forty-six-page letter—it would later be widely distributed as a slim volume—that sought to lay bare the many fallacies of colonization as a strategy for ending slavery. Like Garrison, whose strident style of abolitionism he had always opposed, Birney concluded that colonization was not only ineffective in removing freed Black people from U.S. soil, it acted as a protective guard for the bondage system, and thus had served only to prolong slavery's sinful sway for at least another generation. He wrote: "It is to be feared that we, who have been supporters of colonization, have, thro' ignorance, been instrumental in prolonging, at least through one lifetime, the dark reign of slavery on the Earth, and in sending one generation of our fellow men, weeping witnesses of its bitterness, to a comfortless grave!" Birney added that the colonization scheme had effectively "paralyzed" the Southern clergy from playing its rightful moral role as a critic of slavery. And he argued that the removal approach played upon what modern Americans would recognize as racism in seeking to coerce Black people into a lifetime exile to Africa "among savage men and in a deadly clime." Colonization was, as Garrison had concluded before him, an atrocious sham.

Birney's letter landed with explosive force. Here, after all, was a former slaveowner and avowed gradualist renouncing his old positions to embrace the radical approach of abolitionism. The letter was printed and reprinted in religious and antislavery publications and created a sensation across the North, where the anti-abolitionist mobs in New York had recently trashed Lewis Tappan's house. Birney's former colleagues in the Colonization Society attacked him, while Weld exulted in the likely boon his letter would spell for the abolitionist movement, especially among former supporters of colonization. Closer to home, Birney found himself "much vilified and abused" in Danville, shunned even by his friends. Resistance grew during the ensuing year as Birney signed on with the American Anti-Slavery Society to open an abolitionist newspaper in Danville. (The delighted Tappans agreed to keep their financial support to Birney secret for as long as he was in hostile territory.) He was attacked by newspapers across the South and targeted by a pressure campaign in his hometown that made it impossible for him to find anyone willing to print such a paper.

In July 1835, nearly three dozen Danville residents, including members of the colonization society, sent Birney a letter urging him to postpone publishing his newspaper, to be called the *Philanthropist*, until the state legislature was given an opportunity to weigh in on whether such a publication would be allowed in Kentucky under the broad leeway that the states assumed over the press. The letter warned that a newspaper printing opinions on abolition could spark turmoil and prompt slaveholders to clamp down more harshly on their slaves. "You injure yourself. You injure society at large. You injure the slaves themselves. *You do good to none,*" the group warned. The letter hinted at possible personal danger to Birney if he pressed forward, saying its signers were moved by "our unfeigned desire to avoid violence—to shun a storm of which you seem to know not." The letter writers then turned to another argument that was being wielded increasingly during the 1830s as the South looked for ways to defend slavery against its critics: agitation on the issue imperiled the slave's "happy and contented" life in bondage.

Birney pressed his right to free discussion but, hemmed in on all sides, finally decided that it was fruitless to try to start an abolitionist paper in a slave state such as Kentucky. He would have to go north to a free state. In late 1835, he moved with his family across the Ohio River to Cincinnati, where he had met with the Lane rebels a year earlier. Even as Birney prepared to publish his new paper there, detractors on the Kentucky side kept up their jibes. "We have little doubt that his newspaper will be torn down," sneered the *Louisville Journal*. "Not having been permitted to open his battery in this State, he is determined to cannonade us from across the river. Isn't it rather too long a shot for execution, Mr. Birney?"

Birney, the neophyte editor, was about to find out that his newspaper writings would be equally unwelcome in Cincinnati.

CHAPTER TEN

INCENDIARY
MISSILES

A S THE CALENDAR TURNED to 1837, Lovejoy could sense a strait-
jacket of censorship tightening around him. Although he had steered
a relatively careful course in the *Observer* since his arrival in Alton in July, a
pair of worrisome moves—one on each side of the Mississippi—left little
doubt that an offensive by Southern states to limit public criticisms of
slavery had arrived at his doorstep. In early January, a select committee
of the Illinois legislature reported out a set of resolutions that broadly
condemned abolitionists and the "doctrines promulgated by them," and
pronounced that the antidote to these dangerous ideas would be found in
a "rebuke which is so richly merited," delivered by the court of public
opinion.

In approving the resolutions, the Illinois lawmakers in Vandalia were
expressing their solidarity with the South's hardening position on speech.
They said that they appreciated "the feelings of anxiety and alarm that
have been produced in the slaveholding states by the misguided and
incendiary movements of the abolitionists," whose actions could only

result in the "most deleterious consequences to every portion of our Union." In denunciatory language, the legislators asserted that the anti-slavery societies had only "forged new fetters for the black man" while feeding bitterness in the South and igniting the "turbulent passions of the monster mob." If the abolitionists continued, the lawmakers agreed, the result would be bloodshed and the end of the Union. The General Assembly's resolutions took no binding action, but they offered a near-full endorsement by a free state's legislature of the suppression approach taken by slavery forces elsewhere. The measure passed unanimously in the Senate and would gain approval in the state House of Representatives, with all but six votes in favor. One of those dissenters was Abraham Lincoln.

Across the river, Missouri lawmakers at the same moment were weighing their own crackdown on antislavery publications. Lovejoy had known about this for weeks, and, displaying a bit of political smarts, took the opportunity to mail to every member of the legislature a pamphlet celebrating free expression that had been adapted from a much-publicized open letter written by the famed Unitarian preacher William Ellery Channing to James Birney. Channing had previously criticized abolitionists as extreme and confrontational, but in this letter, the Boston cleric adopted a new stance. He lauded the abolitionists for their defense of enslaved Black people and for standing up to the bullies and attackers he believed were trying to deprive free white people of their "sacred rights" to speak. The abolitionists "are sufferers for the liberty of thought, speech, and the press; and in maintaining this liberty amidst insult and violence, they deserve a place among its most honored defenders," Channing wrote. The letter, a remarkable show of respect from an abolitionism skeptic and a ringing defense of free speech, was reprinted widely.

Lovejoy had already splashed Channing's letter across nearly a full page of the *Observer*, with an accompanying editor's note arguing that the right to speak and print "on any subject whatsoever" was divinely granted and subject to no man's tampering. Any legislative attempt to restrict the freedom to debate slavery, Lovejoy argued, "would not only be unconstitutional, but immoral; and every man would not only be at liberty to disregard it, but he would be bound to resist it." One of the Missouri lawmakers who received the Channing letter, a state senator named R.B. Dawson, sent the pamphlet back to Lovejoy with a tart letter noting that the state Senate had passed a bill to criminalize the publication or circulation of antislavery materials. He said the House of Representatives was expected to follow suit. "You would do well, therefore, to withold any further publication upon the same subject from the state of Missouri or its citizens," Dawson warned the editor.

If he felt threatened by that message, Lovejoy did not sound it. He printed Dawson's letter in the *Observer*, then attached his own dismissive rejoinder. "It would seem that the legislature of Missouri are really determined, Don Quixote like, to run a tilt against a free press. They might just as well attempt to stop the circulation of the air over their prairies as to prohibit the dissemination of newspapers, whether proslavery or anti-slavery, through their mails," he wrote. "People will laugh such a law to scorn." It was too late. A day earlier, the Missouri House had proven Lovejoy grievously wrong by approving the bill on a 61-to-0 vote, imposing fines and a possible life sentence to anyone who would "publish, circulate, or utter, by writing, speaking, or printing any facts, arguments, reasoning or opinions" that might be seen to incite slaves to "rebellion, sedition . . . or murder."

The legislatures' actions in Illinois and Missouri marked an inauspicious start to a year—1837—that would grow only more contentious for Lovejoy. During the trouble-filled months to follow, the editor would assume a more insistent, indignant posture in the pages of his frontier newspaper. Lovejoy's commitment to the cause of the slave would deepen. And that cause would become increasingly difficult for him to keep separate from that of a freely operating press. It was possible to detect, here at the outset of 1837, early signs that forces were gathering in opposition to each other, sliding toward collision—at least outside the halls of the state legislatures. Anyone in Alton who thought Lovejoy had pledged his silence on slavery months earlier was in for bitter disappointment.

* * *

ALTHOUGH STILL A NEWCOMER in Alton, Lovejoy wore many hats. He was a husband and a father of a toddler. He was a man of the cloth and, as of January, the pastor of the newly organized Presbyterian church in Upper Alton—a project that had been spearheaded by his friends Enoch Long, Thomas Lippincott, Frederick Graves, and Thaddeus Hurlbut (who was now also helping Lovejoy get the *Observer* out every Thursday). Lovejoy remained a temperance crusader and spiced up the *Observer* with cautionary tales of alcohol-related excess meant to convey the life-threatening perils of drink. (A typical parable called "The Drunkard's Grave," reprinted from Gilman's temperance newspaper, told of a promising young Massachusetts congressman whose life comes unraveled thanks to social drinking among Washington's power set, leading him eventually to the poorhouse, madness, and death.) Lovejoy was also a part-time teacher—he led Sunday school classes, speaking "with fine expression of countenance and a voice as soft and tender as a woman's," one of his students would later recall. In dispensing with the customary fire and brimstone about God's wrath, Lovejoy was, his pupil remembered, "like an 'oasis' in the desert of Calvinism."

Lovejoy also hoped to foster in Alton, with its desire of one day becoming the "Queen of the West," an intellectual and cultural life like that of other great cities. By early 1837, residents were proposing the creation of a reading room that would be called, with perhaps exaggerated grandeur, the Alton Atheneum. By then, Lovejoy had already joined with other local citizens to establish the Upper Alton Lyceum, a club that would meet weekly at a brick schoolhouse to discuss issues of the day, including some that might sound familiar to modern-day Americans—capital punishment and controls on immigration, for example. Lovejoy was among the Lyceum's original members when it organized in October 1836, and he held the post of president for a couple of months. Meetings opened with a prayer and attendance was a serious matter: members were fined 12.5¢ for each absence.

In this setting, too, Lovejoy seemed eager to promote the discussion of slavery. In January, the group agreed to schedule its next debate on this loaded question: "Does the principle of the Right require the immediate emancipation of the slave?" There, in plain English, was the question now weighing heavily on Lovejoy, and surely on others of Alton's most thoughtful citizens. In a miniature version of the Lane sessions that had been held in Cincinnati three years earlier, the lyceum debate on slavery would stretch over the next several of its weekly sessions, with Lovejoy leading the argument in favor of immediate emancipation.

But there was discord from the start. Lovejoy's newly elected replacement as lyceum president, William Clark Jr., resigned as soon as the slavery topic was chosen because of the "delicacy" of the matter. Not surprisingly, the resulting discussions proved contentious. In early February, during the third session devoted to the slavery debate, a motion was made to bring it to a halt. Lovejoy objected, but the vote to squelch further discussion went against him. Another brick wall—Lovejoy had lost his bid to argue his case against slavery to completion. Gone with it was his will to remain in the lyceum. He quit the group soon after. In Alton, it seemed, a debating society was no place to discuss slavery.

But Lovejoy didn't need the lyceum to air his views—he, too, was a man who bought ink by the barrel. Although it would be difficult to prove that his setback at the lyceum marked a turning point in his militancy on slavery, it came at a moment when Lovejoy noticeably began to turn up the volume and frequency of his antislavery writings in the *Observer*. On

the same day the lyceum debate was ended, Lovejoy declared in the newspaper that the colonization scheme he had once championed was "utterly
inadequate" as a remedy for slavery. "As well might a lady think to bale
out the Atlantic with her thimble, as the Colonization Society to remove
slavery by colonizing slaves in Africa," he wrote. Emancipating slaves
only to deport them to a far-off continent stuck Lovejoy as "an enormous
injustice" and was the reason so many had abandoned the scheme.

Having thoroughly washed his hands of colonization, whose claimed virtues had already faded for many antislavery-minded Americans, Lovejoy
began to go to work on the clerics he believed were helping to prop up
the slavery system. For many years, pious men and women—Lovejoy
included—had tended to spend more energy worrying over the health
of the slaves' souls in bondage than in actively trying to set them free.
Lovejoy's own Presbyterian church was no exception. In 1818, its leaders
adopted a statement condemning slavery as "a gross violation of the most
precious and sacred rights of human nature; as utterly inconsistent with
the law of God," and committing the church to working for its "complete
abolition." But in reality, church leaders hedged by endorsing the American Colonization Society and its gradualist approach.

During the 1820s, the Presbyterian church—and other Christian
denominations—went largely silent on slavery as a way to maintain unity
between their Northern and Southern wings. By the time Lovejoy began
preaching in the early 1830s, church conservatives were determined to
skirt any discussion of the divisive issue. That was especially true in the
South, but even some Northern Presbyterians were among the fiercest
critics of abolitionists. But antislavery opinion would rise inside the
church, a by-product of the same revivalist spirit of moral reform to which
Lovejoy and so many others had been drawn. The slavery issue became
caught up in wider differences over theology that divided the Presbyterians
into factions, a more conservative Old School and liberal-influenced New
School. Those divisions would prove unbridgeable.

Those fault lines showed during the church's 1835 General Assembly in Pittsburgh, at which the Lane rebel Theodore Weld pushed an abolitionist viewpoint that slavery was a sin and emancipation a duty. The assembly ultimately sidestepped the issue by assigning it to a committee to study the matter. When the General Assembly returned to Pittsburgh the following year, Lovejoy was there, part of a contingent of clergymen hoping for a strong church position against slavery. But he and the other slavery critics were thwarted when the committee recommended avoiding the matter altogether—a decision backed by a wide margin in a vote by the full body. (This was the vote over which Lovejoy joined a protest.) The slavery issue remained a key reason—scholars argue over whether it was *the* key reason—the U.S. Presbyterian church split in two a year later.

The question before Christians in America was not merely one of the convenience of remaining silent about slavery. At the heart of the dilemma was a growing chasm between two radically different religious views of the institution—a division of no small importance in a deeply pious nation. To reformers in the North such as Weld and the Tappans, slavery was a terrible sin against God that demanded immediate redress by each and every moral person. But as abolitionists' criticism of slavery mounted during the 1830s, its defenders in the South and North leaned increasingly on a biblical justification: that descriptions of slavery in the Old and New testaments implied that the practice was permissible from a scriptural point of view. (In particular, the "Curse of Ham" story told in Genesis served for centuries as the basis for justifying Black African slavery and racism against Black people in general.) This thinking allowed apologists in various Christian churches to evade the matter of moral wrong in the institution of slavery and instead focus on how enslavers treated their slaves and whether those slaves' souls were being properly nourished through religious teaching. (At the same time, laws aimed at preventing slave incitement in the South made it illegal to teach slaves to read, even the Bible.)

By early 1837, Lovejoy's dual roles as antislavery editor and clergyman were coming into conflict. As editor, he was seeking—and practicing—more public discussion over slavery, even inviting pro-slavery viewpoints into his paper as a way to spur debate. Although Lovejoy had grown frustrated as he watched his own church and others tiptoe around the moral questions that consumed him, he took a measure of cheer when, a few months earlier, Presbyterian leaders had voted to approve a resolution seeking to "convince" fellow church members that owning slaves was a "heinous sin against God," and to bar from preaching any ministers who held slaves.

Still, as Lovejoy cranked up his assault on slavery in the spring of 1837, some of his sharpest jabs were directed at his fellow clergymen. In letters and published columns, the editor took aim at a religious hierarchy he portrayed as quiescent and enabling when it came to human bondage. (On the East Coast, Garrison and others had for two years been attacking the churches for much the same reason.) From where Lovejoy sat, a lack of clerical outrage increasingly came to appear as a form of moral abdication and towering hypocrisy, and he seethed at the notion that the Bible could sanction the buying and selling of human beings. To draw attention to the domestic slave trade, Lovejoy reprinted a short advertisement from the *Missouri Republican* that offered for sale a Black woman and her nine-year-old daughter. "How long are ministers of the gospel to hold their peace while members of their church thus 'buy and sell and make gain' of their fellow-men and women—it may be brethren and sisters in the same church?" Lovejoy asked.

The eight years that Lovejoy spent living in a slave state had given him a bird's-eye view of the slavery system and its injustices—and he employed this experience in his increasingly regular public commentaries. Stymied at the lyceum, Lovejoy employed the *Observer* as his own forum for debating slavery with clergymen and editors in other states. In one such exchange with the editor of the *Christian Mirror*, a religious paper in

Maine, Lovejoy said that during his time living alongside slavery, he had watched slaves wait outside church in a carriage while their owners prayed "with great devoutness" inside. He had seen slaveholders sell their slaves "into distant captivity . . . yet never did I hear the pastor rebuke the deed."

Lovejoy acknowledged the perils of speaking out against slavery in a state where it was practiced, recalling how his friend David Nelson had been run out of Missouri. Still, he said, silence for ministers was no longer possible. In Lovejoy's open letter to the Maine editor, the Reverend Asa Cummings, he expressed sorrow for the hostile line toward abolitionists that was taken by the editors of some Northern religious newspapers who considered slavery only in the abstract, "when the living and awful reality was before them and around them." Then, in one of the most raw and affecting passages he had written on slavery up to that point, Lovejoy adopted the perspective of the slave to help Cummings envision the "naked facts" of slavery. "I speak in behalf of more than two millions of my fellow-beings, who are not permitted to open their mouths," he said. Lovejoy structured his argument around a simple question: "What is Slavery?" He then proceeded to answer, in the imagined voice of an aging male slave: "It is to have my back subjected to the cowhide or the cart whip, at the will or caprice of my master, or any of his family. Every child has a right to curse, or kick, or cuff the old man. It is to toil all day beneath an almost vertical sun, with the bitter certainty always before me, that not one cent of what I earn, is, or can be my own." Lovejoy continued with the bleak tableau:

My first-born son, denied even the poor privilege of bidding his father farewell, is on his way, a chained and manacled victim, to a distant market, there to be disposed of in shambles, where human flesh and sinews are bought and sold. It is to enter my cabin, and see my wife or daughter struggling in the lustful embraces of my master, or some of his white friends, without daring to attempt their rescue;

for should I open my lips to remonstrate, a hundred lashes would
be the consequence; and should I raise my hand to smite the brutal
wretch, nothing but death could atone for the sacrilege. . . . It is to
be degraded from a man to a brute.

"Such, brother Cummings, is Slavery, not that Slavery such as you
imagine or hope might exist, but Slavery as it actually now exists in
eleven of these United States, nay, such as it exists IN THE CHURCH,"
added Lovejoy. Then he went a step further. It was bad enough that
fellow churchmen, of various denominations, failed to recognize the
naked fact of slavery. But in criticizing the antislavery movement
seeking to topple it, Lovejoy had come to believe, these clerics were
not merely harmless bystanders to an atrocity—they were complicit in
it. By opposing antislavery activists, he warned Cummings, "You are
fighting against GOD."

Through open letters like this one and the vigorous exchanges of
newspapers, Lovejoy was able to convert the *Observer* into a megaphone
whose range now stretched far beyond his local subscriber base, which by
now stood at about two thousand, the most of any of Alton's four weekly
newspapers, by his tally. Lovejoy's name and voice were known to editors,
particularly those of religious newspapers, throughout the Northern states
and into the South. Although his name may not have carried the same
notoriety in the South as that of Garrison or the Tappans, among the newspapers most committed to covering moral questions, Lovejoy's profile rose
as his stance on slavery hardened. Which is not to say he was becoming
popular. Lovejoy's criticisms of the clergy, including church leaders in
the North, were unsparing, and he was unafraid to name names (though
he always made sure to use "brother"). In a column called "The Right
Remedy," Lovejoy took to task, by name, a minister who had suggested
in a Boston journal that sending more clergy to the South to preach would
produce better treatment of slaves. "The gospel of the 'Son of God' requires

not 'the good treatment of the black man as a *slave*, but as a MAN . . . and the first step in this good treatment is to SET HIM FREE," Lovejoy wrote.

Asking enslavers to treat their slaves more humanely or to teach them to read the Bible was just the sort of solution that Lovejoy himself might have once suggested. By this time, however, he saw godliness not in palliative half measures, but in speaking harsh and difficult truths. For the Lovejoy of 1837, the gospel carried only one suitable message: "Restore the slave to HIMSELF; give him back those rights which belong to him." Closer to home, some residents were taking a leery view of Lovejoy's growing assertiveness in the pages of the *Observer*. A Missouri state senator named Abraham Byrd from Jefferson City—the same town where abolitionist materials had been discovered in the box of Bibles—wrote to Lovejoy to protest after receiving a copy of the paper criticizing slavery. Byrd's spelling was atrocious, but his displeasure shone through clearly. "Noperson but a unprinsiabled man would persume to offer such, a man that has injuered his Country as have and have been trying to Incurage things that would End in murder and I have good reasons to beleve that was and is your intentions," Byrd wrote. "[A]nd sir I wish you to keep your self out of my Sunshine."

* * *

IN CHOOSING TO ABANDON Kentucky for the free state of Ohio as the site for launching his abolitionist newspaper, James Birney had jumped, if not from the frying pan into the fire, then into another very warm skillet. The earlier eruption over the Lane activists—the very people who had converted Birney to antislavery—made plain that Cincinnati had no appetite for agitation when it came to race. Like Lovejoy's Alton, Cincinnati was a bustling border city with sisterly ties to a slave state. Its perch on the Ohio River and the Mississippi beyond meant access to important trading centers in the Deep South such as Natchez, Mississippi, and New Orleans far beyond.

Stevedores loaded meat, flour, and lumber onto river flatboats for transfer south, while municipal leaders hatched plans for a railroad link that would connect the "Queen City of the West" with Charleston, the Southern Carolina port. The 475-mile rail link—one of a slew of rail projects taking shape across the country—was seen as a game-changing commercial artery that would join the populous coastal South with nearly a dozen states across the nation's northern interior. Meantime, Cincinnati served as a hot-weather refuge for several dozen slave-owning families who would arrive each summer with their trunks and children and squads of servants to await cooler fall temperatures. Trade and cultural influences lent Cincinnati a strongly Southern flavor—so much so that one writer dubbed it a "Southern city on free soil."

Antislavery activists may have found fertile ground for their message in northern Ohio—the area where Oberlin College had been founded a few years earlier—but Cincinnati promised to be a harder sell. Already, Birney had reason to expect that his plan to establish an abolitionist paper might be greeted with something less than enthusiasm. During a visit to Cincinnati in August 1835, a few months before he and his family moved there for good, Birney was treated to a burst of commentary in the local newspapers assailing abolitionists as "fanatical" and "misguided" and their materials as "vile incendiary publications."

In November, soon after the family's move, Cincinnati's English-born mayor, Samuel W. Davies, showed up at Birney's home, along with the city marshal, county sheriff, and a prominent newspaper editor. The men were there to complain about the publication of a handbill titled "Declaration of Sentiment of the Cincinnati Anti-Slavery Society" and to impress upon the newcomer the very real possibility that violence might be directed that night against Birney or the print shop where the 250 copies had been struck. Birney, summoning "great calmness and self possession," thanked his visitors and told them that the documents were not handbills, but rather copies of the newly formed antislavery group's constitution and principles. More to the point, Birney told the men, he had no plans to cede his civil rights, "whatever might be the madness and folly of those who might choose to assail them."

No mob came that night. But a few days later, Mayor Davies, a fervent Whig whose main claim to fame was that he had once supplied Cincinnati's water, told Birney that the authorities could not protect him or his property if he persisted with plans for an antislavery newspaper. Birney took the mayor's disclaimer to heart. He turned his home into a miniature fortress, placing forty muskets and double-barreled shotguns at the front stairs landing and elsewhere around the house. Birney was an abolitionist, but not a pacifist—he rejected the no-resistance pledge that had been adopted by many antislavery activists in the Garrisonian wing. "There was never a time when he would have refused or neglected to defend his wife and children," Birney's son William would remember.

One of the men who accompanied the mayor to Birney's home that first evening was Charles Hammond, a lawyer and journalist who was one of the most esteemed figures in Cincinnati. Hammond was editor of the *Gazette*, one of a handful of papers that jostled for the bustling city's attention. Hammond had grown up in a slave-owning family in Maryland and Virginia, and established himself as a talented writer as a teenager—the poems he got published in a local paper were signed "The Plough Boy." Hammond was seen as a rising star, and served as state lawmaker and reporter for the Ohio Supreme Court for years. He argued before the U.S. Circuit Court, and some people saw in his intelligence and bearing the makings of a future Supreme Court justice. The pig-tailed Hammond had a national reputation as a pugnacious political writer, with a cutting wit and a virulent distaste for Andrew Jackson and his allies. He had been editor of the *Gazette* for ten years before Birney's arrival.

The fifty-six-year-old Hammond was known as a straight-shooter who didn't scare easily. By one account, Hammond once faced down a group of angry men who showed up outside his newspaper office with a bucket of tar and feathers to punish him for a sarcastic piece they found offensive. Hammond waved his cane at the tools and said, "Take those filthy things away and be gone." As the story goes, he went back to work and the mob vanished. As a journalist, admirers saw in Hammond an editor with a sharp eye and steady hand. As one admirer put it, he "always had a mark, and his editorial revolver, carefully loaded, was leveled steadily; the aim was sure, and the charges were lodged in the precise spot for which they were designed."

* * *

BIRNEY HAD ALREADY IDENTIFIED Hammond as a possible ally, or at least someone with whom he could reason. Hammond was opposed to slavery, but he reserved no love for abolitionists, either. Nonetheless, he was known to strongly defend the free exchange of opinions. Hammond had given Birney a pleasant surprise by agreeing to publish a speech by Birney's friend Gerrit Smith, a philanthropist from upstate New York who had recently joined up with the abolitionists after watching the mobbing of the antislavery convention in Utica. In Cincinnati, a place bristling with potential peril, Birney saw Hammond as like-minded when it came to civil liberties. He called Hammond "our only hope here for the advocacy of the principles of our Constitution."

Birney felt certain that if given the chance to present his views in a sober, respectful manner, he could defuse some of the community's antipathy toward abolitionism, which he viewed more as a product of misunderstanding than of deep opposition. To this end, Birney had an idea: He would try to shield himself against further trouble by explaining to the entire city *why* he was launching an antislavery newspaper there, and ask Hammond to publish his declaration in the *Gazette*. He sat down and composed a long, detailed statement explaining his flight from Kentucky following his inability to find a willing printer there, not to mention the extended harassment he had suffered at the hands of the Danville postmaster. In the statement, Birney said he chose Ohio as his new base because of its strong state constitutional defense of a person's "*indisputable* right to speak, write, or print upon *any* subject as he thinks proper." Birney explained, "I had determined to establish a Press here, that I might '*write and print*' on the 'subject' of Slavery, '*as I should think proper.*'" He said any opposition to his project was probably just a misconception over what he would say and how he would say it. Birney assured residents that he would refrain from insults and "an intolerant spirit."

Birney then turned to his reasons why an abolitionist paper was so sorely needed. There were three. First, as a son of the South, Birney had a long familiarity with slavery and an understanding of the perspective of slave owners that would allow him to write, he said, with "candor and fairness." He was not like Garrison—he knew how to talk about slavery in a way that Eastern abolitionists did not. Second, slavery was immoral and a violation of the Golden Rule—a society based on oppression could not long prosper or survive. Third, it was pointless to avoid discussing the issue of slavery, which was already on the nation's tongue. No mobs could stifle free debate or a free press forever. It was time for an abolitionist press in the West to track the growing movement (Ohio by this point boasted forty to fifty local antislavery societies) at a moment when other newspapers around the country were effectively denying such activists "access to the public mind"—that is, they were acting as censors. In short, Birney wrote, abolitionists needed a way to explain themselves to the public without being branded as fanatics, race-mixers, and insurrectionists—or mobbed by thugs dispatched by "gentlemen of property and standing."

Birney's statement was a thorough presentation of the man, his backstory, and goals—and Hammond said no. The *Gazette* editor found the letter too "inflammatory," as Birney later explained, and asked instead for a series of articles "beginning a long way back" that would trace Birney's thinking "so artfully that nobody can see where I am at." Doing so would be "a waste of time," the abolitionist told his New York sponsor, Lewis Tappan.

With that avenue now closed, it was time for Birney to get on with opening the *Philanthropist*. Birney set as the launch date the first week of the new year. Still, he remained fretful about the possibility of a mob attack. For safety's sake, he decided to print the paper about twenty miles away from Cincinnati, in a town called New Richmond. His worries seemed justified, given how hard some of the Cincinnati papers—with the exception of the *Gazette*—appeared to be trying to stir up local passions against his project. In December, the *Whig*, for example, charged that Birney's newspaper was an effort to "insult our slave-holding neighbors" and "browbeat public opinion." It warned that the abolitionist paper's "pestiferous breath" would "spread contagion among our citizens."

Birney pressed ahead, anyway. On January 1, 1836, the first issue of the weekly *Philanthropist* appeared, a newspaper whose sole purpose was to rid the nation of chattel slavery—the only one like it in the West. And it would be published, in the face of resistance, by a man who once owned human beings as personal property.

* * *

BIRNEY'S *PHILANTHROPIST* WAS NAMESAKE and philosophical descendant of the antislavery newspaper that a Quaker editor, Charles Osborn, had published nearly two decades earlier in the Ohio town of Mount Pleasant. The new version was no innovator when it came to layout and composition—Birney crammed five columns of type densely across four broadsheet pages, with small-font headlines and so little free space that the overall visual effect was that of a bleak gray Sahara. The paper, which went for $2 a year (too little, Birney knew, to produce any profits in the near term), carried no illustrations and very few advertisements beyond notices of abolitionist society meetings or lectures. The snazziest design element was the occasional table showing slave populations by state, or the expenses of the Cincinnati Anti-Slavery Society.

In actual content, Birney attempted to show that he did not intend for the *Philanthropist* merely to assail slavery from a single, militant perspective. Rather, he would open the discussion to all viewpoints, including those of Southern slavery backers and their allies in the North. Birney organized the paper into "departments," with each reflecting news or viewpoints from a different angle. The "Slave-Holder's Department," for example, offered speeches or commentary from the South, which he earnestly mined from the piles of papers that Hammond shared with him (the second such "Slave-Holder's Department" piece, from the Richmond *Enquirer*, painted the Tappans and other Northern abolitionists as fanatics and hypocrites). Articles about mobs and Northern political supporters of the South, who were known as "Doughfaces," got their own department. News about advances by the abolitionist movement was filed under the recurring "Northern Spirit" heading, while the words and actions of anti-slavery clergy appeared in a column called "Anti-slavery Ecclesiastics." (A separate "Pro-Slavery Ecclesiastics" heading captured news about churches that were resisting abolitionism—a topic that would later consume Lovejoy.)

Birney freely sprinkled in his own commentary and even added that of his detractors, such as the item from the *Louisville Journal* predicting that "his office will be torn down." (The same piece allowed that, apart from Birney's "mad notions" on slavery, he was "an honest and benevolent man.") Every issue of the *Philanthropist* contained a slavery-themed poem, such as "The Climber's Complaint," which conveyed the lowliness of the slave's standing: "No! Not the very breath I draw / These limbs are not my own / A master calls me his by law / My griefs are mine alone."

The paper tracked slavery-related debates in Washington, including President Jackson's proposal to censor the mails and efforts in Congress to gag antislavery petitions. It took note when the South Carolina legislature passed a law barring even free Black people from carrying out work "on their own account."

The earliest issues in January were sober, workmanlike. The inaugural edition displayed across most of the front page a speech by South Carolina governor George McDuffie, a ferocious pro-slavery spokesman, demanding harsh punishments for spreading abolitionist opinions—an address that also caught Lovejoy's notice in St. Louis. Devoting such prime real estate to a Southern politician in the paper's maiden issue was a remarkable show of Birney's determination to appear open to all viewpoints. Birney devoted a hefty share of the second and third pages to his reply to a public meeting in Alabama that had created a vigilance committee to ferret out abolitionists who the attendees claimed were engaged in a plot to foment slave insurrection. It named Birney among a group of "abolition fanatics" that also included Garrison and one of the Tappans.

Birney's lengthy reply to the Alabama gathering revolved around the idea that reducing people to property violated Christian principles, and he also accused the South of threatening the basic liberties of free citizens in the North, including that of a free press. "The South say they will hear no argument in the subject of slavery. Why not? Does it not concern them?" he asked. He then made the pro-slavery forces an offer. "You cannot escape the guilt of a refusal. I invite you, without cost, to the use of the *Philanthropist*. Through its columns your voice may be raised, and your arguments carried to the remotest corners of the land." Driving home his point, Birney in his second issue again gave over half of the front page to the Richmond *Enquirer* piece, which warned that abolitionist "fanatics" and their "poisonous presses" in the North threatened to destroy the Union.

Opponents were unmoved by Birney's show of fair-handedness. Editors of rival newspapers tied to both political parties in Cincinnati—Democrats and Whigs—kept up a drumbeat of ill will toward the *Philanthropist*. On January 16, just fifteen days after the *Philanthropist*'s appearance, the Cincinnati *Republican* blasted Birney in a long column, characterizing him as an "unholy and unpatriotic" radical worse even than the widely detested Garrison or George Thompson, the English abolitionist. "The editor rings the changes upon 'incendiary missiles' and 'the dissolution of the Union,'" charged the column, which was reprinted the following day in the *Whig*. The next week, the *Republican* and prominent Cincinnati residents, including the major newspaper editors—minus Hammond— were calling for a community meeting at the local courthouse to address this threat among them.

The hurriedly arranged January 22 meeting was shaping up to be an explosive affair. As city fathers made preparations that day, runners scurried among Cincinnati's foundries, machine shops, and docks, and across the river to Kentucky, to gather up a mob that would meet at a store on Front Street before the courthouse meeting. Once the formal meeting was ended, the roughnecks were to do their work. The city crackled with the potential of an impending clash, and Birney's friends offered to shelter him away from his home. Black residents who had remembered the trauma of the 1829 rioting feared violence would again spill into their precincts; some left town, while others locked themselves inside their homes.

Amid the building tensions, Birney took his tea as normal that afternoon and retired to his study. His son William joined him in hopes of persuading Birney to flee to the countryside. But before the son could speak, Birney announced a different plan: he was going to the meeting. William accompanied his father on the walk to the courthouse, where between five and six hundred people had already gathered, spilling out the doors. "The approaches were thronged," William would recall. "Men stood on the window-sills and looked through and talked in groups in the yard. Inside every place was filled, from the judge's bench to the gallery." Birney and his son made their way through the horde to the steps in front of the bench. There, Samuel Davies, the mayor who had said he could not protect Birney, sat presiding over the assemblage, flanked by a handful of local politicians from both of the city's main political parties. A committee of fifteen men, headed by surveyor-general R. T. Lytle, was dispatched to another room to consider resolutions for the full body.

At this point, a motion was made for the reading of the constitution of the abolitionist Cincinnati Anti-Slavery Society—Exhibit A in the case alleging that Birney was behind dangerous stirrings. A copy of the document was passed to Davies and he began to read aloud. But what the crowd heard next was not the dry text of the group's constitution, which in reality was little more than an organizational chart. Instead, Davies began by reading its preamble, or "declaration of sentiments," a much juicier bit of writing that had been put together by the ubiquitous Theodore Weld to lay out a ringing case for liberation of the nation's enslaved people. A visitor suddenly plunked down in the courthouse would have been treated to a most incongruous tableau: Here was an assembly of angry men, who had been called together to smother the subversive words of abolitionism, listening enrapt as their mayor pronounced those very words. Davies got through reading most of the declaration when one of the attendees made a motion to stop—this was an abolitionist document! Then another asked that the reading of the declaration continue. Some in the crowd so far had found nothing in the declaration that they found objectionable. ("If this be abolition, I have nothing against it," one man was reported to have said as he up and left the packed room.)

Amid this confusion, a man named Charles Hale—a colonel in the militia, stablekeeper, and ward heeler who peered from under a flowing white mane—clambered onto a table to jerk the meeting back to its original purpose. Hale could not read, but he was an effective speaker, and soon had tugged the crowd back on track, drawing applause as he hurled a string of accusations at Birney, charging him with everything from miscegenation to treason. Hale waved a copy of Garrison's newspaper, the *Liberator*, as proof of the abolitionists' alleged plans to break up the country. He then called on the group before him to block this "miscreant Birney" from carrying out such designs from his base in Cincinnati. "The roughs cheered him wildly, and, at the close of his peroration, were ready to rush to the work of destruction," William Birney would write later.

But then, as the din subsided, a voice rose from in front of the bench. "Mr. President, my name is Birney," the man said. "May I be heard?" The courtroom went mute. "My personal character and my cause have been unjustly attacked. May I defend them?" Birney's sudden appearance set off an explosion of shouts.

"Kill him!"

"Hear him!"

"Down with him!"

"Hear him!"

"Drag him out!"

"Tar and feather him!"

The white-haired Hale lunged toward Birney, but others blocked his path. "Fair play," they urged. At last, Lytle, the leader of the anti-abolitionist forces, brought quiet. "My friends, hear before you strike. Don't disgrace our city and our cause before the nation," Lytle pleaded. "I oppose abolitionism, but I honor a brave man, and Mr. Birney has tonight shown himself the bravest man I have ever seen." He turned to Birney and asked him to speak, once the resolution committee had read its completed report to the assembly. Birney waited.

The resolutions were an unsurprising litany of the charges typically lodged against the abolitionists: that they represented an extremist fringe at odds with the needs of the rest of society, that they endangered the economic health of the community, that they were abusing the liberties of speech and the press to interfere with the legal property rights of slaveholders. Of more immediate relevance to Birney, the committee finished by condemning the work of the abolitionist society in Cincinnati and announced the assembly's intention to "exert every lawful effort to suppress the publication of any abolition paper in this city." Birney had been put on notice.

It was his turn to speak. For the next forty-five minutes, Birney held the floor. He explained that he had grown up in the South and, until about a year and a half earlier, had owned slaves himself. He had lived in Alabama and seen slavery in all its forms—he understood it as few residents of a free state could. He pointed to the rising portion of the South's population that was represented by Black slaves and warned of an inevitable "ruinous explosion" there if slavery were to continue to fester. Thus, he said, persuading slaveholders to free their slaves reflected his Christian duty to fellow Southerners. Shouts and catcalls interrupted Birney's delivery, forcing him to pause until they died down. He pressed forward with a more general attack on slavery, arguing that the Constitution had offered no guarantee of its continued protection.

The yelling started up again. "Stop him!" "Put him down!" came the shouts. Then one stood out from the rest: "Put him to death!" Birney soldiered on, his words swamped by the crashing waves of the crowd's fury as soon as they were uttered. He pivoted to the question of press censorship and began to castigate Jackson and others for what he said were growing attempts to squelch the rights of Americans to criticize slavery.

At last, the growing commotion overwhelmed Birney's ability to be heard at all. Davies suggested that he stop, and Birney agreed. He gave thanks and stepped down. A few other men rose in an effort to revive the assembly's wrath, but the earlier air of frenzy was ebbing. As Birney made his way slowly out of the courtroom, the crowd yielded respectfully before him. Birney arrived home and made a check of the arsenal he had placed around the house. The weapons were at the ready, if needed, and William took a position in an upstairs window in case a mob appeared. But nobody showed up.

The local press, which had played a role in summoning the meeting, would report on it with grudging praise for Birney's display of nerve, if not for the antislavery ideas that they considered extremist. Charles Hammond's *Gazette* offered a colorful account of the courthouse scene, and it treated Birney's abolitionist remarks with a laudable even-handedness, despite the fact that Hammond would not publish Birney's own declaration. By the end of the evening, the paper noted with what sounded like frank admiration that "his conduct had disarmed the madness of the multitude."

But there was no mistaking the toxicity of the climate in which Birney now operated. The assembly had approved a resolution calling for "lawful" steps to suppress abolitionist writings, but anyone reading the local newspapers in the ensuing days might have gotten a different idea. The *Whig* warned a few days after the gathering that if Birney and the Cincinnati antislavery group persisted, "they assume an awful responsibility, and the *consequences* must be on their own ill-fated heads." Some days later, the *Republican* tossed in its own veiled threat. "Every American patriot is called upon by the ties of humanity, patriotism and honor, to put down abolition and abolitionists *peaceably* if we *can* and *forcibly* if we *must*."

Birney wondered in print who would come to his aid, if any of these threats came to pass. "Where is the mayor of this city when his authority is thus set in open defiance?" he asked. "Does he go to these editors and caution *them* against such expressions? Does he advise *them* against such law-breaking attempts? We fear not." Birney was right about one thing: The mayor would not prove a helpful presence when things heated up again.

CHAPTER ELEVEN

THE SOUTH BUILDS A BARRICADE

T HE IDEA OF PUBLISHING antislavery viewpoints—even in the South—wasn't always the risky proposition that Lovejoy and Birney were finding it to be. For nearly two decades, certain men of conscience had rolled ink across their presses to decry human bondage—all without causing much of a stir in the communities where they lived. Admittedly, these antislavery editors were operating in border states along the slavery divide, rather than in the Deep South, where the attachment to slavery was uniformly stronger. Nonetheless, it is fair to say that antislavery opinions were freely expressed in slave states such as Tennessee and Birney's Kentucky during the opening decades of the 1800s, so much so that there were even newspapers devoted to the topic.

That all changed after 1830, however, when events would convince nervous defenders of slavery that the best way to preserve their peculiar institution—and maintain peaceful coexistence between the states—was to clamp down on any speech or writing attacking it. Pro-slavery forces would spend considerable energy during the 1830s trying to construct a form of ideological cordon aimed at keeping out abolitionist expression in all its forms—a barrier they sought to stretch even to the free states of the North.

This clampdown was not always effective in silencing abolitionist speech, but it ushered in an exercise in censorship unlike any in peacetime American history by seeking to suppress a broad array of expression: newspapers, literature sent by mail—even whether slavery could be discussed in the halls of Congress. Lovejoy and Birney made the decision to attack slavery through their journalism at precisely the moment when doing so became taboo—and, in some places, unlawful—across much of the country. But they were not the first to do so. Although editors in major slave-owning communities such as Virginia stepped gingerly, even conventional newspapers in some parts of the South once freely published articles that dared to imagine a future free of the "evil" of slavery.

The honor for the first editor of an antislavery newspaper in the United States goes to Charles Osborn, a white Quaker minister raised in eastern Tennessee. Although his section of the state tended to be more receptive to antislavery opinion than elsewhere in Tennessee, Osborn's distaste for slavery led him to move to Ohio, where in 1817 he established his version of the *Philanthropist* (this paper was separate from Birney's subsequent paper). Osborn's own views were radical for the time when it came to emancipation— he supported immediate, unconditional freeing of the slaves—but his religiously themed paper took a more tempered stance, going only as far as to support gradual abolition. He also opposed colonization, the foundational principle of the American Colonization Society, which had been formed a year before the launch of the *Philanthropist*. Among the people who worked for the paper was another Quaker, Benjamin Lundy, a sales agent and sometime contributor (and later editor). Lundy would go on to play an important role as an antislavery editor in his own right. (It was Lundy who, in Baltimore in the late 1820s, would convert still another printer to the budding abolitionist cause: William Lloyd Garrison.)

While Osborn published from Ohio, a free state, yet another Quaker, Elihu Embree, opened an antislavery paper at around the same time in eastern Tennessee, the same region where Osborn had grown up. The Embree paper, eventually known as the *Emancipator*, promised "to advocate the abolition of slavery" and to serve as a clearinghouse for speeches and tracts on slavery and slaveholders, which the paper once referred to as "monsters in human flesh." In a sign of the appetite for antislavery commentary in eastern Tennessee at the time, the *Emancipator* managed to gain two thousand subscribers before Embree died in 1820. Opposition existed, though. Tennessee governor George Poindexter returned a sample of the *Emancipator* that had been sent to him, saying that the paper was "mischievous in its tendency: designed to sever the bonds of social harmony." Still, there did not appear to be any concerted efforts to stifle the paper's work. Other newspapers pressing for Black emancipation were published in Kentucky and New Orleans, though apparently without wide readership.

Lundy was by far the most consequential antislavery editor of the 1820s—indeed, probably no other white American did more during that decade to promote freedom for the enslaved, thanks to Lundy's writings and personal campaigning across thousands of miles of travel. Following the death of his old boss, Osborn, Lundy decided in 1821 to launch his own paper dedicated to ending slavery. He called it the *Genius of Universal Emancipation*, a name that stuck even as he moved it to four different cities in the North and South during the next fifteen years. The New Jersey–born Lundy was a saddlemaker by trade and already had been busy trying to set up antislavery societies in Ohio when Osborn first asked him to get involved with the antislavery *Philanthropist*.

Now on his own, Lundy quickly sought to use the monthly *Genius* to prescribe a step-by-step program for checking the spread of slavery to new states, ending the trade of slaves within the country and scrubbing from the Constitution the three-fifths provision that tilted power to the Southern states with slave populations. He was uncompromising in denouncing slavery, but seemed to lean to a gradual form of emancipation. And he promoted a variation on the colonization scheme by personally traveling to Haiti and, in later years, Texas, to search for possible alternatives to Liberia for the removal of freed Black people. (During the 1820s, Lundy personally lobbied slave owners to release their slaves, then traveled with the freed people to Haiti to ensure that the government there made good on its promises of land for them.)

Lundy, whose own awakening to the cause of slavery came during a stretch of time when he lived and made saddles in what is now West Virginia, set the bar high: He sought to rally public opinion during a period when, it seemed, the nation had stopped thinking and debating much about slavery after its first years of independence. He believed that the most important thing was to "arouse and awaken the American people to a sense of the inconsistency, the hypocracy [sic] and the iniquity of which many of them are chargeable in suffering this foul blot to remain upon their national escutcheon." He would use the Genius and his unapologetic truth-telling to keep the curse of slavery before Americans until they could avert their gaze no more.

Lundy shifted from the free state of Ohio to Tennessee and then Baltimore, Maryland, another slavery state. It was during a fundraising trip to Boston in 1828 that Lundy met Garrison, who at the time was working as an editor of a temperance newspaper. It was an encounter that would change Garrison's life and alter the path of the antislavery cause. Garrison biographer Henry Mayer writes that Garrison saw in the reed-like Lundy an older version of himself: "slender and quick, with abundant energy and sharp talk that testified to his righteousness with every gesture and syllable."

It was this meeting with Lundy, Garrison would recall, that "opened my eyes" and "inflamed my mind" about slavery. Garrison was converted. In the next issue of his temperance paper, he hailed Lundy's Genius as "the bravest and best attempt in the history of newspapers." Within months, Garrison had swapped his own gradualist view for a full embrace of immediatism. In 1829, he decamped for Baltimore to join Lundy in publishing the *Genius*. It would be a learning laboratory for Garrison on two fronts. Garrison would live among Black people in a slavery state—Baltimore alone was home to about five thousand slaves and nearly three times as many free Black people when he moved there—and he would cut his teeth as an antislavery propagandist.

Lundy and Garrison practiced a no-holds-barred style of newspapering and were unafraid to name names in criticizing the domestic slave trade, in which Baltimore played a key role as a transshipment port. (Baltimore, as we know, was the origin of many of Captain Benjamin Godfrey's slave-trading trips to New Orleans in the years before he abandoned his seagoing life and later moved to Alton.) This pugnacious style had its downsides. Lundy was beaten badly by a slave trader he had criticized in print. For his part, Garrison found himself facing criminal prosecution for libel in 1830 after he denounced a Massachusetts ship owner for being part of the slave-trading system in Baltimore.

The prosecution seemed to Garrison a naked attempt to muzzle such criticisms in a slave state. Even though the core facts of his news item were true—the Massachusetts ship owner's ship had, indeed, ferried a load of slaves to the South—Garrison was convicted of libel. The sentence was six months in jail or a $50 fine that Garrison couldn't afford to pay, so he chose jail. From behind bars, Garrison wrote copiously, including about the use of the libel law to crimp press freedom. One of the pamphlets produced from his incarceration happened to catch the eye of none other than Arthur Tappan, who promptly offered $100 to free Garrison after forty-nine days. For his part, Lundy would continue publishing the *Genius* from various spots, with periods spent in the District of Columbia and Philadelphia. (He even hired presses to print from the road as he traveled around the country.) Lundy and his newspaper had kept the antislavery flame burning during the moribund years of the 1820s, and he would ultimately outlast Lovejoy and Birney as an abolitionist editor. He died in 1839.

Free Black people in the North were also sounding the call for slave emancipation during the 1820s. Northern Black people had organized early in opposition to the nascent colonization campaign, arguing for slave liberation on U.S. soil, rather than deportation to a far-off land. Organizers gathered three thousand free Black people in Philadelphia in 1817, in an early demonstration of antislavery activism. During the 1820s, Black clergymen in New York and Pennsylvania helped seed dozens of Black abolitionist groups—several years before white activists like Garrison would launch organizations that would become the main channels for the larger abolitionist movement.

The first Black antislavery newspaper was *Freedom's Journal*, a New York publication founded by John Russwurm, a Bowdoin College alumnus who had been the first Black student to graduate from an American college. Russwurm and his co-editor, Samuel Cornish, launched *Freedom's Journal* in response to the racist diatribes of a separate pro-slavery newspaper, and published material reflecting the interests and tribulations of Black readers. In so doing, the paper was a natural vehicle for the antislavery views of free Black people in New York, which had the largest Black population in the North. *Freedom's Journal* circulated throughout the Northeast and as far south as North Carolina, but it lasted only two years. It closed in 1829 after Russwurm switched positions and joined the colonization movement, to the dismay of former colleagues. He eventually moved to Liberia. Cornish started a new paper instead, a radical publication called the *Rights of All*. It also wouldn't last long. But Cornish would remain active in the wider abolitionist movement, and his early newspaper ventures helped pave the way for subsequent Black abolitionist publishers, including the most famous, Frederick Douglass.

Black readers in the North also would make up the bulk of subscribers for Garrison's *Liberator*, which launched with a bang on New Year's Day, 1831.

Following his printing stint with Lundy in Baltimore, Garrison had come to believe that the only answer to the moral wrong that slavery represented was immediate emancipation, a term that over the years would mean different things to different people. For Garrison, it spelled an urgency that would not brook shades of gray or politeness. In the Liberator's inaugural issue, Garrison recanted his own remarks backing the "popular but pernicious doctrine of *gradual* abolition" and excoriated his own "timidity" in earlier writings in Lundy's *Genius of Universal Emancipation*. His new publication would pull no such punches, Garrison promised in his main editorial. "I am in earnest—I will not equivocate—I will not excuse—I will not retreat a single inch—" He then notched up the volume with the printer's equivalent of a bellow. "AND I WILL BE HEARD."

Garrison's combative approach, which in the minds of many Americans came to define abolitionism as a whole, would for some time generate within Lovejoy a deep disdain over tone and what he saw as a view out of touch with the realities of slave states. Across the South, it would contribute to rising fear that freely expressed criticisms of slavery represented a threat to the stability of the slavery enterprise, as well as to the understandings that undergirded the Union itself. The South's answer was a stunning effort by pro-slavery forces to make sure that no one would be able to read such words.

* * *

IN THE OPENING WEEKS of 1832, at around the same time that Lovejoy was attending revivals in St. Louis that would lead to his religious conversion, an extraordinary event was taking place far to the east in Virginia. There, lawmakers in a Southern state were having a wide-ranging discussion that boiled down to a simple question: whether or not to free Virginia's slaves. The fact that such a debate would be taking place at all was a measure of the shock and consternation among white people that had followed the slave rebellion led by Nat Turner a few months earlier. The attack by Turner's band had killed about sixty white people, including children. Turner's subsequent capture and execution by hanging did little to relieve the sense of alarm in Virginia.

To many white people, the episode was proof of the grim dilemma that fellow Virginian Thomas Jefferson had succinctly laid out on several occasions. In living with slavery, Jefferson had warned in 1820, "we have a wolf by the ear, and we can neither hold him, nor safely let him go. Justice is in one scale, and self-preservation in the other." Jefferson, a slave owner himself, and others of the nation's founders, had long recognized that slavery represented a moral stain on a nation built upon the rights of man, but left for another day the decision of whether to risk the national marriage to remove that blight. Now an act of appalling violence was once again thrusting the issue to the fore.

Jangled white Virginians hurriedly circulated petitions, gathering more than two thousand signatures that called on legislators to craft a solution to the suddenly urgent matter of slavery in the commonwealth. The petitions reflected a wide range of proposed solutions that spoke to the fractured views held among Virginians. (Those in the eastern region, which held most of the state's slaves, were more heavily pro-slavery, while those in the west looked more favorably on plans to free slaves.) Some petitions proposed the wholesale removal of free Black people, revealing deep worry over their potential to disrupt white society. Others backed gradual emancipation and deportation of Black people to Liberia, while still other petitions, pushed by Quakers, decried slavery as an "evil" and called for its abolition. Influential editors also called upon lawmakers to take action, with Thomas Ritchie of the Richmond *Enquirer* ultimately arguing in favor of "gradual, systematic, but discreet" emancipation.

In January 1832, the Virginia House of Delegates, after some parliamentary jousting in committee, placed the question of emancipation before the full body in a stunning form—with an open debate before spectators and the press. For weeks, lawmakers argued back and forth on emancipation, a discussion that swept in broader questions of morality, efficacy, and competing rights. Abolition-minded delegates who saw in slavery a moral wrong wondered aloud if a dependence on unpaid Black labor was producing a torpor among white plantation owners that would prove a long-term drag on Virginia's economic competitiveness (a concern similar to the one Lovejoy would voice about Missouri). Conservatives defended slavery on the grounds of private property rights, saying the U.S. Constitution protected slaveholders against "usurpation" by the government.

Virginia newspaper editors could barely contain their glee over the spectacle of an unfettered discussion, following long years of official silence on slavery that went back to the country's founding. "The seals are broken which have been put for fifty years upon the most delicate and difficult subject of state concealment," proclaimed Ritchie, whose newspaper printed the legislators' speeches and found room for the opinions of others on both sides of the argument. "[T]he press fearlessly speaks its own sentiments—unawed by the tocsin of denunciation or the menaces of proscription." Another editor, John Hampden Pleasants of the Richmond *Whig*, also saw in the legislative debate an important breakthrough: "In a free land, with a free Press, one subject was prohibited and guarded from free discussion with Turkish jealousy. Nat Turner, and the blood of his innocent victims have conquered the silence of fifty years."

In the end, the House of Delegates rejected the move to free slaves through legislation, claiming that "a further action for the removal of the slaves should await a more definite development of public opinion." The decision dealt a permanent setback to antislavery Virginians who had spotted a glimmer of hope. For the newspapers that had zealously thrown themselves into the struggle, however, the mere fact of a free airing of opinions provided a sign of hope that slavery's fate was sealed. "The moment statesmen were permitted to examine the moral foundation and the pernicious effect of slavery, and the press was unshackled to proclaim their sentiment and to combat in the cause of reason, justice and the common good," wrote Pleasants, "that moment the decree of abolition was registered in the book of fate. It must be so, and it cannot be otherwise."

His prediction would prove wildly optimistic, at least in the short term. Equally misplaced was the burst of elation among journalists over the atmosphere of freedom that seemed to have suddenly blossomed in their midst. The historic Virginia debate did not usher in a new era of openness—rather, it spelled the brief last throes of unhindered speech and writing on the matter of slavery in the South. Turner's rebellion in August 1831, was, in the minds of many Southerners, warning enough. But the printing press also posed a threat. Many in the South believed that Turner had been inspired to violence by the printed word coming from people like Garrison, who had launched his *Liberator* earlier that year. Even before that, signs of menace had already spilled off the press in the form of an explosive pamphlet published by David Walker, a free Black man in Boston, who tapped a wellspring of Black anguish in calling for equal rights and urging enslaved Black people to liberate themselves from oppression.

Walker's seventy-six-page *Appeal to the Colored Citizens of the World*, published in three editions beginning in 1829, stirred wide panic across the South after police in Savannah, Georgia, discovered sixty copies that had arrived by a white crew member of a ship in December of that year. The Savannah mayor appealed to his counterpart in Boston, Harrison Gray Otis, to arrest Walker. But Otis replied that there was nothing he could do because Walker, a transplant from North Carolina who sold used clothing, had broken no laws in his city. Georgia was determined to stanch further pamphleteering. The state clamped a forty-day quarantine on ships carrying Black sailors, and it enacted a law imposing the death penalty on anyone who circulated material seeking to incite rebellion. Virginia's House of Delegates met behind closed doors in 1830 to discuss how to smother distribution of the *Appeal* after a copy was found in Richmond.

Here was a turning point: For the rest of the 1830s, the South's stated fears of servile insurrection became the fuel for a regionwide effort to squelch the words of critics. In the aftermath of the Virginia debate on emancipation, a writer called "Appomattox" published a thirty-page letter that saw nothing but peril in the airing of views by an antislavery press. "Let us pay no regard to the claim which may be asserted for the independence of the press," Appomattox wrote. "[I]f in the exercise of *their* independence, they choose to print, we, in the exercise of *our* independence, may choose to suppress, to the uttermost of our power, what we deem inflammatory, dangerous, mischievous." Appomattox made clear he was calling for individual actions, such as to cancel a subscription to a newspaper (or, ominously, "to discourage the circulation of it"), rather than laws to punish speech aimed at "sedition."

But editors and activists would encounter a mixture of actions against open expressions of opposition to slavery—through laws, indictments, threats, and strong-arming by mobs—in what amounted to a vast, and largely unchallenged, regime to suppress speech. Nearly every Southern state enacted laws prohibiting the circulation of "incendiary" materials, or those deemed likely to incite slaves to revolt, and broadly interpreted what was meant by those terms. Alabama's law, as in Georgia, included the death penalty for publishing papers likely to produce "conspiracy or insurrection" among slaves or free Black people. South Carolina governor George McDuffie told his state's lawmakers that publishers of abolitionist literature should face death "without benefit of clergy." A North Carolina law imposed lashing for circulating dangerous materials—or even for teaching slaves how to read and write—while Mississippi, South Carolina, and Louisiana provided fines and jail terms for violations of their laws aimed at blocking writings and speech deemed likely to stir up slaves. Maryland, Virginia, and Tennessee had similar versions of laws on the books to keep out antislavery speech. (Missouri, where Lovejoy was still based in St. Louis at the time, would not put such a law on the books until closer to the Civil War, but relied instead on an 1804 law that imposed the death penalty for conspiring to encourage slave rebellion.)

These draconian suppression laws were seldom enforced, perhaps in part because so few abolitionists ventured to proselytize in person in the slavery South in the face of a hardening barrier to their words. (The whipping of Amos Dresser would confirm the perils of carrying abolitionist writings into slavery country.) Such suppression laws were seen as thoroughly legal in the South, where leaders held the view that criticizing slavery from other states represented an unconstitutional interference in their affairs. Following this line of reasoning, many in the South hoped to attack the plague of antislavery materials at their source: several slave-state legislatures urged Northern states to pass their own measures to clamp down on antislavery publications. But none of the states in the North would agree to go along, despite the widespread hostility toward abolitionists that ignited violent mob actions in places such as New York, Boston, and Utica.

Likewise, the North failed to act on Southern reward offers for the capture and delivery of Arthur Tappan, or to arrest a man named Richard G. Williams, the publishing agent of the New York–based *Emancipator* newspaper, after his indictment in 1835 by a Tuscaloosa County, Alabama, grand jury on charges of circulating "seditious and incendiary" pamphlets. A Virginia grand jury separately targeted the leadership of the American Anti-Slavery Society by demanding the extradition of its entire executive committee. But these charges came to naught. Slavery interests would have to erect a protective barrier at their own border if they were to hold the accursed abolitionists at bay.

* * *

THE SAME U.S. POSTAL system that ferried tons of bundled newspapers— including Lovejoy's *Observer*—all across the country had, by the middle of the 1830s, become an important cog in the abolitionist movement's nationwide publicity machine. The American Anti-Slavery Society was producing four separate monthly journals—the *Emancipator*, *Human Rights*, the *Anti-Slavery Record*, and *Slave's Friend*—and publications were pouring off its steam-powered presses in vast numbers by 1835. The trick was to put these implements of moral suasion into the hands of clergymen, opinion makers, and slave owners in the South. And that's where the U.S. Post Office came in.

The Tappan brothers and the antislavery society's leaders hoped that mailing the materials in bulk to named recipients would help the cause of freedom find purchase among society's elites of Southern society, including among the slave owners themselves. Reformers had used the mails before to promote their varied crusades—temperance, for example, and Sabbatarianism—but this would be the first time the postal system had been employed systematically as a means to combat slavery. It was an audacious gambit—targeting twenty thousand Southerners who had not asked to receive antislavery publications—and a clever way to avoid the South's feared vigilance committees. The antislavery group launched the mail strategy in 1835, and by the peak of its campaign in summer, it had bundled and sent 175,000 separate pieces around the country.

The postal campaign served to aggravate the paranoia in slavery states that had grown, tumor-like, since the Nat Turner rebellion and the acceleration of the abolitionists' activities. In Charleston, South Carolina, a vigilante group called the Lynch Men decided to take matters into their own hands. On the night of July 29, 1835, the men broke into the post office and located a bag of American Anti-Slavery Society literature that had arrived aboard the steamship *Columbia* and been set aside by the city's postmaster, Alfred Huger. The vigilantes crept out with the bag and, the next day, burned the antislavery journals in front of a noisy crowd of two thousand people who had gathered on a parade ground next to the military academy known as the Citadel.

The resulting controversy over the use of the mails to promote abolitionism would capture in miniature some of the dynamics roiling the country over slavery. That included a hysteria in the South that was producing calls for greater censorship and a deep suspicion of any action by Washington that might be seen to open the way for the federal government to regulate slavery in any way. Huger was caught between his fear of leaving the mails naked to future mob attacks and that of spreading literature that would be seen in South Carolina to promote slave rebellion. He appealed for help to the postmaster in New York, Samuel Gouverneur, who in turn asked the antislavery society to halt its mailings to the South. The group refused. Gouverneur, employing a novel reading of the law that essentially used South Carolina's ban on abolitionist materials as his guide, decided to block further mailings by the activists from New York until the U.S. postmaster, Amos Kendall, decided how to proceed.

Kendall, the Jacksonian former newspaper editor, delivered wishy-washy guidance to the local postmaster: He could not lawfully block the offending materials from the federal mails, but would not order that they be delivered in contravention of state laws barring the circulation of "incendiary" materials. The local postmasters were on their own to decide how to proceed, but with the knowledge that the federal government would look the other way if their solution was to purge antislavery journals—at least until Congress took up the matter. As Kendall told Gouverneur, "You and the other postmasters who have assumed the responsibility of stopping these inflammatory papers will, I have no doubt, stand justified in that step before your country and all mankind."

Gouverneur and Huger were effectively shutting off the flow of abolitionist materials at the tap, a policy that was met with loud but mixed reviews in the North. While some editors and citizen groups in Northern states supported actions aimed at cleansing the mails of publications that they viewed as toxic, the idea of placing such power in the hands of postmasters made defenders of a free press more than a little queasy.

William Leggett, the editor of the New York *Evening Post* and no fan of the abolitionist strategy, said Kendall's approach effectively handed the South the ability to impose a "censorship of the press . . . by allowing every two-bit postmaster through the country to judge of what species of intelligence it is proper to circulate." Those free-press concerns would grow sharper over time.

President Jackson, who viewed the abolitionists with contempt, at first suggested that federal postal authorities expose the names of anyone found to subscribe to the offending journals and let the local communities deal with them. Then he shifted gears by proposing that Congress outlaw mailing offensive matter, thus injecting the federal government into the matter. But other Southerners, such as Senator John C. Calhoun of South Carolina, who were obsessed with any possible federal encroachment into the slavery issue, feared that a national postal ban on abolitionist materials might lead to a more general erosion of states' rights. Calhoun proposed that if anyone was to restrict published materials, it should be the states, not Congress. This was in keeping with a widely held view that while the First Amendment barred the federal government from regulating speech on public issues, the states were free to do so.

In the end, though, the two positions effectively canceled each other out—Congress left press rights untouched and expressly prohibited local postmasters from interfering with the flow of the mails. Nonetheless, postmasters continued to hand abolitionist journals over to local authorities for destruction under state laws barring incendiary publications. (In Kentucky, for example, Birney discovered that the local postmaster was intercepting antislavery newspapers addressed to him, based on Kendall's instructions to Gouverneur. For two months before leaving Danville for good, Birney received letters, but no abolitionist literature.) The South's barricade against abolitionist ideas was holding firm at the same time its leaders—people such as Governor McDuffie and an increasingly shrill Calhoun—were trying a new, aggressive tack in the defense of slavery.

They were dropping their defensiveness and fighting back in earnest by depicting slavery not as some unavoidable evil, but rather as a "positive good" for the nation and its 2.5 million enslaved people.

Thanks to the exchange newspapers that were delivered to him, Lovejoy was able to monitor these far-off debates from his perch on the frontier. His reaction was growing dismay. When a feverish-sounding McDuffie delivered a highly publicized speech in December 1835, proposing that abolitionists—those "wicked monsters and deluded fanatics"—face execution "without benefit of clergy," Lovejoy ran the text in the St. Louis *Observer*. The address included the contention that slavery was sanctioned in the Bible. As McDuffie put it, "the patriarchs themselves, those chosen instruments of God, were slaveholders." Lovejoy published the address without editorial comment but fired back at McDuffie the following week. Lovejoy wrote that the idea of divine sanction for human enslavement was "unworthy of the Christian name, and worthy only of the darkest ages that ever brooded over a wretched and sinful world."

A few months later, Lovejoy waded into the postal controversy—taking aim, in particular, at Calhoun's bill to allow local postmasters to suppress antislavery mailings—and let fly his disdain for the notion of government censors in America. "How many censors of the Press would it require in the Charleston P.O. to examine, closely enough to decide whether or not they are 'incendiary publications,' all the printed documents delivered in that city?" Lovejoy asked. "The whole plan is less absurd than wicked. . . . It might answer for the meridian of Persia or Russia, but it cannot live in the atmosphere of this republic." Lovejoy ended his brief, three-paragraph attack on the Calhoun postal measure by arguing that the country stood at a crossroads. Calhoun's bill was evidence, Lovejoy said, "that either the system of slavery or the Constitution of this Republic, with all its free institutions, must soon come to an end. There is no other alternative."

* * *

EVEN AS CALHOUN AND his allies in Congress frantically plugged holes to stem the flood of antislavery propaganda in the mails, a fresh breach in the dam demanded their urgent action. Alongside its postal campaign in 1835, the American Anti-Slavery Society had launched a companion effort that would prove equally vexing to the South's attempts to silence condemnations of slavery. The weapon in this offensive was the humble petition, a tool for expressing the public's will since the time of English kings. Starting in late 1834 and continuing through the next year, the Anti-Slavery Society sent printed petition forms to hundreds of its branches and other societies in towns and cities across the North, such as the group that Lovejoy's mother, Betsey, had joined. The petitions employed stock language prepared by the society (at times with wording borrowed from Theodore Weld) urging Congress to pass legislation to abolish slavery in the District of Columbia and the territories and to halt the domestic slave trade. Canvassers, who often were women, were instructed to leave no stone unturned: "Follow the farmer to his field; the wood-chopper to the forest. Hail the shop-keeper behind his counter . . . forget not the matron, ask for her daughter. Let no frown deter, no repulses baffle. Explain, discuss, argue, persuade." More than half of the petitions bore women's signatures.

The idea was to inundate Congress with hard evidence of antislavery opinion and to keep the slavery issue constantly on its members' lips. Congressmen, one at a time, would present the petitions they had received from their home states, starting with Maine in the extreme north and then working southward. During the congressional session that began in late 1835, the abolitionists would present petitions carrying more than thirty-four thousand signatures that had been collected by the grassroots activists. The new petition campaign recalled a drive during the late 1820s that also had asked Congress to end slavery in the District of Columbia. (The capital was a logical target for such action because, unlike the states, it fell under federal jurisdiction and therefore was subject to congressional action on all matters, including slavery—at least on paper.) In that earlier case, Congress declined to act following a bitter floor debate, but the episode encouraged the antislavery society to reprise the strategy as a means of agitation on the issue. If the plan now was to keep the slavery question boiling, it succeeded wildly, aided by the panic-stricken South's attempts to muzzle not just the odious abolitionist press but also ordinary Americans in their exercise of the First Amendment right to petition.

U.S. Representative John S. Fairfield, a Mainer from the coastal town of Saco—some one hundred miles south of Lovejoy's home town of Albion—stood in the House of Representatives on December 16, 1835, to open the 25th Congress. Fairfield read a petition that had been signed by 172 women in his district calling for the abolition of slavery in the nation's capital. Every one of the House's 242 members would have the opportunity to stand and read any petitions they had received, but Maine's customary position at the head of the petition agenda meant that the thirty-nine-year-old Fairfield got to go first. Fairfield noted that he did not necessarily agree with the sentiments of the women who had signed the petition, but was obliged to share it as part of his congressional responsibilities. And so he did.

Fairfield's brief presentation that day marked the first salvo in what would turn into a years-long parliamentary tug-of-war over whether such petitions—and, by extension, slavery itself—could be discussed by the people's elected representatives in the halls of their Congress. Led by Calhoun and Representative Henry Pinckney, a fellow South Carolinian, slavery's defenders sought to erect the same kind of blockade on slavery talk in Congress that they had thrown up against abolitionist newspapers in the mails. The right to petition, although enshrined in the First Amendment, represented a public relations headache for pro-slavery politicians of the South and their allies in the North. Petitions in Congress threatened to open discussion about slavery in the one place where it would be impossible to ignore. Aside from their usual fears of slave insurrection, Southern members of Congress had no interest in indulging the abolitionists' desire to make points by slandering them as monsters and man-stealers. But they needed to find an acceptable way to smother the petitions without infringing on First Amendment guarantees of "the right of the people . . . to petition the Government for a redress of grievances."

The answer arrived after some back and forth, and would become known as the "gag rule." Under this device, crafted by Pinckney, the House would summarily dispose of any petitions related to slavery without printing or discussing them—the petitions would instead be "laid on the table" and "no further action whatever shall be had thereon." Through this tabling stratagem, Congress would meet its Constitutional obligation to receive citizen petitions, while relegating them instantly to the parliamentary equivalent of suspended animation. Its members would never have to discuss the petitions nor fear their ever coming to life. It was a bald use of the South's inflated clout in Congress, with the help of Northern votes, to prevent members from bringing up a topic that most of them preferred to leave unmentioned, anyway. For his part, Pinckney was clear about the gag rule's purpose: "to arrest discussion of slavery within these walls."

Despite tireless, and often ingenious, efforts to subvert the gag by opponents such as John Quincy Adams, the former president now representing Massachusetts in the House, the gag rule would survive in one form or another for eight years. In a larger sense, however, it backfired. Abolitionist groups mobilized to gather mountains more petitions in hopes of embarrassing the would-be censors. And Adams's mischievous parliamentary ploys—he once presented a petition purportedly signed by twenty-two slaves to ask if it fit under the gag rule—would thrust the topic of slavery before the House again and again, to the great fury of his Southern colleagues. (A separate gag in the Senate, authored by Calhoun, is thought to have been more effective at stanching discussion.)

The House's gag rule ultimately would be repealed at the end of 1844. That shift came about as a result of dwindling votes among Northern Democrats in support of the gag, which had to be fought over and approved each time Congress convened for new session. By the time of its repeal, many Northerners—even those once hostile to abolitionism—were feeling increasingly resentful over the slavery camp's continued efforts to stifle expression. And it was the South itself that had managed to feed the growing view that its suppression tactics now threatened the civil liberties even of white Americans. There was a certain measure of Aesopian turnabout here, of overreach producing loss. But the North's darkening mood on such questions didn't form all at once—this took years to evolve. By that time, the Northern scorecard of condemnable acts would reflect the cases of the editors Lovejoy and Birney.

CHAPTER TWELVE

A RIGHT TO INTERFERE

I N THE SPRING OF 1837, Alton's soaring prosperity came crashing down as spectacularly as it had once taken flight. A years-long festival of giddy lending and exuberant investment in land and minerals had fed a go-go economy whose expansions owed more to fevered speculation than actual growth. It was a classic bubble, and it popped with disastrous results. The area's galloping land prices stumbled and fell. Meanwhile, the lead trade that Gilman and Godfrey had worked to corner through the purchase of mines in the area—heavily leveraged investments staked by the state bank that they controlled—fell victim to a national collapse in lead prices.

It was all part of a bigger, dismal story playing out across Illinois and the rest of United States. The bottom fell out of the national economy, which had been propped up artificially by the policies of state banks that printed and lent money with little regard for how much gold or silver they had to back it, and with no national bank or oversight to apply the brakes. Land peddlers had been hawking entire towns to Easterners. As

Illinois governor Thomas Ford would later assert, "our people surrendered their judgments to the dictates of a wild imagination. No scheme was so implausible as not to appear plausible to some." Collapse was foretold. The value of currency plummeted. Many of the banks that had suddenly sprouted overnight in preceding years crashed just as quickly.

Almost no sector of the nation's economy was spared, from agriculture to manufacturing. Debts went unpaid. The price of the South's cotton fell. Northern merchants like the Tappans watched their trade wither. (Lewis Tappan would later start a business, the Mercantile Agency, that was a forerunner to modern credit-rating companies.) The crisis marked the worst of America's early brushes with economic downturn and would come to be known as the Panic of 1837. Those living through it applied a more prosaic moniker: "hard times."

The depression hit Alton and its population of twenty-five hundred as hard as if a swollen Mississippi had jumped its banks. Lovejoy's friends Gilman and Godfrey were at the heart of a local economy that relied heavily on their lead monopoly for its trade with the outside world. When the price of lead began to tumble on the East Coast, they would try to prop it by stockpiling their supply, but this was to no avail. The pair had borrowed $800,000 from the state bank to buy mines and smelting operations in Galena, sending land values there zooming. When the price of lead ultimately hit rock bottom, so did their ability to pay. The bank had also lent liberally to other Alton businesses, including a pair of large produce shippers. All told, by one estimate, it would end up losing $1 million in bad loans.

The nationwide downturn also hurt Alton's river trade, including the freight-forwarding operations carried out by Godfrey, Gilman & Co. As their enterprise edged toward distress, others fell completely. Business owners were unable to pay their bills. Building projects stalled. The pounding of Alton's hammers dimmed. Harm rippled out in unexpected ways. Enoch Long, the barrel maker who was a close friend of Lovejoy and Gilman, scrambled to cover various of his friends' debts, including more than $5,000 in commitments they had made toward the construction of the new Presbyterian church in Upper Alton. The loss of that money, plus the failure of other Long investments during the panic, would leave him penniless by the following year.

Lovejoy had spent much of the spring beseeching his fellow clergymen to take a stand on slavery, but he also was watching as the economic damage piled up. By May, he had seen enough of this calamity to detect the hand of God at work. It was time to pick up his pen. There were many targets at which to take aim, many lessons to draw. To Lovejoy, the economic depression was offering what a later generation might call a teachable moment, and he had no intention of squandering it. On May 25, he published a blistering column called "The Bubble Burst," in which he took the occasion of economic pain to make larger points about morality. Lovejoy attributed the depression to a litany of social ills: the soul-wasting effects of wealth, an excessive "love of money," too many feckless churchmen and—naturally, since he was compiling a litany of moral offenses—the existence of human bondage.

"For the past three or four years the people of this nation have been pursuing after wealth, as their chief good, with an eagerness unknown before in our history," Lovejoy began. "Wealth has been the God after which this nation, in the language of the Scripture, has gone a whoring." He took aim at the embarrassment of "luxury, licentiousness, and immorality" that had been unleashed in the rush for "bubble wealth." Pious Christians had proved just as vulnerable to the temptations of fast money, he charged: "We are all verily guilty in this matter."

He turned to the question of slavery, saying that money lust had "blunted" the nation's moral senses to the evident atrocities of slavery. Even worse, Christian clerics had looked the other way or sought to brandish the Bible to justify "this horrid business," Lovejoy said. "Men were either too busy in making money themselves, or too desirous to get a share of that earned by the forced labour of the poor slave, to hear his groans. His tears, mingled with his blood drawn by the whip of his merciless taskmaster, fell unheeded to the ground." And, Lovejoy added, anyone who dared speak up against this injustice risked community derision or the violent reactions of the mob—those "gentlemen of property and standing" who tore down abolitionists working "in behalf of bleeding humanity." If the nervous citizens of Alton had looked to Lovejoy's paper for words of comfort during hard times, what they got was a parson's wagging finger. And there was enough slavery talk to catch the eye of Alton's own gentlemen of property and standing. For some of these men, who looked to the South for trade and profits, it was not a wild stretch to wonder if Lovejoy's writings themselves were a cause of their mounting economic troubles.

* * *

IT BEGAN WITH WHISPERS. Even before Lovejoy's searing rebuke on the economic downturn, his antislavery commentary had begun to generate the sort of rumors that would likely spell trouble in a town like Alton. It was bad enough that some locals had grown weary of his regular moralizing on drinking or violating the Sabbath. He was a tiresome teetotaler and Yankee scold—that was one thing. But as the *Observer*'s circulation climbed, hardly an edition passed that didn't include news about the antislavery movement, such as the creation of new societies in other states and even elsewhere in Illinois. As the spring season unfolded, so did a local anti-Lovejoy campaign conducted sotto voce.

By one account, Lovejoy had said that anyone who opposed abolitionist lectures should be "hung up without judge or jury." This was patently false. Lovejoy was never known to promote extrajudicial punishment or violence of any manner. But in suggesting that he backed vigilante violence in the pursuit of radical antislavery aims, such an allegation served to undermine Lovejoy's standing as an advocate of free discussion and rule of law. It made him look no better than the mobs who had tormented him in St. Louis. ("It seemed to declare to the world that you, too, approved of violence and bloodshed," a worried friend wrote to the editor.) Lovejoy's alleged declaration gained wide enough local circulation that one of the competing Alton papers, the *Spectator*, was moved to issue a disclaimer.

Even more potentially dangerous, however, were murmurings that Lovejoy supported miscegenation. A report was making the rounds that Lovejoy had told parishioners at the Upper Alton Presbyterian church one Sunday that if his wife should die that day, he would marry a Black woman within a week's time. The idea of such a declaration from a white minister of the 1830s—from the pulpit, no less—was preposterous on its face. But the rumor helped tar Lovejoy without bucket or brush by linking him with one of the most explosive tropes employed against antislavery activists at the time—that they favored interracial marriage, or amalgamation.

The New York City riots that targeted abolitionists in 1834 owed much of their furious energy to paranoid beliefs—fanned by certain newspaper editors—that the activists' radical agenda included marriage across racial lines. After the attacks on the Tappans during New York's three days of violence, the white mobs had inflicted their worst damage by invading homes and smashing property in the city's Black precincts. White residents were ordered to light up their windows to avoid trouble—the mob would pass them by in order to attack homes where darkened windows suggested Black families lived. Painting abolitionists as crazed race-mixers was also a common theme in the South.

Lovejoy was all too familiar with the amalgamation charge against people who opposed slavery. He crafted a forceful rejoinder when a Kentucky newspaper called the *Baptist Banner* accused abolitionists of advocating interracial marriage, and thus defying God's purported plan to separate Black people from white people ("much as he has separated midnight from noonday," it said). Lovejoy countered that there was no evidence for such a wild assertion. Moreover, he asked, if God had meant to keep the Black and white races apart, how to explain the abundant proof that slave owners had fathered children with their Black slaves?

Lovejoy pointed to the case of the nation's unmarried vice president, Richard M. Johnson of Kentucky, a Jacksonian Democrat, who had fathered two daughters during a long-term, open relationship with an enslaved woman, Julia Chinn. "Is not the Vice President of the United States, and one of your own citizens, an 'amalgamator,' as you phrase it?" Lovejoy asked the Kentucky editor. Lovejoy said the scarceness of Black people with the "pure gloss of an African complexion" was confirmation enough that extensive miscegenation had taken place in the South. He left unmentioned that such mixing was typically the product of sexual violence.

Lovejoy surely was aware of the whisper campaign around him—he was even asked once whether he really *had* promised to marry a Black woman. (His exact answer went unrecorded.) But if he felt twinges of worry, Lovejoy kept them to himself. His brother Owen had moved to Alton to join him and Celia several months earlier and was studying to be an Episcopal minister. (Sister Elizabeth would make the same journey West later in the year.) Lovejoy exulted in the growth of his thirteen-month-old son, Edward, "a very healthy, fat, large child" with "blue eyes, rosy cheeks" who seemed on the verge of talking. And the editor was feeling optimistic about the *Observer*, whose numbers were moving in the right direction and, he said, "gaining favor daily with man, and I hope with God."

Lovejoy detected progress, as well, in the antislavery cause that was sprouting around him in Illinois. "Antislavery sentiments are becoming more prevalent here and we shall soon have societies multiplying all around us," Lovejoy predicted in a letter in April to his brother Joseph in Maine. Thanks to his earlier series of published exchanges with the Reverend Asa Cummings of the *Christian Mirror* in Portland, Lovejoy knew that his antislavery opinions were circulating far beyond Alton. He was mindful of how they were coming across. Lovejoy asked Joseph in closing if his jousting with Cummings on the failure of the clergy to confront slavery had appeared "un-Christian in spirit or unkind in manner." The letter may have been the last time the two brothers communicated—if Joseph wrote back, his reply never surfaced.

* * *

BY EARLY SUMMER, LOVEJOY began to see his newspaper not only as an outlet for news about the abolitionists' war on slavery but also as part of the army. Specifically, he was taking up ranks with the American Anti-Slavery Society, in which Birney and Weld were also playing key roles, and his ties increasingly twined with theirs. In late June, Lovejoy printed news of the latest round in the group's year-plus-long campaign to bombard Congress with petitions calling for an end to slavery in the District of Columbia. This time, the Anti-Slavery Society was seeking the names of two people in every county in the North who would spearhead petition drives in their home communities. Lovejoy announced that he would forward names of people he knew, and he urged *Observer* readers around Illinois to nominate other "friends of humanity" to rally to the cause.

Lovejoy adhered to the conventional abolitionist view that Congress exercised no constitutional authority over slavery, since that was understood to belong to the states alone. But the nation's capital was a different matter, he believed. Because it belonged to the whole country, the moral burden for what happened there lay with all Americans and with their elected members of Congress. Lovejoy hoped to appeal to his readers' sense of shared culpability. "[L]et every freeman in this republic remember, that so long as Slavery exists in the District of Columbia, he is himself a slaveholder, and a licenser of the horrid traffic in slaves, carried on under the very shadow of the Capitol's walls," the editor wrote. "We have a right to interfere there."

Lovejoy said that the petition effort, which as before was being shep-herded in the House of Representatives by John Quincy Adams, was in search of one million signatures. But such work would not be for the faint of heart. Lovejoy warned the prospective organizer that the business of circulating antislavery petitions "will cost him some time, some trouble and the good will of every advocate of Slavery." Nonetheless, he proposed that with enough volunteers and "proper effort," Illinois could provide as many as thirty thousand signatures. This was no minor step. Lovejoy was not only aligning his newspaper with the nation's largest abolitionist organization, he was thrusting the *Observer*—and himself—into the realm of direct agitation on slavery. The *Missouri Republican* and Alton *Spectator* were clearly displeased by Lovejoy's call for volunteers and published comments that appeared to be intended to "excite public indignation."

Then, a week later, on the Fourth of July, Lovejoy sat down and penned a piece titled "Illinois State Anti-Slavery Society." The headline was drab, but beneath it thundered what one of Lovejoy's friends would later call his "most obnoxious editorial." Taking note of the symbolism of Indepen-dence Day, Lovejoy decried a bitter irony—that white Americans would be basking in "the declaration that 'all men are born free and equal' . . . while our feet are upon the necks of nearly THREE MILLIONS of our fellow men! Not all our shouts of self-congratulation can drown their groans— even that very flag of freedom that waves over our heads is formed from materials cultivated by slaves." As Lovejoy summoned his readers to join the fray, he suddenly sounded a lot like the Boston rabble-rouser Garrison: "The voice of three millions of slaves calls upon you to come and 'unloose the heavy burdens, and LET THE OPPRESSED GO FREE!'"

But how could his readers contribute to such a lofty goal? Lovejoy had an answer. He said the time had come to organize a statewide antislavery society in Illinois like those that abolitionists had formed in other Northern states. His regular mentions in the *Observer* of such organizations were an indication that he had been tracking their growth. As well, Lovejoy was broadening his connections with established abolitionists—such as James M. Buchanan, a recent transplant to nearby Carlinville—who were also associates of James Birney. When the time came to organize the inaugural meeting of the Illinois society, Lovejoy would invite the Ohio activist James Thome, a well-known veteran of the Lane battle, and Birney himself. Although Lovejoy and Birney had spent only limited time together (Birney had hosted him in Cincinnati), they now inhabited different corners of the same universe of Presbyterian churchmen who had turned their energies to antislavery.

At the same time, Lovejoy's success as a newspaper editor seemed increasingly to hinge on antislavery sentiment: the most loyal pockets of the *Observer*'s subscribers were in Quincy, the abolitionist hotbed where David Nelson lived, and in Jacksonville, the home of Illinois College and Lovejoy's friend Edward Beecher. Lovejoy was aware that his call for a statewide antislavery group could provoke ill will, even if he could not yet fully anticipate the backlash it would engender. "With many we are already a 'fanatic' and an 'incendiary,' as it regards this matter, and we feel we must become more and more vile in their eyes," Lovejoy conceded, with what sounded like tacit acceptance. "We have never felt enough, nor prayed enough, nor done enough in behalf of the perishing slave." And in case proposing formation of such a group wasn't a bold enough step, Lovejoy suggested that a suitable headquarters for it might even be Alton itself.

This was all too much. Certain businessmen and residents who earlier had looked the other way when Lovejoy inveighed against alcohol or profane language now confronted the unnerving possibility that he was about to turn their community into a base for antislavery activity. Such a move would be terrible for the city's image and could only serve to complicate ties with its slave-state trading partners, including those just across the river in Missouri. This was already unwelcome in prosperous times, but simply anathema to many in the town during an economic downturn. Words needed to be said before Lovejoy's growing pugnacious-ness threatened what remained of the city's economy and its reputation for relative order. On the morning of July 8, two days after Lovejoy's published call for a state antislavery society, anonymous handbills appeared on the streets of Alton, calling residents to a public meeting at an establishment called the Market House. The purpose of the gathering was to discuss the *Observer* and try to prevent it from printing and spreading what a local paper labeled "the odious doctrines of abolitionism." The tranquil period of Lovejoy's new life in Alton was coming to an end.

The Market House meeting took place three days later. Among the organizers were several of Alton's physicians, including J.A. Halderman, who was elected as meeting chairman. Another doctor, Horace Beall, was appointed to a three-member committee that wrote up a set of strongly worded resolutions, which were unanimously approved by the larger group. The assembled men included John Hogan, a voluble local wholesale mer-chant who was a Whig member of the Illinois legislature. Hogan, whose face seemed forever reddened, was known around town for a boisterous manner and dogged optimism. He was a former Methodist pastor and had earlier worked with Lovejoy as part of the local Bible society and Sunday school union. But Hogan now hoped that the *Observer* editor would agree to put down his pen once he had learned the opinions of some of his fellow Altonians—and respected ones, at that.

The group had little trouble deciding on the points it wanted Lovejoy to hear. For one, his public writings were exposing the community to "Abo-litionist doctrines of a most inflammatory nature"—ideas that, even in a free state, were "improper as well as impolitic." In publishing columns about slavery, the group charged, Lovejoy had trampled on the "sacred pledge" he had once made to leave the subject out of his newspaper. In the statement it approved, the group also made clear that it feared that further antislavery agitation would jeopardize Alton's economy "by eliciting from our sister states, a feeling towards us highly injurious to our community."

Moreover, the group asserted that Lovejoy's troublesome words risked stirring up mob violence in Alton.

Halderman noted with satisfaction that the gathering demonstrated to slaveholding states that they had friends who would defend them, even in non-slave-owning corners. The assembly stated in boilerplate fashion its opposition to slavery but quickly turned from that, declaring that any solution would, of course, require the approval of the slave-owning states. The preferred answer, at least for the men who gathered at the Market House that night, was colonization or gradual emancipation. They baldly rejected the "misrule of Abolitionism." In a bit of rhetorical sleight of hand, Halderman framed the effort to quiet Lovejoy as entirely consistent with the country's legacy of free speech, saying that it was the group's "duty" to "act and speak on all questions" when it saw the need.

The job of offering up the resolution that mattered most fell to "Colonel" Alexander Botkin, a former butcher who also was a local Whig activist. Botkin wore the bulbous nose of Shakespeare's Bardolph, as one friend put it, as well as the bloated features of someone a bit too fond of drink. But his resolution sounded lawyerly in its careful wording. (One chronicler later suggested that it wasn't his work at all.) Botkin said that Lovejoy's paper spelled harm to the overall community and that, "as we deprecate all violence of mobs," the group's members "politely request a discontinuance of the publication of his incendiary doctrines." The group, claiming to speak for Alton, was formally asking Lovejoy to stop talking about slavery.

A committee was named to meet with Lovejoy but instead sent him a politely worded letter thirteen days later, along with the various resolutions that had been passed during the Market House session. The committee asked him, "with the utmost deference to your feelings as a man, and your rights as a citizen," for a prompt reply to the central question: Would he keep writing about slavery? The representatives indicated that the stakes were high on all sides. "Nothing but the importance of the question which the meeting was called to consider, and the dangers which its unwise agitation threatens . . . could have induced us to take the step we have," said the letter, which was signed by all five committee members, including Halderman and a second young physician, Benjamin K. Hart, a thirty-year-old Harvard graduate who was also president of the Alton's town board.

The Market Street group's letter was respectful in tone and carried not a hint of a threat. But the contents of the accompanying resolutions clearly amounted to an ultimatum, and they put Lovejoy in a difficult spot. First, he was suddenly placed in opposition to his own purported vow to avoid writing about slavery—a characterization that he thought wise not to litigate at the moment. (Lovejoy's friends would later deny that he ever made such pledge, but his decision to remain silent here left him open to this continued line of attack.) More consequentially, though, the group's condemnation of his slavery columns forced the editor to decide now just how committed he was to continue with his newspaper writings. Even if he had been aware of the earlier whisper campaign, Lovejoy was now being put on notice in the black and white of resolutions that a certain number of fellow Altonians had gathered to consider. The decision before him was one Lovejoy had not anticipated facing when he scurried to Alton nearly a year earlier. How far was he willing to go to publish what many around him clearly did not want to hear?

* * *

LOVEJOY'S REPLY CAME IN the form of two resounding blasts. One arrived on July 20, nine days after the Market House meeting aimed at getting him to desist. Lovejoy wrote and published a long, blistering column that occupied a hefty chunk of page 2, under the headline "What Are the Doctrines of Anti-Slavery Men?" If the editor had once denounced abolitionists as wild-eyed extremists, this piece of writing was unmistakable

proof that he was now fully one of them. He fiercely defended the abolitionist position and the people who advocated it, arguing that abolitionists
had been unfairly tarred by misrepresentations and untruths, including
the shopworn charge that they were champions of amalgamation.

The case for abolition rested first and foremost, Lovejoy argued, on
the belief that all men were created free and equal, a condition that was
impossible to honor so long as any man was permitted to turn another
into merchandise—"a 'THING,' a 'CHATTEL,' an article of personal
'PROPERTY.'" American slavery was "a legalized system of inconceiv-
able injustice, and a SIN," Lovejoy wrote. He warned that the "political
evil" represented by bondage was not merely a bane to the nation's slaves.
It threatened the wider society as well and would soon bring about "the
downfall of our free institutions, both civil and religious."

Lovejoy also sought to turn the words of Southern politicians like Calhoun against the slavery cause they so ardently defended. Calhoun, in
arguing about the former tariff issue years before, had declared that "he
who *earns* the money—who *digs it out of the earth* with the sweat of his
brow, has a *just title* to it against the Universe," Lovejoy wrote. It was just
such a liberty—the right of a man to keep what he earns—that abolitionists
were defending now. And because the Bible offered only one remedy for
sin—to repent immediately—the same held true for the sin of slavery.
"Abolitionists believe that all who hold slaves, or who approve the practice
in others, should immediately cease to do so," the editor argued. Emancipation might spell economic harm to slave owners, but it would be as
worthwhile as to deprive a rum seller of his profits, he said.

In this remarkable column—part self-criticism, part war cry—Lovejoy
was openly embracing a fiery approach that he had, not so long before,
denounced as dangerous for the country. Gone were the weasel words of
gradualism, the paternalistic concern for souls over the lived existences
of breathing people. The time for half measures had passed. Lovejoy may
not have directly applied the abolitionist label to himself—his detractors

had done this for him, after all—but the volcanic July 20 column was the closest he would come to a personal manifesto on the crime of slavery. His conversion to abolitionism was complete.

A second, more pressing matter still remained: the Market House group's ultimatum. The polite, almost deferential, tone of the committee's letter aside, there was no avoiding the question: would he stop publishing on slavery? Six days after his stunning "Anti-Slavery Men" column hit the streets, Lovejoy put quill to paper again. He thanked the committee's members for the courteous tone of their message, then promptly went to work dismantling any hope they had for a smooth resolution. He could not recognize the authority of the Market Street assembly when it came to "the public newspaper of which I am Editor," Lovejoy said. "By doing so, I should virtually admit that the liberty of the press and freedom of speech, were rightfully subject to other supervision and control than those of the land. But this I cannot admit."

Lovejoy borrowed from Dr. Halderman's own clever turn to argue that yes, the country's founders had conveyed a liberty of speech to act and speak on "*all questions* concerning this great commonwealth." But, he added, this freedom was bestowed not by the nation's forefathers but rather "from our Maker." Employing the right of expression on the matter of slavery was not "unwise agitation," as the committee had suggested in its letter. Rather, it was essential. "It is a subject that, as I apprehend, must be discussed, must be agitated." Should the would-be censors want to test the validity of his opinions, Lovejoy offered in closing, they could find them clearly stated in his July 20 column about the doctrines of antislavery men.

His answer to the group, then, was an emphatic no.

CHAPTER THIRTEEN

THE ODIOUS DOCTRINES OF ELIJAH LOVEJOY

T HE *OBSERVER* EDITOR'S INCREASING defiance had caught the attention of many in town. One man who surely was keeping an eye on the events beginning to roil Alton was Usher F. Linder, the newly named Illinois attorney general, who had moved there a few months earlier. Linder, a lanky, politically hungry transplant from Kentucky, was a strong defender of slavery. He believed that hurried emancipation would mean the ruin of the white man and saw abolitionists like Lovejoy the same way many of his fellow Southerners did: as peddlers of a dangerous dogma whose logical outcome would be slave rebellion and untold violence. Linder, only twenty-eight years old, had been named as the top law-enforcement official in Illinois by the legislature a few months earlier, in February. By law, he was supposed to be working from the capital in Vandalia but opted instead to base himself in Alton. The striking topography of the Alton area had captured his fancy. "I have never been in any country more striking and bold than the bluffs of the Mississippi," he would later recount.

Linder was an unalloyed Southerner, the son of a tavern owner, raised in a meadow-covered region of central Kentucky known as the Barrens. By happenstance, he and Lincoln were born just a month and seventeen miles apart and would cross paths, professionally and politically, in Illinois through much of their adult lives. (Seventy miles to the east of their birthplaces in Kentucky was the Birney plantation in Danville.) Linder grew up to believe in the supremacy of white people and to favor the lesser-evil argument when it came to slavery. He was trained as a lawyer and worked a short while in Kentucky. Linder and his young wife, Elizabeth, then made the move with their two children to Charleston, Illinois, about 140 miles east of Alton, traveling the National Road that was the pipeline to the West. In Illinois, Linder eked out a living as a so-called circuit lawyer, arguing cases as he made the rounds on horseback. Linder became known as a captivating speaker and was said to be "almost irresistible" to juries.

Linder was a political climber and won election to the state legislature in 1836, running as a Whig. (He would later switch to the Democrats for good as their party became the main defenders of slavery.) His colleagues in the House of Representatives included "Honest John" Hogan, the ruddy merchant from Alton, and Lincoln. Linder, standing over six feet tall, was described as "one of the most picturesque figures in the House" and a "terror on the stump"—a nod to his oratorical charms. He amassed enough clout among his colleagues in the legislature to win their approval for the attorney general's post, though the vote was closer than it probably should have been because some of his fellow Whigs declined to support him.

Although slavery was not Linder's primary issue, he, like many cautious politicians at the time, saw emancipation as a potential disaster for white people and the Union. As he would later describe it, a press that cranked out abolitionist writings was nothing more than an instrument of slave insurrection and murder, operating in the guise of religious devotion. Linder was also a shrewd politician. Although antislavery opinion in Illinois was growing, he knew that abolitionists as a rule were widely disliked.

It was not difficult to see the potential electoral benefits in standing against these activists in a state where lean times seemed invariably to revive calls for legalizing the ownership and sales of slaves.

Linder may have been encouraged in this direction by a political mentor and housemate: Theophilus W. Smith, an ardently pro-slavery judge and former state senator from Madison County, who was frequently neck-deep in intrigue and once drew a pistol on then governor Ninian Edwards. (Smith had been impeached for corruption and abuse-of-power charges while serving as a justice on the Illinois Supreme Court, but he was acquitted after the state senate fell short of the required two-thirds vote to convict.) Previously, as a state senator in the 1820s, Smith had been a prominent backer of the proposed 1824 convention to legalize slavery in Illinois. Smith also had little use for Lovejoy's friends, Gilman and Godfrey. The judge was on the losing end when the Gilman and Godfrey investment group won the contest for control of the State Bank of Illinois in 1835. So when Linder won a seat in the legislature, the judge persuaded him to introduce a series of resolutions in the House calling for an investigation into the group's running of the bank. In Linder's telling, the resolutions "fell like a bombshell" in the chamber, but an investigation eventually cleared the bank's management of wrongdoing.

Linder was admired for his way with words, but he also possessed a belligerent side that could quickly turn violent. According to one account that gained publicity at the time, soon after being named as attorney general, Linder burst into a barber shop to confront a senator, John C. Reilly, a fellow Whig who had not voted for him. The two exchanged sharp words as Reilly finished his shave. As Linder turned to leave the shop, he drew a pistol and fired several times at his colleague, wounding him slightly, according to a letter to one of the newspapers. Linder wrote a letter of apology, and the matter was dropped. The *Missouri Republican* summed up the episode by calling Linder a "noisy" choice for the job of top lawyer. The newspaper also said Linder was "not so regular in his habits" as might be expected for that position—a thinly veiled reference to his reputation for drinking.

Linder's name did not appear on the Market House resolutions asking Lovejoy to bring a halt to his antislavery writings or in the letter that followed. It has been suggested that it was Linder who ghost-wrote the lawyerly sounding resolution that Alexander Botkin introduced, mentioning the risk of mob violence in Alton. That scenario seems entirely possible, though there is no hard evidence that Linder was the brains behind any aspect of the meeting. But as the struggle over a free press in Alton escalated during the many weeks to come, Linder would take on an increasingly prominent role as Lovejoy's main nemesis. No one among Lovejoy's critics would prove more eloquent, more pugnacious, or more wily. If Linder's work lay in the shadows until now, it would soon be plenty visible to all.

* * *

HART AND THE OTHERS at the Market House meeting had failed to win Lovejoy's promise to steer clear of the subject of slavery—anyone who read the *Observer* could plainly see that the editor and his allies were proceeding with plans for a statewide antislavery convention. Lovejoy served as chairman of a newly formed Madison County Anti-Slavery Society, which started meeting in the Upper Alton Presbyterian church in early August to begin sketching plans for a statewide convention in late autumn. Lovejoy openly posted notices of the meetings and their outcomes in the *Observer*, alongside other local news items.

It was clear that the hoped-for gathering was stirring considerable interest among antislavery-minded people in Illinois—by the middle of August, more than two hundred people had indicated their support. But Lovejoy knew there were yet more souls to round up. "Now is the time for every man whose heart is in the work to come forward and give it an impulse that shall be felt from one end of the state to the other, yea, in every county of our sister state across the river." The Alton area was emerging as the favored site for such a statewide convention. Indeed, the Madison County society approved a motion by Lovejoy's friend Enoch Long to host it in Upper Alton, a stone's throw from the slavery South.

More broadly, Lovejoy had come to see that "this great movement" of antislavery should attract—indeed, would attract—all moral people to its side. Still to be drawn were the "conservatives of church and state" who, Lovejoy said, could not be bothered so far to take sides in this epic struggle. "They cannot bear the idea of being disturbed, and compelled to take sides in this contest," he wrote. Lovejoy was also flashing signs of a remarkable loosening in his own rigid views of some of the abolitionist movement's key figures, including his old foil, William Lloyd Garrison. In a column called "Fault-Finders," Lovejoy urged wary readers to look past their differences with some of the more controversial abolitionists. He specifically urged leeway for the iconoclastic Garrison, who was embroiled in an all-out war with mainstream Protestant leaders over his attacks on clergymen who remained silent in the face of slavery, as well as over his rejection of the institution of the Sabbath and skepticism toward the Bible itself. But Lovejoy now argued that too many moral-minded people were keeping themselves from the slave's cause just because they disagreed with certain beliefs held by its better-known advocates, thus "converting mistakes into crimes."

As a further example, Lovejoy pointed to the case of the colorful Grimké sisters, Sarah and Angelina, converted Quakers from the South who had taken on a controversial role as roving lecturers for the East Coast–based antislavery movement. The presence of these women speaking in churches before mixed crowds of men and women was horrifying to traditionalists, who saw in such behavior the eventual breakdown of society. Lovejoy allowed that he, too, opposed the Grimkés' public role. But he argued that philosophical nitpicking over "trifles" was getting in the way of the greater struggle they shared. For Lovejoy, who once scolded his own mother for her support of the "wicked" Garrison, this was a stunning show of pragmatism over purity and a sign of how he now viewed the stakes in the crusade against slavery. "All good men will come over—those who possess the greatest simplicity of Christian character will come first, and the rest will follow, as the truth reaches the heart," he wrote.

Lovejoy was now coming under attack from newspapers on the Missouri side of the slavery divide. The *Missouri Republican*, which never was much help to Lovejoy when he faced mobs in St. Louis, was zealously covering his latest controversies across the river in Alton. The newspaper had cheered on the Market House gathering in July, saying Lovejoy was finally getting his just deserts for "his adhesion to the odious doctrines of abolitionism." The *Republican*'s coverage of the meeting carried more than a whiff of menace as it considered what lay ahead for Lovejoy. "The editor of the *Observer* had merited the full measure of the community indignation; and if he will not learn from experience, they are very likely to teach him by practice." Lovejoy's continued agitation, the *Republican* charged, had cost him "all claims to the protection of that or any other community."

Then, following the formation of the Madison County Anti-Slavery Society, critics speculated that it would inspire many other such groups to spring up around Illinois. One Missouri newspaper referred to the *Observer* as "the minister of mischief" and said the time had passed for the community to eradicate it. "Something must be done in this matter, and that speedily! The good people of Illinois must either put a stop to the efforts of these fanatics, or expel them from the community." If this were not accomplished, it said, the answer for Missouri and other slaveholding states might be to stop doing business with Alton.

Not surprisingly, words began bleeding into action. On the evening of August 21, Lovejoy had gone to a friend's house to perform a marriage ceremony. On his way home, at about nine P.M., he stopped at a drugstore in Alton to get some medicine for Celia, who was ill. As he made his way toward home, Lovejoy was stopped on the outskirts of town by a group of men who didn't appear at first to recognize him. When they did, the men began to throw clumps of dirt. One of them ran up alongside him, wielding a club. "It's the damned abolitionist!" the man shouted. "Give him hell!" The mob threatened to tar and feather Lovejoy. He soon found himself surrounded, the men's arms linked to form a blockade, as shouts rang out. "Rail him!" "Tar and feather him!" "Tar and feather him!"

Lovejoy was certain that he was about to meet the tar brush (a humiliating ordeal that usually spelled burned skin and the painful removal afterward of the wood tar and coating of feathers). It was then that he spoke. Lovejoy conceded that the mob could do with him what it pleased. But he had a request: would one of the men take the medicine to his ailing wife without frightening her? A member of the group agreed to do so, and set out. Lovejoy then turned to the mob and asked to be released. "You have no right to detain me," he said. "I have never injured you." This drew grumbling and curse words from the group. Lovejoy concluded, "I am in your hands, and you must do with me whatever God permits you to do." In Lovejoy's retelling of the encounter, the men conferred briefly and agreed to let him go. The party included the doctor Horace Beall, a Maryland native who had been part of the Market House bid to get Lovejoy to drop his slavery commentary, as well as another Alton physician, James Jennings, a Virginian. Concerned about possible legal action by Lovejoy, the men went to consult with their lawyer, George T. M. Davis after the episode. There, "they expressed their amazement that he was ready and willing to suffer the worst possible indignity, and, if need be, give up his life rather than surrender 'the chimerical idea of emancipating the niggers of the South,' which they persistently maintained could never be accomplished," Davis would recount.

That was not the end of the vigilante activity that night, however. After Lovejoy was freed, fifteen to twenty people made their way to the *Observer* office and began pelting it with rocks. One of those rocks crashed through a window and hit one of the printing workers in the head, severely injuring him. In a short while, several members of the mob rushed inside and started trashing what they could see. They grabbed up metal type and broke the heavy press to pieces, then carried the debris into the street and scattered it for all to see. It was a spasm of destruction that many had been waiting for in recent weeks—twice before mobs had appeared in front of the *Observer*, but each time turned away before any attack could take place.

For the second time in thirteen months, Lovejoy's press was destroyed. On the Missouri side, the latest sacking of the newspaper elicited little sympathy for the *Observer* editor. Rather than condemn an attack against a fellow newspaper, the *Missouri Republican* fretted that the incident would generate negative press attention elsewhere that would unfairly stain the reputation of Alton—the same instinct it had displayed after the McIntosh slaying in St. Louis a year earlier. Alton's citizens "abhor disorder as much as any other community, however fastidious," the newspaper argued, "but there is a point beyond which endurance may cease to be a virtue."

Instead, it turned blame on Lovejoy and his newspaper, saying that Lovejoy had "justified the harsh measures" because he had violated his pledge to avoid discussing slavery. A day later, with more to say on the matter, the *Republican* claimed that Lovejoy had previously been impervious to the "mild means" aimed at persuading him to desist. "In fact, he exhibited a stubbornness that surprised even his friends," the *Republican* sniffed. "The result has been seen, and although regretted because of the violation of law involved, is condemned by but few, if any." Another St. Louis paper, the *Missouri Argus*, likewise suggested that Lovejoy had it coming to him. "This terminates the existence of a print which has for a long time been disseminating doctrines peculiarly hurtful to the domestic institutions of this state," the *Argus* declared.

On the Illinois side, the reaction was somewhat more sympathetic to Lovejoy. The Alton *Telegraph*, the paper where his brother John worked, ran a terse, just-the-facts account of the destruction but topped it with a one-word, all-caps headline obviously meant to convey dismay: "OUT-RAGE." The short piece predicted that a criminal investigation would follow, but there is no evidence that local authorities looked into the matter with any intention of criminal prosecution. In any case, Alton, which had just been incorporated as a city, didn't have a professional police force. For its trouble, the *Telegraph*, soon after publishing its article on the sacking of the *Observer*, received an anonymous threat that it, too, would face attack.

The destruction of Lovejoy's press meant that he was now the editor of a newspaper with no means to publish. There were few places to turn for help. Alton was in the final days of its first political campaign as a city, and there was little sign that anyone in the local establishment would be willing to stick their necks out for an abolitionist. Benjamin Hart, the Harvard graduate who was one of the leaders of the Market House gathering, had been an early favorite to become Alton's first mayor, but he turned down the nomination. Another candidate for the top office, Charles Howard, took pains to counter rumors that he was soft on abolitionism: he placed a statement in at least two Alton newspapers to state that he opposed the movement. Howard noted that he had not even attended the meeting with Lovejoy a year earlier at which the editor made his purported pledge to stay clear of slavery. Meanwhile, Halderman, the physician who chaired the Market House meeting and a Whig, would win a seat as an alderman.

The man who prevailed for mayor in the late August vote was a lawyer and transplanted New Yorker named John M. Krum. He was a Democrat and had moved to Alton from St. Louis two years earlier. Krum represented a possible source of hope for Lovejoy in one sense: He had not been active so far in the campaign to silence the *Observer*. The twenty-seven-year-old mayor was worried more about local issues—upgrading Alton's steamboat landing on the Mississippi, raising the property tax rate, and creating elementary schools—than about slavery or freedom of speech. However, he was not unaware of the tensions in his city. In his inauguration message, Krum said that establishing a well-regulated police force would be a top priority in his administration—in part to protect any citizen's "right to act and speak according to the dictates of conscience." Krum did not mention mobs or the recent publicized actions against Lovejoy and the *Observer* in his speech, but that was probably unnecessary. It was obvious to many in Alton that frictions were mounting over the limits of expression. The issue was about to topple Krum's mayoral agenda.

* * *

LOVEJOY WAS NOW IN much the same beleaguered position he'd occupied when he arrived in Alton thirteen months earlier. His press, as Lovejoy told his mother, had once again "been mobbed down." His tormenters showed no signs of laying off. And any hope of starting anew was going to depend on the generosity of others. Lovejoy decided to borrow a voice to get his own back. He persuaded the *Telegraph* to print a one-page extra edition, in the form of an open letter, in which he appealed to his two thousand or so subscribers to help him round up the money to buy a new press and get the *Observer* up and running again. He needed $1,500.

Lovejoy's appeal was titled "To the Friends and Subscribers of the Alton Observer." It sounded like an 1830s version of a public broadcasting pitch. "We need your help, and we must have it or sink," he wrote. The editor said that what was at stake was nothing less than "whether the liberty of speech and of the press is to be enjoyed in Illinois or not." He called upon new subscribers to send their names, old ones to pay overdue charges, and everyone to contribute what they could to help fund the purchase of a new press. "Everything depends on you," Lovejoy pleaded. "If you take hold like men, like freemen, like Christians, all will be well; if you do not, mobism will triumph, but I shall be guiltless."

His strategy worked. Soon, pledges in denominations of $10 and $20 were rolling in from ministers and others around Illinois. But funds also came in from other parts of the country—a measure of Lovejoy's lengthening reach in the antislavery community. A supporter in Galena wrote to offer $50 after hearing of Lovejoy's plight from a friend. "He is not much of an abolitionist but he thinks we ought to protect the liberty of the press," the donor wrote, promising more money if needed. Lovejoy also received $20 from longtime Ohio abolitionist John Rankin, a towering figure in the antislavery movement now working for the Anti-Slavery Society in New York. He got a separate donation from David Lee Child, a well-known East Coast activist (his wife, Lydia Marie Child, was famous in her own right as an antislavery writer and lecturer in the Garrisonian mold). Even though Lovejoy operated quite apart from the core of the abolitionist movement headquartered back East, he was not altogether without support. In a matter of days, Lovejoy had gathered up enough funds to allow him to dispatch Owen to Cincinnati to buy a new press. It would be his third.

Lovejoy's apparent resoluteness of action during these late-summer days belied the creeping doubts that now darkened his thoughts. For one thing, Lovejoy was about to host a statewide antislavery meeting—most likely during the first week of November—that he had little idea how to carry out. It was obvious to all that such a gathering would be less than welcome by many residents of Alton, to put it mildly. And that was not to mention those looking on from across the river in St. Louis. Lovejoy was a preacher and a newspaperman—not an organizer. His links to the abolitionist movement were certainly better developed than even months earlier, but Lovejoy's work on the frontier was hardly a top priority for the antislavery groups agitating from places like New York and Boston, whose work was focused primarily in the Eastern states and on Congress.

Lovejoy sat down in early September, at around the same time his appeals for funding help were reaping results, and wrote a letter seeking guidance from his friend Gerrit Smith in upstate New York. Smith had converted to the antislavery cause after the Utica mobbing two years earlier and, because of that trouble, seemed a good person to ask about navigating the impulses of a hostile crowd. Lovejoy began his "Dear Brother" letter by noting that he had recently been the "victim of Lynch law," apparently referring to his recent encounters with local vigilantes. He then invited Smith to attend the November gathering in Upper Alton and to offer whatever expertise he could. "We need help greatly," Lovejoy wrote. "Many of our friends are inexperienced, we have a dreadful opposition to encounter, and we need the advice, the counsel, and the encouragement of those older brethern and friends, who have dealt with mobs and braved a vicious public sentiment."

More immediately, however, Lovejoy was discovering that his stewardship of the *Observer* itself had become a source of discord not only among his foes but among his friends as well. Since his arrival in Alton, Lovejoy had counted on the bedrock support of a coterie of Alton's pious elite: Presbyterian pastors and churchgoers, anti-alcohol activists, and businessmen, such as Gilman, with deep pockets and a social conscience to match. But that web of backing had begun to fray amid the latest challenges from respectable critics and thuggish vigilantes alike. Lovejoy still had die-hard backing from some of his benefactors, but others had started to consider the possibility that, in the face of so much controversy, he might no longer be the best choice to run the *Observer*.

Winthrop Gilman canvassed some of the paper's other backers about the state of affairs and came to a painful conclusion: for the sake of unity and the greater cause of freedom, the best course might be for Lovejoy to step aside. "I find so little union among our brethern in regard to re-establishment of the *Observer* with yourself as Editor that I think it becomes a very serious question whether duty should induce you to retire from it," Gilman wrote on September 8. The businessman said he would make good on a $100 commitment he had made a day earlier to support the *Observer*, but that would be it for him. "From conversations with several dearly beloved & highly respected brethern, I have come to the conclusion to do nothing more in aiding the paper," Gilman wrote.

This note came like a gut punch. Just a day earlier, Gilman had been busily trying to save the newspaper. He crafted an open letter in his own script to "our fellow citizens of the State of Illinois," announcing that the *Observer* would be revived with a new press, and assuring all that its supporters would "guard the freedom of the press without reference to the fact whether we agree or differ with doctrines of it." The public statement forgave those who had trashed the *Observer* office and vowed not to seek vengeance. "We deprecate violence but are determined to yield to nothing but Law," it said. Never, the letter said, would the group cede the "rights secured to us by our fathers of freely speaking and publishing our opinions various and diversified as we know them to be."

The declaration did not mention slavery—or Lovejoy—but it seemed a sturdy enough assertion of freedom of the press to justify the *Observer*'s resurrection. Lovejoy immediately set to work mailing copies of the statement for signing in several cities outside Alton, including Quincy, Jacksonville, and Springfield. But no sooner had he begun this than Gilman's letter arrived, asking Lovejoy if he should consider quitting. It is unclear whether Gilman had a sudden change of heart after writing up the group's free-press declaration, or was all the while working on two tracks: saving the *Observer* from its enemies while at the same time easing Lovejoy toward the exit. In either case, the result was the same: The ranks of Lovejoy's backers, multiplying elsewhere in the country, were shrinking in Alton.

The loss of Gilman's support represented a painful blow to Lovejoy. If one of Lovejoy's earliest backers was questioning whether he should remain as editor, how many others might back out? Was Lovejoy helping to advance the antislavery cause he had come to adopt so fervently, or was his continued tenure as editor merely serving to splinter it and galvanize the opposition? Would leaving now add up to surrender? Even before the latest Gilman wrinkle, Lovejoy's brother John had been in touch with the owners of the Quincy *Argus* newspaper about a possible purchase of the business, with its Smith Imperial press and assorted styles of type. It was not specified whether John was considering making the purchase for himself or inquiring on his older brother's behalf. (It would not have been the first time Lovejoy had pondered moving to Quincy, a town receptive to the abolitionist message and the largest single base of *Observer* subscribers.) Nothing came of the exchange, however.

Lovejoy spent three days searching his soul for the best next step. On September 11, he emerged with a decision: He would leave it up to the others to decide whether he should remain or quit. In a letter addressed to "Friends of the Redeemer in Alton," Lovejoy said he would "most cheerfully" step down if the *Observer*'s supporters decided that "the cause we all profess to love will thereby be promoted." He urged his fellow religious to ignore personal feelings in making their decision. "I am ready to go forward if you say so, and equally ready to yield to a successor, if such be your opinion," Lovejoy wrote. He said he had done his best, warning that "if I am to continue [as] Editor, you must not, on the whole, expect a much better paper than you have had."

Lovejoy set only one condition: If the *Observer*'s supporters asked him to resign, they would cover any unpaid bills he had incurred as editor and pay him to move with his family to "another field of labour." Lovejoy was broke. A balance sheet that he drew up to accompany his letter showed the *Observer*'s finances in a precarious state. The paper was $1,000 in the red, with a variety of outstanding charges. In addition, Lovejoy's associate editor, Thaddeus Hurlbut, had been working for months and had yet to be paid. On the bright side, Lovejoy had compiled a list of more than two thousand subscribers. The editor expressed his wish for a unanimous decision from the paper's supporters.

The result of the meeting to consider the *Observer*'s future was less than satisfying. The backers came to a swift—and unanimous—agreement on the first question they took up: whether to reestablish the newspaper. The answer to that was yes. But the second, of whether Lovejoy should remain as editor, proved stickier. The supporters met three different times to discuss the matter and each time failed to agree, postponing the matter for another day. On leaving one of these sessions, a participant remarked jokingly to one of the Lovejoy brothers, "We have been trying to kill your brother all the afternoon, but we cannot succeed."

Politically speaking, Lovejoy was in an exceedingly awkward position. He had enough loyal support, even if not unanimous, to hold the helm at the newspaper and pursue the activist course he had begun. But he was nowhere close to the sort of full-throated expression of civic support among Alton's elites that would likely be needed to protect him from potential harm. The political class was, at best, an unreliable force. And some of its canniest players, Usher Linder high among them, were downright hostile to Lovejoy's antislavery publishing. Newspapers on both sides of the river ranged from antagonistic to merely timid. Lovejoy's core of friends—people such as Enoch Long, Royal Weller, and the Reverend Frederick Graves—had certainly demonstrated their steadfastness. But they were few in number and had limited financial means.

To make matters worse, a visiting preacher from New Orleans, the Reverend Joel Parker, was bowling over many people in Alton at this same moment with an influential religious tract arguing once again for the idea that the Bible blessed slavery. The tract, written by a Mississippi clergyman named James Smylie, plus Parker's promotion of it, had struck Alton at a particularly sensitive moment. The biblical argument won over some believers, confused others, and generally served to sap the antislavery ardor of some of Lovejoy's erstwhile allies.

Even as Lovejoy prepared to receive a new press with which to relaunch the beleaguered *Observer*, he and his newspaper were gravely exposed. In fact, at that moment there was no abolitionist—or editor—anywhere in America who faced a more serious threat to their right to free expression. The last who had been in such immediate danger was Lovejoy's colleague in Cincinnati, James Birney, a year earlier.

CHAPTER FOURTEEN

A BAND OF
LAWLESS MEN

B IRNEY'S SHOW-STOPPING APPEARANCE BEFORE the unfriendly
crowd in the Cincinnati courthouse had ended, remarkably, largely
without further event. His check of the muskets and rifles inside his house
proved to have been unnecessary—the mob that gathered earlier in the
evening did not turn up at the Birney home, as had been feared. As well,
the clamorous scene at the courthouse had done nothing to dissuade Birney
from his course: He would continue to publish the *Philanthropist* and its
abolitionist message. But unlike Lovejoy, who edited a religious newspaper
that happened to run articles against slavery, Birney was a full-time
antislavery activist. This meant that he carried a diversified portfolio—he
was an organizer, lecturer, administrator, fundraiser, and editor.

Soon after arriving in Cincinnati in late 1835, Birney was named to the
executive committee of the Ohio Anti-Slavery Society, which had expanded
to include around 120 affiliate groups, with ten thousand members statewide. Among Birney's tasks was the job of choosing suitable lecturers
from the ranks of the society's devotees and assorted eccentrics—men who

dressed like Christ or sported Mexican sombreros and hanging beards, others who had adopted a Spartan diet of coarse bread and fruit. Birney's task was to apply a measure of discipline to the society's operations and public image. He, too, was a lecturer, and would spend much of the spring of 1836 traversing Ohio on horseback, organizing antislavery talks in churches and barns in a state that sported a powerful streak of abolitionist sentiment. (The Ohio movement included John Rankin, the Lovejoy donor, who had made his name as a minister and pioneer abolitionist and would turn his home in Ripley into a stop on the Underground Railroad.) In some places, Birney drew audiences of two hundred or more, even when he spoke on consecutive days.

But anti-abolition feeling in Ohio ran strong, as well. Birney found himself beset by opponents who interrupted his talks by shouting from the doorway or hurling eggs, apples, and small stones. Mobs were sometimes able to break up the meetings, and one group once hounded him to the home of a friend with whom he was staying. During a visit to a coarse-mannered town called Granville, a pack of men who Birney described as "beastly drunk" disfigured half a dozen horses outside his lecture by shearing the hair from their manes and tails. The attacks and harassment may have been the handiwork of louts, but they were orchestrated by "leading men in Granville," Birney was sure. "Although they would not, and on the present occasions did not, partake of the disgraceful deeds of the ignorant and the openly vicious, yet no one can doubt of their having incurred the deep guilt of the instigators and abettors," he wrote, a day after the confrontation. He was speaking of Granville's gentlemen of property and standing.

Yet, Birney's primary tool for spreading the word of abolitionism was the *Philanthropist*, and he managed to keep up with the weekly publication schedule alongside his myriad other duties. Despite the unmistakable condemnation of slavery that came through in the paper, Birney's generally mild tone during its early months seemed to have played a role in defusing the tensions that had threatened to explode in January. It was starting to look as if the worst of the storm had passed. An ally in Kentucky wrote to Birney to report that "much of that heat manifested on the first appearance of the *Philanthropist* has cooled."

By March, Birney believed that the conditions in Cincinnati were safe enough to allow him to move the paper's office there from its home in New Richmond, whose remote location had made it seem less vulnerable to attack. Even so, he recognized that the risk of a mob violence against the *Philanthropist* was real. For one thing, he deeply mistrusted the Cincinnati mayor, Samuel Davies—a man he described as "a poor creature and much opposed to us." (Birney's son William had an even lower opinion of Davies, labeling him a "servile parasite.") Nonetheless, Birney decided there could be political profit for the movement, even if it were struck by vigilantes. "It will be difficult to mob it—yet it may be done," he told Lewis Tappan in March, as he prepared to move the paper. "But let them mob it—as sure as they do, it will instantly make throughout this State *Five* abolitionists to one that we now have." The idea that an attack on the antislavery press could help win over skeptical Northerners was a variation on one of Birney's core beliefs: that the South's tooth-and-nail defense of slavery was a threat to the civil liberties of white people in the free states. "The contest is becoming—has become,—one not alone of freedom for the *black*," Birney had written to Gerrit Smith in New York several months earlier, "but of freedom for the *white*."

The *Philanthropist*'s new office in Cincinnati made no attempt to hide its purposes as a wing of the abolitionist crusade. It occupied the upper floors of a building in the corner of Main and Seventh streets, in the heart of the business district. Even a casual passerby would know what went on inside—an eighteen-foot sign on the Main Street side proclaimed "Anti-Slavery Office." The shelves were stocked with pamphlets and books on abolition for sale, and the place carried the feel of a busy storefront as *Philanthropist* subscribers and others came and went. Birney was in the office most days and became a fixture among the world of merchants downtown. He was also a familiar face at the Presbyterian church on Sixth Street.

Coming only two years after the Lane fiasco, this open embrace of abolitionism might have been read as a brazen display of cheek. But instead, Birney and his printer, a Quaker named Achilles Pugh, enjoyed a few months of relative calm. For more than two months, not a single local newspaper mentioned Birney or the *Philanthropist.* By summer, subscriptions had risen to 1,700, from just 700 at its start. Birney's fledgling newspaper had even won the hearty admiration of Benjamin Lundy, the battle-toughened abolitionist editor, even though the two had never met. Lundy, writing as he prepared for a fact-finding trip to Mexico, said he was so impressed by Birney's work that if he were not already busy, he would move his *Genius of Universal Emancipation* to Cincinnati to join with the *Philanthropist* as part of an effort to proselytize the West. In a matter of six months, then, Birney's newspaper project appeared to have threaded the needle. He had found a market for his antislavery ideas and garnered the respect of dyed-in-the-wool abolitionists. At the same time, his foes, apparently placated, had receded into the background. They were leaving Birney alone to publish his antislavery news and commentary freely. Until they weren't.

* * *

THE MOOD SHIFTED ABRUPTLY in July, for reasons that are not entirely clear. A mob of thirty to forty men moved against Pugh's print shop on Walnut Street late at night on July 12. Some stood as lookouts while the others used a ladder to scale a wall and climb onto the roof. From there, they entered through a window and encountered a boy sleeping on an upper floor. The men commanded him to stay quiet and covered his head with a sheet to prevent him from identifying them. The group proceeded then to ransack the place. They ripped up copies of that week's issue of the *Philanthropist* that sat ready for distribution. They ruined the ink and broke apart the press, and then carted off its pieces. Pugh lived at the site, and the mob posted sentries at his door to keep him from alerting neighbors. Despite the ruckus and the location of the assault in the middle of downtown Cincinnati, not a single peace officer appeared during the mob's two-hour fit of destruction.

The midnight raid on Pugh's press was hardly the end of it. Two mornings later, residents awoke to find handbills posted on the street corners with a message aimed at the antislavery activists. "Abolitionists Beware," the flyer warned. It said that citizens of Cincinnati had become convinced that the "wicked and misguided operations of the abolitionists" were hurting the city's business, and that the wrecking of Pugh's press "may be taken as a warning." Any attempt to revive the press, it threatened, would be interpreted as an "act of defiance to an already outraged community, and on their own heads be the results which follow." The message ended by noting that foes of the *Philanthropist* already had prepared a plan to "eradicate an evil which every citizen feels is undermining his business and property."

But who were the people behind these actions? The handbill was in part the work of a man named Joseph Graham, a trader who did business with the South and belonged to the Texas Aid Committee, which sent men and arms to white Texans to support their war for independence from Mexico. Graham had also been a key player in the sacking of the press two nights earlier. Birney and his allies believed that the attack on the press was engineered by members of the city's wealthy elites, though carried out by roughnecks they had hired, including several from across the state line in Covington, Kentucky. And it could certainly be argued that the wording of the handbill reflected the concerns of Cincinnati's business community more than those of its foundry workers and common laborers. There was an additional, shadowy force in town that seemed likely to have backed any actions aimed at stifling the abolitionists: the dozens of Southern slaveholders and their families who had come to spend the summer. The antislavery camp feared that the presence of so many members of the Southern planting class there encouraged Cincinnati natives to do their bidding in seeking to shut down criticism of slavery.

Anti-abolitionist sentiment was amply represented by the local newspapers, in particular the *Evening Post*, the *Whig* and the *Republican*, which served as mouthpieces for those who saw Birney's *Philanthropist* as a noxious troublemaker and hazard to the city's continued prosperity. (Charles Hammond's *Gazette*, however, took a more tempered approach to the growing controversy.) The *Post* reacted to the appearance of the July 14 handbill to warn that "an act disgraceful to our city"—violence—would greet any attempt by the abolitionists to reestablish the press. Meantime, an ominous note turned up on the scales of a local merchant asking him to post a sign in his storefront to indicate—yes or no—whether he supported the abolitionists. It was signed "Anti-Abolition."

The cascading events prompted Birney, Pugh, and another member of the antislavery group's executive committee to call on Mayor Davies in hopes of persuading him to support a public appeal to reduce the tensions. The trio handed Davies $100 to offer as a reward to anyone with information on the perpetrators of the press assault. The next day, on July 16, Davies indeed issued a public statement with the reward offer and a businesslike appeal to the public to obey the law. But in a jab at the abolitionists, Davies ended his pronouncement by noting that it was their acts that allegedly had been the spark for the riot at Pugh's office. In closing, the mayor urged the antislavery activists to put a halt to "such measures as may have a tendency to inflame the public mind, and lead to acts of violence and disorder, in contempt of the laws and disgraceful to the city." To Birney and his supporters, the net effect of the mayor's words was to signal that the onus for a future outbreak of violence would rest on the *Philanthropist* for what they might have called "provocation," rather than on the mob.

A fresh round of handbills sprouted the following morning, this time naming Birney directly. "A Fugitive from Justice, $100 Reward," the posters offered. "Said Birney in all his associations and feelings is *black*; although his external appearance is white," the handbill said. It offered to pay the $100 with "no questions asked." It was signed "Old Kentucky." The danger to Birney seemed to be growing more immediate. As a precaution, Birney sent his wife to stay with her family in Kentucky. Meanwhile, Birney's own father in Kentucky, who had never approved of his son's antislavery activities, sent Birney's brother-in-law, John J. Marshall, to Cincinnati to persuade Birney to put a stop to his abolitionist activities.

Marshall's pleas went nowhere, although Birney did agree to abandon his well-armed home temporarily and move into a boarding house called the Franklin House. But there, Birney's arrival sparked a minor uprising among the other boarders, more than a dozen of whom signed a letter to the proprietor demanding that the abolitionist leave, or else they would. The Franklin House owner, a man named William Johnson, ignored the demand and, as a result, twelve of the signers—most of them young clerks employed in nearby stores—ended up checking out. The *Whig* took note of the boarder revolt, saying there existed an "overwhelming majority in the city opposed to the wild schemes of the abolitionists."

* * *

THE DAYS-LONG DRUMBEAT OF bullying and threats could not go unanswered. By July 18, less than a week after the assault on the *Philanthropist* press, Birney and his fellow members of the antislavery society had devised a response. In an open address to the residents of Cincinnati, Birney's group ran, one by one, through the litany of affronts that had been waged against it, charging that a "secret confederacy" aimed to "put down the liberty of the press and the freedom of speech." The *Philanthropist*, it said, was trying, through argument and facts, to end slavery by peaceful means, and to demonstrate the need to free the slaves "if we wish to preserve our own liberties." The address laid out the threat in stark terms, arguing the rights of all of free society were on the line in this tug-of-war. It was becoming Birney's mantra—that the rights of free white people were being sacrificed to protect the South's oppression of enslaved Black people. "A band of lawless men array themselves against the Constitution, declaring that *their* will and not that of the *People* is paramount," the message declared. "What Fellow Citizens, ought we to do in such a case?"

In the days that followed, the *Whig* and *Republican* answered Birney's salvo with a renewed bombardment against his camp. The *Whig* ran an item accusing the Cincinnati abolitionists of being led by an "English emissary," repeating the old canard that antislavery activists were traitorous foreign agents. It published a separate piece, signed by "Public Sentiment," that compared the Cincinnati mob to the patriots who took part in the Boston Tea Party. The *Whig*, which aligned itself with the party of the same name, warned "abolitionists and amalgamationists" that they were viewed by residents as "enemies of America" and would have no home in Cincinnati. A few days later, the paper editorialized that "self preservation" reasonably could be placed ahead of written law. "We are perfectly justifiable in arresting the hand of the assassin even though in doing so we find it necessary to proceed to the severest extremities," the *Whig* argued. "If, then, the abolitionists place themselves in the position of the assassin, what can they expect?"

The *Republican*, which backed Andrew Jackson's Democrats, added its voice by publishing a menacing "word of advice" to three of Birney's allies in the antislavery society, businessmen who had joined Birney in signing the July 18 address. "Publish no more cards or addresses about midnight invasions," it warned. "Eschew the society of James G. Birney. Avoid him as you would a viper." There was no mistaking the business community's preoccupation over how the work of the abolitionists might injure its prospects for continued trade with the South. Two days later, the *Republican* wrote, "Cincinnati is intimately involved with the slave states, in business and social intercourse." Its recommendation, then, for dealing with the activists was "not hang them, tar and feather them, quarter or drown them." Rather, the newspaper continued, the answer was to unveil to all their abolitionist leanings—and to ostracize them. "We would say to our southern brethren—here is Mr. _____, an extensive merchant on _____ street. He is an enemy to your institutions. He would persuade your slaves to cut your throats," the *Republican* proposed. "If you visit our city do not trade with that man."

The rising passions could not long be contained solely on the pages of newspapers, however. On July 23, the same city fathers who had organized the January courthouse meeting summoned a new gathering at a place called the Lower Market House. The purpose, announced in several of the local papers, was to decide whether the people of Cincinnati "will permit the publication or distribution of Abolition newspapers in this city." The list of leaders of the session was a Who's Who of prominent city residents. Included among them were Nicholas Longworth, the city's biggest landholder; Robert Buchanan, a well-known banker; and David T. Disney, a businessman who had served in both chambers of the Ohio legislature. The city's postmaster, a minister named William Burke, was chosen as president of the gathering.

The session attracted "not more than 1,000" attendees, including two hundred to three hundred from what Birney tersely called the "mob-party." And although it lacked the noise and drama of the January assembly, its participants were no less determined to shut Birney and his newspaper down. They agreed that "nothing short of the absolute discontinuance of the said abolition paper in this city, can prevent a resort to violence," and promised to suppress it through the use of "all lawful means." An additional resolution stated that if Birney and his supporters continued publishing the *Philanthropist*, "we cannot hold ourselves responsible

for the consequences." The group named a committee, led by the highly
accomplished Jacob Burnet, a former U.S. senator who had served as a
justice on the state Supreme Court, to meet with Birney and to discuss the
assembly's decision that the *Philanthropist* must cease.

But Birney was having none of it. He replied to the committee that the
newspaper was the official organ of the twelve-thousand-member Ohio Anti-
Slavery Society—it had been so since March—and that he was not empow-
ered to discuss its fate with the group on his own. The Burnet committee
would have to take the matter up with the society's executive committee, of
which he was a member. So the two committees prepared to meet. Burnet
said it would be pointless to ignore the fact that 95 percent of the city's population opposed Birney's cause. "It is to be feared that this excitement cannot
be kept down much longer," the former senator told Birney. Meantime, the
city's newspapers kept up their own pressure, with one piece in the *Whig*
charging—falsely—that Birney had made a "solemn pledge" not to publish
in Cincinnati.

The meeting of the two camps, on July 28, didn't settle much. Judge
Burnet's delegation trooped to the home of Birney associate Isaac Colby
for the sit-down. Burnet appeared genuinely shaken by the feverish sentiments crackling across the city and warned that there was even worse
news: 160 men in the Cincinnati region had already gathered and held
drills to prepare for an assault on the *Philanthropist*. And still others on
the Kentucky side were ready to join them in any effort to put down the
newspaper. Other members of the Market House delegation echoed Burnet's dire assessment—one who owned a business among the foundries
and boat yards along the Ohio River told Birney's group that emotions of
the workers there were nearly ready to explode.

Not surprisingly, the theme of the session turned to business and the
share of Southern trade that Cincinnati might lose if it continued to be
associated with abolitionism. Buchanan, the bank president, said his con-
tacts in the South were not necessarily aware of the *Philanthropist* but were

generally concerned that the city was known to be entertaining antislavery talk. This much became clear: nothing short of a complete shutdown of the *Philanthropist* would satisfy the men who claimed to speak for the community. When asked by Birney's team whether they would support the newspaper's publication as long as mob violence could be prevented, Burnet and others in his delegation were ready with a quick answer: no. It was not the *Philanthropist*'s tone on slavery that was the problem—it was that it spoke at all.

* * *

THE ABOLITIONISTS ANSWERED BURNET'S committee in writing the next day. No one could accuse them of burying the lede. Right in the first sentence of the antislavery society's response appeared the critical kernel: The group would "decline complying" with the request to halt production of the *Philanthropist*. Birney's group went on to explain. It was not for fear of abandoning the cause of the slave that the society was persisting, it said. Rather, shutting down the newspaper would spell "a tame surrender of the FREEDOM OF THE PRESS—THE RIGHT TO DISCUSS," the group said.

Birney's camp explained that the *Philanthropist* was the only medium in Cincinnati where readers had access to an antislavery viewpoint. Further, the abolitionists asserted, during six months of publication, the newspaper had steered a civil course—Birney had even invited slave owners to make their arguments in its columns. To silence the *Philanthropist* would represent a "base and unmanly" surrender to the South's demand to remain mute on a matter of deep concern to the entire nation, the antislavery group said. "We believe, that a large portion of the people of Cincinnati are utterly opposed to the prostration of the liberty of the press," it declared. Responsibility lay with city authorities to uphold the law, the statement concluded. (For some reason, these last two points were omitted when the text of the abolitionists' response was published in the *Whig*.)

The Burnet committee threw up its hands at this message of defiance and countered with its own public statement saying that it had done every-thing it could to avert further trouble. All the town elders could do now was to make clear their "utmost abhorrence of every thing like violence" and urge their fellow citizens to avoid it. Hammond, who had steered a more or less neutral course as the battle lines grew increasingly stark, was mindful that the failure of the meeting carried the potential for disorder. He opted to delay publishing his report until after the weekend to avoid dropping the news when the chance for mayhem was highest. But the *Whig* and *Republican* could not wait. On Saturday morning, July 30, both papers printed items that were certain to fan the growing public excitement. The *Whig* asked, "Are the abolitionists in this city mad? Will they not take counsel of what had occurred? Or will they persist in contemning public sentiment until they bring upon themselves the excited vengeance of the multitude?" By nightfall, the multitude was stirring into action.

Once again, it was Joseph Graham, the man behind the earlier threat-ening handbills, who was at the forefront of the effort to silence Birney's newspaper. Graham had taken part in the assault on Achilles Pugh's press and home three weeks earlier and now stood before a crowd in front of a downtown hotel. This time, Graham was urging the passage of a pair of impromptu resolutions that, in essence, sought to dress vigilantism in the garb of democratic decision-making. The first item was to destroy the press and scatter its type in the street. The second was to notify Birney that he had twenty-four hours to leave the city. (The *Gazette* would report later that the second item was to tar and feather Birney, but Graham wrote to the paper to deny that part.) With those votes taken, the crowd of fifty or so well-dressed young men—probably clerks and store workers from Cincinnati, plus some others from Kentucky—had their plans, which were said to include the tarring and feathering of various people associated with the antislavery movement. Birney's son would later note that several of those who gathered were "stout workmen" who did not vote, but rather looked like "men receiving orders to do work for which they were paid."

The party later made its way to the site of the antislavery society's office on the corner of Main and Seventh, where the *Philanthropist* was housed. There it went to work. Darkness was settling as the group broke open the office door and rushed inside, aiming for the press. The vigilantes smashed everything in sight. They tossed the type out the window into the street, along with books and other office materials. They attacked the press as if it were some hulking beast, pounding it to pieces, then hurling them outside. In the end, they managed to dismantle the entire *Philanthropist* office and reduce it all to a pile of wreckage strewn on the street. Just as during the July 12 attack on Pugh's home, not a single police officer appeared to stop the destruction. One city official was looking on quietly as the mob worked, however—the mayor, Samuel Davies.

The mob, now thoroughly energized, wasn't done for the night. From the antislavery society's office, the party moved to Pugh's house in search of more printing equipment to wreck, but found none. Then the throng trooped to the home of William Donaldson, a member of the antislavery society's executive committee. He was not at home. Someone then proposed heading to Birney's residence, and the mob soon showed up at the front door. Again, the men would be frustrated—only Birney's teen son, William, was at home. (The elder Birney was away delivering an antislavery lecture in the town of Hillsboro.) Graham, at the head of the mob, took charge of questioning the son.

"Who are you?" he asked.

Young Birney answered.

"Where is your father?"

"In Warren County."

"In anybody else in the house?"

"No."

Graham turned away to speak with his comrades, and William ducked inside quickly, locked the door, and ran to the first-floor landing, where he took up position with a weapon and about forty rounds of ammunition, in case the men should break in. The teen waited while Graham and his followers spoke outside, then he heard the crowd move from the house. The mob, stymied in its hunt for abolitionists, surged back to the site of the *Philanthropist* office on Main Street, where someone proposed piling the debris left from the earlier attack and setting the whole mess ablaze. But Graham jumped on top of the heap and persuaded his men that doing so risked setting fire to the surrounding buildings. Instead, the mob wrestled the mangled body of the press down Main Street and tossed it into the Ohio River.

The men briefly retired to the Exchange for drinks and then shifted their attention to a predominately Black section of town called Church Alley. The mob rampaged through the neighborhood, entering empty buildings and destroying them. (The mayhem caused no injuries to residents, but it came only two months after a white mob burned down five tenements in a predominately Black neighborhood and, by one account, opened fire on residents with guns, leaving at least one person dead.) Hours had passed since the original attack on the *Philanthropist* office. At around midnight, back in front of the newspaper office, Davies called for an end to the night's activities. "We have done enough for one night," the mayor said to triumphant cheers from the mob, according to one observer. "The abolitionists themselves, must be convinced themselves by this time, what public sentiment is, and that it will not do any longer to disregard, or set it at naught." Even as Davies finished his remarks, the exultant crowd was drowning them beneath chants of "Home! Home!" Not long after, the men had faded into the darkness.

The mob's chief quarry—Birney—remained at large, however. The following night, Sunday, a group gathered near the Franklin House, where Birney was said to be lodging. Three men, led by none other than

Mayor Davies himself, authorized themselves as a "domiciliary committee" and proceeded to the boarding house to look for the abolitionist. They conducted a search of the property but left, persuaded that Birney was not to be found there. Tensions spilled over into the next day, and Davies, citing fears of "violence and disorder," issued an official appeal for calm. Several groups of volunteers stepped forward to help keep the peace. Mobs clustered again that night, including a group of two hundred men who appeared determined to renew attacks on the homes of Black residents. But the volunteer peacekeepers managed to douse the flare-ups and prevent further mayhem.

Birney, who was returning on horseback from his lecture outing, was unaware of the chaotic goings-on in Cincinnati until he stopped on Tuesday night at a friend's house around fourteen miles outside the city. There, he learned that the *Philanthropist* office had been sacked and the press destroyed three days earlier. Birney's own safety would surely be in question. He packed up not long after midnight and rode through the quiet of the wee hours toward Cincinnati, arriving shortly after sunrise without encountering anyone. Birney would write later that if he had entered town during daylight hours, "I would have been instantly seized and lynched."

Allies quickly spirited him from his home to a friend's farm several miles outside Cincinnati. But that friend already had been threatened earlier for his ties to Birney, so they shifted the editor to the home of yet another acquaintance for the rest of the week. By the following week, Birney had come out of hiding and was back in Cincinnati, taking care to throw off any would-be assailants by switching where he slept. Birney was able to walk the streets again openly, though he was watchful enough to avoid the boisterous precinct next to the river. "I have been brought into such notoriety that I hate to go out," Birney wrote to his friend Lewis Tappan in New York.

The month's paroxysm of mob violence might well have spelled the end of the *Philanthropist*, whose ruined press lay at the bottom of the Ohio River. Birney remained surrounded by business and political elites bent on shutting him down, and a corps of vigilantes clearly willing to break the law to do so. And all were spurred on by certain local newspaper editors who saw nothing incongruous in pronouncing dismay over Birney's exercise of a printing press. The standoff seemed certain to be the source of continuing tensions, if not outright violence against Birney and his friends, along with other vulnerable city residents. Something had to give. The brutality of Cincinnati's riotous past was, from all available evidence, destined to play out again. The only question was when.

CHAPTER FIFTEEN

THE WISE
AND GOOD

L OVEJOY'S FRAYING SITUATION IN Alton, following the destruction of his own press, was about to go from bad to worse. His brother Owen had managed to secure a replacement press in Cincinnati, thanks to the success of the fundraising campaign in the religious and antislavery press outside Illinois. During his trip to Cincinnati, Owen arranged to ship the press by steamboat to the Alton dock, where Lovejoy's helpers would be waiting to receive it. (Lovejoy was away at the time.) From there, the plan was to store the press in a warehouse owned by two friends, Reuben Gerry and Royal Weller, and then to await Lovejoy's return. Owen and the press arrived by steamboat around sundown on September 21, and a number of Lovejoy's friends took delivery of the crate, as planned.

But Lovejoy's foes were also keeping an eye out for the arrival of a new press. As the editor's allies moved the crate through downtown on the way to the Gerry & Weller warehouse, voices called out from the street: "There goes the abolition press, stop it, stop it." John Krum, the mayor, also knew the *Observer* press was coming and was aware there already had been threats against it. Krum reassured Lovejoy's men that the press would be protected that evening, and that they should leave him in charge of safeguarding it. They agreed. The supporters tucked the press into the warehouse, and Krum posted a constable at the door to keep away potential vandals, with instructions to stay until eleven P.M. The constable took his post. But soon after he left later that night, a group of twenty to thirty men masked with bandannas forced their way into the warehouse. They located the box containing the press and wheeled it out of the building and across the street to the river's edge. There, they began cracking it open to get at their prize.

By this time, someone had run to summon Krum, who rushed to the scene while the mob was at its destructive work, breaking apart the press and tossing pieces into the Mississippi. Krum ordered them to disperse. The men were calm in their response: they would go as soon as they had finished. It took the mob less than an hour to complete its task. Lovejoy's new press was reduced to pieces on the river's muddy bottom, silenced before it had birthed a single offending issue. Mayor Krum turned for home, the limits of his authority laid bare by the vandals' casual disregard. The damage that night was limited to the press. The group had found its target and dispatched it with a businesslike efficiency. Krum's words would sound almost admiring when he reportedly declared later that he had never witnessed "a more quiet and gentlemanly mob."

The assault meant that Lovejoy lost his newest press before he had even laid eyes on it. Reactions to the attack in the newspapers were free of the crowing that had greeted earlier attempts to muzzle Lovejoy. "However worthy of censure the Abolitionists may be for persisting in the propagation of their tenets . . . [o]ne wrong never can justify another; and violence never should be tolerated in a country of laws and equal rights," pronounced the Alton *Telegraph*. On the opposite side of the river, the usually antagonistic *Missouri Republican* managed a backhanded condemnation of the violence. "We regret, exceedingly, these violations of the law and if Mr. Lovejoy has any regard for himself, he will not continue the unequal contest," the paper counseled. For its part, the antislavery press in other states used the incident to rally abolitionists to stand up against lawlessness and the ongoing offensive against civil liberties. One such paper, the *Michigan Observer*, said there was "double occasion" to support Lovejoy's newspaper. "The anti-slavery cause has arrived at a crisis in Illinois," it warned.

Lovejoy was also using "crisis" to describe the atmosphere around him. By early October, the editor was as gloomy as he'd been all year, feeling abandoned by most of his friends and quite alone. If the assault on the new press weren't worrisome enough, Lovejoy suddenly found even his family under threat. On October 1, a little more than a week after the attack on his press, Lovejoy was serving as guest preacher for a minister friend, William Campbell, in St. Charles, Missouri, the town where Celia Lovejoy's family lived. The couple and young Edward were staying with her family there. As Lovejoy ended his evening sermon and prepared to head to his in-laws' home, a young man slipped him a note. It said: "Mr. Lovejoy, Be watchful as you come from church to-night." The warning was signed, "A Friend." Campbell and his brother-in-law agreed to accompany Lovejoy, and the short walk to Celia's family home went without incident. Campbell stayed a while as the two men talked. Lovejoy had forgotten the threatening note when a knock drew Celia and her mother to the front door at around ten P.M. Lovejoy took up a candle in the darkness to check for himself. The living quarters were on the second floor above a store. A group of men had gathered in front on the ground level.

"We want to see Mr. Lovejoy. Is he in?"

"Yes, I am here," Lovejoy answered.

At that, some men rushed up the stairs to the second floor and inside the family's quarters. Two of them—a man Lovejoy knew only as Littler, from Virginia, and a second man, from Mississippi—grabbed him. Lovejoy asked what they wanted. "We want you downstairs, damn you," one of the men answered. The attackers struggled to pull Lovejoy from the room, and

Littler took to punching in an effort to subdue him. At this point, Celia, who was pregnant, struggled to reach her husband. She pressed through the crowd of intruders on the second floor but was forcefully pushed back. One of the men in the crowd pulled a short dagger threateningly. Celia answered by slapping him in the face, and then rushing past to where Lovejoy sought to fend off his attackers. Celia threw her arms around her husband as the men yanked him in the other direction, ripping his clothes and shouting profanities as they struggled. Finally, she began striking them in the face and shouted that they would have to seize her first. Celia's mother and a sister joined in the fray, adding to the commotion.

At last, the invaders released their grip on Lovejoy and eased out of the room. Celia collapsed and was taken to bed, only to awaken later in an eruption of shrieks and hysterical moans. Lovejoy was shuttling between his wife and infant son when the mob returned. The men burst into the room and grabbed Lovejoy in a renewed effort to tug him away. They gave up only after Campbell showed up to help his friend wrestle free. By now, the front yard was crowded with armed men and "drunken wretches," a braying assembly that milled and bellowed vows to get Lovejoy. "The infernal scoundrel, the damned amalgamating abolitionist, we'll have his heart out yet," he would recall hearing. At least one shot was fired by the mob, but no one was hit.

One of the original attackers, the Mississippian, fired up the crowd again with a story, whether true or not, that his wife had been sexually violated by a Black man. He said the reported attack had been somehow provoked by Lovejoy. The Mississippi man was now ruined, he told the others gathered on the yard, and might as well die. But first, he "would have my blood," Lovejoy recalled two days later. The mob charged at the house for the third time, this time bearing a handwritten note ordering Lovejoy to leave the next morning by ten. When he didn't answer the message, the group let out a howl "as if so many demons had just broken loose from hell." Lovejoy quickly scrawled a reply: He would be on a stagecoach and gone by nine A.M. The group retreated to a local grog shop for refreshment, but then made two more alcohol-fueled forays to the house that night before ending their fitful siege for good, at around midnight. Lovejoy slipped out while his pursuers weren't looking but later returned to the house.

Lovejoy ultimately sneaked away to the home of a friend outside St. Charles, where Celia would join him the next day for the return trip home to Alton. The trauma of the invasion left Celia badly jangled, and once home, she remained bedridden in a state of near hysteria, haunted by nightmares and "constantly starting at every sound," as Lovejoy put it. During the previous year and a half, Celia Lovejoy had watched her husband be hounded from one city, only to end up as the target of vigilantes again. In just the previous two months, she had watched him lose two printing presses and a hefty share of the support that had nourished the couple in Alton since their arrival. The strain had taken a frightful toll on Celia, and Lovejoy knew it. "What the final result will be for her, I know not, but hope for the best," he confided to Joshua Leavitt, editor of the abolitionist New York *Evangelist*, two days after the terrifying St. Charles attacks.

Lovejoy began keeping a loaded musket near the bed as he slept. Owen and John slept in the adjoining room, also armed with a collection of muskets and pistols. Lovejoy was uneasy with resorting to firearms as a means of defending himself, but could not see any good alternatives amid the darkening climate. "There is at present no safety for me, and no defence in this place," Lovejoy told Leavitt. "I feel I do not walk the streets in safety, and every night when I lie down, it is with the deep settled conviction that there are those near me and around me who seek my life. I have resisted this conviction as long as I could, but it has been forced upon me."

Lovejoy had come to recognize his tenuous political footing. In his own church, he had been informed that certain members were offended by his now-regular prayers on behalf of slaves. His own friend Enoch Long, the parish elder, had recently informed Lovejoy that he was not allowed to preach from the exhortation in the book of Proverbs to speak up on behalf of the poor and needy. One leading Presbyterian had said in front of some others that he would do nothing anymore to protect the *Observer* in the face of a mob. "I have no doubt that four-fifths of the inhabitants are glad that my press has been destroyed by a mob, both once and again," Lovejoy wrote. "They hate mobs, it is true, but they hate Abolitionism a great deal more."

Lovejoy knew that "a few excellent brethren" stood at his side in Alton, people who were "desirous to know their duty in this crisis, and to do it." But he wasn't sure they were as prepared as he to carry on the fight "at all hazards." A make-or-break test of this resolve lay just ahead: The inaugural meeting of the Illinois Anti-Slavery was now set to take place in Alton at the end of the month. There was no telling how his enemies would react, but the marshaling of forces was already under way.

* * *

BY THE THIRD WEEK of October, Lovejoy's opponents were quite aware of his plans to host a statewide antislavery convention, and they had come up with a few countering moves of their own. The first was to reactivate the local chapter of the American Colonization Society, whose effort to deport freed Black people to Africa had lost much of what steam it once generated in previous years. The growth of abolitionism, while still a fringe movement nationally, had left colonization as the refuge for those who wished to proclaim opposition to slavery in the abstract without having to face actual emancipation. The recent presence of Parker, the New Orleans pastor, and the pamphlet he had circulated was helping energize efforts to revive the Alton colonization group as well as to peel community support from Lovejoy and his press. From a political standpoint, Parker's argument that the Bible sanctioned slavery may have been confusing to residents who had stood with Lovejoy, but it was proving an effective means of isolating him.

The reborn colonization society met in the Presbyterian church in Upper Alton on October 24, just two days before the planned start of Lovejoy's own convention. The colonization gathering drew a healthy crowd, pulled to the church by handbills that had been anonymously posted around town. Parker was joined as a featured speaker by two prominent Altonians: the Reverend John Mason Peck, who had never been a fan of Lovejoy, and state senator Cyrus Edwards, a Whig candidate for Illinois governor whose brother Ninian had led the state as governor during the 1820s. John Hogan, the merchant and state legislator, was elected as one of three vice presidents of the group. Although Usher Linder, the attorney general, was not listed officially as part of the colonization society's rebirth, the formation of a strategy to blunt Lovejoy's influence would surely have included him, given the role Linder was soon to play. Interestingly, the man elected to be president of the revived society was Gilman's brother, Benjamin Ives Gilman Jr. Another name stood out on the list of attendees: Enoch Long, Lovejoy's fellow churchman. There is no record of Long's actions at the session, so it's difficult to know why he was there. Was he genuinely drawn to the colonization idea? Was he ready to join Lovejoy's critics? Was he there to keep an eye on the gathering opposition—acting, in essence, as a Lovejoy spy?

The stated purpose of the meeting was to establish a local chapter of the colonization effort, and the men who assembled there approved a number of resolutions endorsing the "benevolent" removal of Black people as a condition of slave emancipation, whenever that happened. (The group described the proposed act of sending freed Black people to Liberia as "providing an asylum" for them.) But amid the votes and speechifying, it was not hard to detect that the real aim of the meeting was to gather Alton's business and civic elites into a common front against Lovejoy and his dangerous insurgency. One resolution, for example, deplored the growing "hostility" toward the colonization approach, as well as what it called the "unchristian and abusive epithets" leveled against slaveholders in general.

Parker and Edwards delivered speeches that were "eloquent, pointed and exhilarating, and well calculated to allay the recent excitements, and unite the feelings and sympathies of all the wise and good on behalf of the colored man," according to one newspaper account. Lovejoy's brothers would see it differently. In their telling, Parker aimed fire at the abolitionists, accusing them of "bustling around with a great deal of ardor but with little discretion." Parker said Black people would never receive fair treatment from white people in the United States, so the best course was to send them where a freed slave might have a chance for respect. "Now this prejudice may be wrong, but so it is, and we must act on it," Parker reportedly told the gathering.

Peck, the Baptist preacher who had chronicled Alton's development as part of his Illinois gazetteer, was even more forceful: He accused the activists of being race-mixers and of using abusive language against slave owners. The *Western Pioneer* newspaper that he edited smiled on the colonization meeting in its write-up, expressing its hope that the session would have a "harmonizing effect" on the city's political tensions and win support for a version of emancipation conditioned on the removal of freed Black people from the United States. In a not-so-veiled poke at the Lovejoy camp, the newspaper warned that "a very few restless spirits" would likely be unhappy with the newly charged colonization movement in Alton, but that they would find themselves outmatched by the "wise and good, the benevolent and real friends to humanity."

Meanwhile, Lovejoy was rallying his own forces. A week before his planned antislavery convention, the editor gathered in Springfield with other Presbyterians for a meeting of the Illinois synod. There, Lovejoy found himself among kindred spirits—men who, for the most part, had been faithful backers of the *Observer* and his use of the press to assail the sin of slavery. Joining Lovejoy in making the trip from Alton was Frederick W. Graves, who had emerged, along with *Observer* associate editor Hurlbut, as the most stalwart of the editor's local supporters. "There is no cowardice in him, no shrinking from duty through fear of man," Lovejoy had written of Graves a few weeks earlier. "I wish I could say as much of our other pastors." Chosen as moderator for the synod meeting was the careful Gideon Blackburn, who had long stood against slavery but was seen by some activists as overly reluctant to jump into the abolitionist movement with both feet. (The abolitionist James Buchanan described Blackburn as being "as wary in relation to slavery as an old bear is of a trap—he vexes me very much.") Despite his reserve, Blackburn, too, would soon be thrust into the heart of the maelstrom now brewing in Alton.

If there was anyone at the clergymen's gathering who was Lovejoy's equal in giving shape to the upcoming antislavery convention, it was Edward Beecher, the president of Illinois College. For several years, Beecher had been a sounding board and protégé of sorts as Lovejoy underwent his own metamorphosis into an abolitionist. It was Lovejoy, after all, who had helped usher Beecher to the belief that gradual emancipation was "fallacious" and to see immediatism as "philosophical and safe." Since then, the pair had emerged as members of a camp among the Presbyterian clergy that sought, mostly in vain, to push the church toward a strong stand against slavery. Both men had watched with dismay five months earlier when the church effectively split in two during its General Assembly meeting in Philadelphia—a schism over church doctrine between "Old" and "New" schools that also reflected the growing regional divide over slavery. Lovejoy and Beecher didn't see eye to eye on everything, but no matter how the antislavery convention turned out, they were in it together.

Born a year apart, both men were sons of New England and of fathers who were Congregational ministers. Beecher had been raised in stately Litchfield, Connecticut, in a pious family whose every member seemed destined for influence—and several would meet that promise. (Among his siblings were Harriet Beecher Stowe, who would go on to write *Uncle Tom's Cabin*; Henry Ward Beecher, who would be an immensely successful Congregational preacher; and Catharine Beecher, a writer who would make a name promoting the training of women as teachers.) Edward, one of thirteen Beecher children, set off on the preacher's path of his father, Lyman Beecher, the Calvinist mover and shaker. Edward entered Yale at age fifteen and graduated four years later as valedictorian. After a stint as a school headmaster and Yale tutor, Beecher landed a spot as minister of the famed Park Street Church in Boston—an appointment that probably owed more to his father's clout in the church than to Edward's readiness for such a duty. Beecher, only twenty-three, had little in the way of formal religious training or preaching experience. He turned out not to be much of a preacher. After three years at the Park Street Church, his parishioners informed Beecher that his sermons weren't of much use to them, and his own spiritual revelations struck even Beecher as too eccentric to speak aloud. At one point in 1828, he took a month-long break from the grueling pace of religious revivals and went to Maine, suffering from "prolonged nervous strain." He finished his church tenure in 1830, after four years at the pulpit.

No doubt influenced by his father's belief that civilization's great moral struggle was taking shape in the West, Beecher turned his attentions to the Mississippi Valley. His previous Yale connections and family name surely helped when Beecher was named president of the newly founded Illinois College in Jacksonville, Illinois, in 1830. The college was founded by a group of former Yale divinity students known as the "Yale Band," whose members had moved to Illinois to work as missionaries. Some had come to admire Beecher during his earlier stint as a Yale tutor, and were eager to name him as Illinois College president. (Lovejoy, who at the time was an editor in St. Louis, did not yet know Beecher in 1830, but he placed a short item in the *Times* noting the college appointment.)

In Jacksonville, Beecher and his wife, Isabella, encountered a rough but booming frontier town where the hardships included rampant malaria and not much interest in the intellect's life. The New York writer and editor William Cullen Bryant would describe Jacksonville as "a horridly ugly little village, composed of little shops and dwellings stuck close together around a dingy square." But the college, designed to produce clergymen and more teachers, proved with Beecher's help to be a cultural oasis amid coarsened surroundings, and some of its faculty members would eagerly join the antislavery fraternity.

In those early days, Beecher's attitude was, in his own words, "decidedly hostile to the doctrines of immediate emancipation." But as the slavery issue began to percolate all around, Beecher had occasion to think hard about abolitionism—undertaking what he called "a careful examination of the history of experiments on this subject." The subject was close at hand. Beecher's father, then still a supporter of colonization, was president of Lane Seminary at the time of the student rebellion that was led by Birney's friend Theodore Weld in 1834. (Two of Beecher's brothers, Henry and Charles, would end up as Lane students after the exodus.) That same year, Edward Beecher and Lovejoy met at the Illinois College commencement and were soon to be regularly in contact.

Beecher's thinking on slavery began to shift. Like many other churchmen in the North, Beecher was appalled by the spate of riots in New York and elsewhere in 1835 that targeted antislavery activists. He offered Lovejoy a pep talk that same autumn when the owners of the *Observer*, at the time still based in St. Louis, were seeking to scrub that newspaper of any talk of slavery. "When I see the demands of the friends of the system of slavery, & their determination to muzzle not only abolitionists, but all who are determined gradually & wisely to remove the system, whatever be their ground, I think the time for silence has gone by," Beecher wrote. He urged Lovejoy to persist. "I say go on. You will find as you have already that the stand you have taken will increase the number of your friends." For the next two years, Beecher and Lovejoy would remain allies and collaborators, never so closely again as they were at that moment.

Beecher had carefully watched the recent attacks on the *Observer* and shook his head over what he saw as the misguided motives of those who would silence the newspaper. Beecher believed that "prejudice and a false sense of their local interests blinded their minds," leaving them vulnerable to the seeming appeal of vigilante justice. "They seemed to regard it as a less evil to have their city become the abode of mob law than the theatre of a fair discussion of an unpopular theme," he would write.

As Illinois College president, Beecher resisted joining any antislavery groups, but he was eager to help Lovejoy with the antislavery convention. He had in mind a significant change in its design, however. Beecher proposed the change to Lovejoy while the editor was in Jacksonville for commencement in September, a month before the convention was to take place. Instead of making abolitionism the focus, Beecher suggested, why not bill the gathering as one that would focus on free inquiry into the subject? Beecher figured that opening the convention to all "judicious and moderate men," and not only those drawn to antislavery, could help lower the flame beneath the recent simmering tensions. This should reduce the possibility of violence and "produce an influence which should restore the supremacy of law in Alton"—as well as to repair some of the public relations damage that the recent mob actions had done to the state's reputation, Beecher believed. He proposed calling the proposed organization a "society of free inquiry."

Lovejoy was opposed to this approach. He saw the convention as a chance to cultivate the cause of antislavery in Illinois and no doubt fretted that a free-inquiry tack might divert the activists from their intended path. And hadn't Lovejoy repeatedly made the point that the two causes— freedom for the slave and for the press—were really one and the same? Moreover, given Lovejoy's own bitter history with mobs in Alton, there was little in the body of evidence to suggest that the men who had sought to silence his newspaper would suddenly embrace an open discussion of slavery now. Beecher, however, thought the wrong element would stay away—it seemed unlikely to him that anyone who had pounded a printing press to fragments would bother showing up for a meeting devoted to free inquiry.

Beecher was badly misreading the terrain, and Lovejoy knew it. ("How correct was his judgment," Beecher was later forced to admit.) Nonetheless, in the interest of unity, Lovejoy yielded to his friend's vision. The convention would be summoned, under Beecher's name, for the purpose of promoting free discussion in Alton. Lovejoy held firm on one aspect, though: Even with a tweaked emphasis, the group would still be called the Illinois Anti-Slavery Society.

Beecher posted a notice of the meeting in the Alton *Telegraph* on October 18, addressing it "to the friends of free discussion." His message played down the slavery issue, explaining instead that the convention welcomed all who supported a free discussion of slavery—even if, he added gingerly, "they are not yet convinced of the safety of its immediate abolition." Beecher laid out two starkly competing visions for what could happen next: a "kindly" search for principles on which "all good men can unite," or a continuation of the tug-of-war over speech that threatened "the harmony and peace of society." Beecher's stratagem was based on his assumption that reason and good will could win out over passion and division, that there remained a body of respected, even-handed leaders who still might prevail. He would have his answer soon enough.

CHAPTER SIXTEEN

EFFECTS MOST HAPPY

B Y HORSEBACK AND COACH, they streamed in. Scores of abolitionists and like-minded clergymen from all over the state answered
Beecher's call to attend the groundbreaking gathering of the Illinois
Anti-Slavery Society on October 26, a Thursday. The parade of activists
included faces and names familiar to Lovejoy from his attendance over
the years at official church meetings and various visits to Illinois College.
David Nelson, the man whose revivals had converted Lovejoy five years
earlier, came in from Quincy. Gideon Blackburn, the cagey "old bear,"
traveled in from Macoupin County, along with James Buchanan, who had
applied that moniker. Both men were friends of James Birney. Asa Turner,
a Beecher ally and member of the Yale Band that had founded the Illinois
College, made the trip. And, of course, many of Lovejoy's backers from
Alton and the rest of Madison County, who already knew their way to the
Presbyterian church in Upper Alton: Graves and Hurlbut, the longtime
abolitionist Thomas Lippincott, warehouse owner Royal Weller, and
numerous other friends and supporters. (Hurlbut had known Beecher's

family for many years: After finishing his theological training at Andover Seminary, Hurlbut took his exam in the Boston home of Lyman Beecher, Edward's father.) All told, about eighty-five abolitionists joined the procession from sixteen Illinois counties. In a sign that Lovejoy's effort had attracted notice within the abolitionist movement elsewhere, two activists traveled from Ohio to represent the antislavery movement there.

Right from the start, however, something was off. As Lovejoy and his supporters arrived at the church, it was apparent they wouldn't be left alone. There, along with the preachers and activists, stood the lanky Linder and florid Botkin, who had taken part in the Market House meeting aimed at silencing the *Observer*. Beecher's move to open the convention to "friends of free inquiry" had handed Lovejoy's opponents just the opportunity they were seeking. The Linder camp, energized by the meeting of the Alton colonization society two nights earlier, had devised a rather ingenious way to thwart the abolitionist convention: they would join it. For the next two days, dozens of these men, led by Linder and his fellow legislator, John Hogan, would throng the church. A number of them, including the physicians Halderman and Beall, had been involved in earlier efforts to quell Lovejoy's press. (Beall, who also had been part of the mob that stopped Lovejoy on the darkened road in August, brought along his business partner, another doctor named Thomas M. Hope.) Also to join was the would-be Illinois governor Cyrus Edwards.

Their gambit boiled down to simple arithmetic—they would attempt to use their numbers to take control of the gathering and foil whatever actions the antislavery activists had in mind. It would amount to a parliamentary hijacking—all the interlopers had to do was say they were opposed to slavery and in favor of free inquiry. The scheme was reportedly Botkin's idea. But as Lovejoy surveyed the surprising tableau of his abolitionist friends and determined foes crowded into the same church, he knew that the much-anticipated convention was in trouble even before it had been called to order.

The opening of the assembly was loud and confusing. Beecher arrived to find one of the men shouting to get seats for himself and friends, while Lovejoy tried to keep out the unwanted guests. Lovejoy called the meeting to order at about two P.M., and managed to tap Blackburn as temporary chairman and Graves as its temporary secretary. But that was the most progress the assembly would make all day. For the rest of the afternoon, the brick church was awash in angry shouting and catcalls. Lovejoy accused Linder and the others of deliberately seeking to undermine a meeting that had been called to discuss slavery. Botkin and Linder jumped up to insist heatedly that they and their friends were eligible to take part as "friends of free inquiry." The debate grew so fiery at one point that Linder, who as state attorney general was the state's top prosecutor, shook his fist in Lovejoy's face.

The essential problem of the gathering had been laid bare. Lovejoy's original public summons had been directed only to abolitionists, but the Beecher revision flung open the doors to anyone who claimed to be in favor of free discussion. For hours, the parties went furiously back and forth. So fruitless were the proceedings that both sides gave up, and the graybeard Blackburn gaveled the session adjourned until the following morning. Once outside the church, Linder clambered onto a woodpile and turned on the oratorical charms for which he was famous. He furiously denounced the activists for having tried to shut his followers out of the meeting and trotted out some of the charges commonly lodged against the abolitionists, including that they were traitorous. Linder then turned his cannons against the "Yankees" who had imposed on Alton their ways and constant moral crusading, including the introduction of Sunday schools and temperance societies. Laughter from the crowd interrupted the harangue after someone remembered that Linder had recently signed a no-drinking pledge following one of his bouts of alcoholic excess. "By the way, gentlemen, temperance is a very good thing," Linder continued, sliding quickly past the embarrassment. Linder's barrage took aim at all abolitionists but were most sharply directed at Lovejoy. The attorney general ended his speech by instructing his audience to return with friends for the next day's session.

Day two, on Friday, was no smoother for Lovejoy and Beecher. After the previous day's fiasco, they settled on a new tack to try to out the interlopers: they would revert to the original design, so that the only people who could sign in were those who declared their moral opposition to slavery. But that tactic, too, soon went awry when Lovejoy's enemies opted to claim that they, too, opposed slavery and simply enrolled. Worse still for the abolitionists, the nervous trustees of the church delivered a message saying that the church must be open to all "orderly well disposed persons" and would be closed to any "one sided discussion." Linder's followers knew this was a win for them, and erupted in noisy cheering.

The abolitionist camp managed to get Blackburn elected over Thomas Hope to serve as permanent president of the convention, while the body elected two competing secretaries—the Lovejoy forces chose Graves, while their opponents chose William Carr, a vociferous, pro-slavery critic of the editor. The job of coming up with an agenda for the meeting fell to a three-person committee that had little hope of reaching consensus: the abolitionists Beecher and Turner, plus Linder. As the morning wore on, the Linder and Hogan forces strengthened their hand by sending runners to recruit men—"certain lewd fellows of the baser sort"—off the street. One of their supporters stood at the church door hailing passersby in the manner of a carnival tout: "Join the convention? Botkin and all our men are joining."

By afternoon, the Linder camp was ready to flex its numerical muscles. As expected, the three-man committee could not agree on a so-called "statement of sentiments" to help guide the convention's discussion on slavery and civil liberties, including the right to a free press. So Beecher and Turner prepared a sweeping majority statement on civil and religious rights that was based upon guarantees written into the Illinois Constitution. Linder, meanwhile, proposed his own set of resolutions that were

vehemently hostile to abolitionism. By the time the three men returned
to the full assembly to announce their competing reports, Botkin and his
men had packed the small church to bursting, with more than one hundred
supporters—easily enough to carry any vote.

The assembly brushed quickly over the statement written by Beecher
and Turner and instead adopted Linder's resolutions, which endorsed
the South's views on slavery so completely they might have been crafted
by South Carolina governor McDuffie himself. Approved were resolutions stating that Congress had no authority to outlaw slavery in the
District of Columbia or in any state, and others saying that the passage
of any law to free slaves would violate the Constitution and "lead to a
civil war between the slave and non-slaveholding states." The convention
further approved Linder statements pronouncing slavery a "political
evil" that was not the burden of the "current generation" to fix, and
another asserting that slave owners should determine if and when any
emancipation would take place.

In all, the assembly's passage of the Linder package amounted to a thorough rout of the antislavery forces. At Hogan's urging, the Beecher-Turner
statement in support of civil and press liberties was tossed aside as no
longer relevant. Blackburn adjourned the session indefinitely. The abolitionists who had journeyed to Alton filed out of the church in failure. They
had been so thoroughly ambushed that they were unable even to establish
their antislavery society—the sole purpose of the gathering. Beecher's
"judicious and moderate men" had been no-shows. Lovejoy's convention,
designed to kindle an abolitionist crusade in Illinois, had through parliamentary trickery produced a full-throated defense of slavery instead. The
defeated abolitionists, fearing further harassment, decided against meeting
again that evening. They quietly scattered to private homes around Alton
to pray and work out a next move.

* * *

BY SATURDAY MORNING, THE activists had a consensus. They would gather on their own in a private setting—away from the Linders, the Hogans, and the Botkins—to continue the work they had come to perform. Fearful of returning to the church, at least fifty-five men crowded into the Upper Alton home of Thaddeus Hurlbut, the *Observer*'s associate editor. (It happened to be Hurlbut's thirty-seventh birthday.) The gathering of ministers and laymen had two matters to decide: whether to move forward with formation of a statewide antislavery society and what to do about the *Observer*. Asa Turner, a member of the Yale Band of Illinois College, was named chairman. Hunkering down in a private home did not guarantee peace and quiet, however. Several men appeared at Hurlbut's door, threatening to break in and to harm him if he stepped outside. Only the appearance of a group of special constables, hurriedly assembled the night before, allowed the abolitionists to resume their meeting unmolested.

On the first question, about creating the antislavery group, the eye-opening experiences of the previous two days had led some in the group to wonder if the wisest route might be to put off the move entirely or change the name of the society to shift the focus from slavery. Beecher, in particular, worried that he might injure his standing as college president by "joining an unpopular and despised minority" on an issue as explosive as slavery. But he also had watched as the horde crushed the group's earnest attempt to organize what was meant to be a civilized discussion.

It was time, Beecher decided, to face cold facts—the common ground on which he had once imagined that "all good men could unite" was a fiction. In its place was, as he saw it now, mob rule. "I therefore felt it to be a solemn duty, situated as I was, not to retreat before the illegal violence which raged around me," Beecher would write, "but to show my abhorrence of it, at whatever hazard." He would join. The assembled men agreed on a constitution—the same set of principles that had been shunted aside by Linder's majority a day earlier—and the Illinois State Anti-Slavery Society was established. Listed among its founding provisions was the state of Illinois's own guarantee that "the printing presses shall be free to every person . . . and no law shall ever be made to restrain the right thereof." Lovejoy would be the group's corresponding secretary.

When it came to the matter of the *Observer*, there was little disagreement on whether to restart the newspaper—the real question was where. Some of the supporters present, including Gilman, favored moving it to Quincy, Nelson's home, which sat on the banks of the Mississippi about 110 miles to the north. Quincy, after all, held the *Observer*'s most loyal pocket of subscribers, and its reputation as a place friendly to the abolitionist viewpoint seemed to make it a natural fit for the paper's intensifying focus on slavery. Moving the *Observer* to Quincy—and away from Alton—might prove the wisest path, these men believed. (Nelson, however, considered Quincy's image as a bastion of liberal-mindedness to be greatly oversold. After a preaching tour of the region a few months earlier, he had declared, "I cannot say that with people who are emphatically ignorant I can as yet see anything encouraging unless it is their bitter malignity, constant lying and hearty execrations.")

But Lovejoy, joined by others in the group, argued against moving the paper. There was more to consider here than the safety of the newspaper. Moving the *Observer* to another county would represent a surrender to mob bullying and a triumph for lawlessness—not only in Alton but elsewhere in the state and beyond, these men felt. Mobs all over would be emboldened by the newspaper's retreat, rendering the press vulnerable wherever a band of vigilantes decided it must be gagged. Fleeing would never redeem Alton's now dented reputation, they said, but staying put could. The rest of the country was watching how this struggle over press freedom, and civil liberties in general, would turn out.

The discussions inside the Hurlbut home that afternoon were about far more than where to house the press of a quirky, four-page religious newspaper—they were about where liberty ended and tyranny began, and when the stakes demanded taking an unwelcome and potentially dangerous

stand. The conversation was, in this sense, a most American one, and it
ended in a near unanimous decision: the *Observer* would be reestablished
in Alton, with Elijah Lovejoy as its editor. Two days later, on October 30,
a man in Cincinnati named J.A. James wrote up an invoice for $275. The
customer was Lovejoy. The sum was to pay the costs of "one medium
double press," bought on credit, plus $19 for shipping, insurance, and
interest. This would be Lovejoy's fourth printing press—his last—and it
represented hard evidence that the lofty words spoken at Hurlbut's were
not merely talk. The new press would be expected in Alton in a week's
time.

* * *

AS THE ABOLITIONISTS HUDDLED in Hurlbut's house that Saturday
afternoon, the *Observer* wasn't the only newspaper under discussion. So, too,
was James Birney's *Philanthropist*. In the course of the discussion, one of
the Ohio activists, a man named Dr. Miles, raised the subject of the Birney
newspaper and its sacking at the hands of Cincinnati vigilantes a year earlier. The paper's sorry experiences might have served here as a lesson on
the dangers of defying a community's repeated warnings. But the visiting
abolitionist instead invoked the *Philanthropist* to tell a different story—one
with a redemptive ending, with "good effects" prevailing over violence.

How was this possible? Hadn't the Cincinnati mob, with the tacit support of certain city elites, ruined the newspaper office and destroyed its
press? And done so with the mayor watching? Wasn't the *Philanthropist*
finished? And Birney's life threatened? What "good effects" was this
Ohio abolitionist talking about? What had converted the *Philanthropist*'s
dreadful woes into the stuff of a happy ending?

The prospects for the beleaguered paper had certainly looked bleak in
July 1836—as dire as they appeared now for Lovejoy's *Observer*. Following

the mob rampage that left the Philanthropist's dismembered press at the bottom of the Ohio River, Birney faced hostility from nearly every conceivable constituency—from the local business chieftains eager to connect their city to the South by railroad, to the local newspapers, reflecting the views of both major political parties, that saw him as a dangerous meddler. In between were many others with an interest in silencing the *Philanthropist*: Southern-born dock workers and factory hands, carpetbagging slave owners, pro-slavery Kentuckians from across the river. But there remained one group in town that had steered clear of the fray as the tensions over the *Philanthropist's* antislavery cause spilled into violence, and that still commanded considerable respect. This faction, represented by people such as the *Gazette* editor Charles Hammond, might be labeled the camp of cooler heads.

Hammond had been appalled by the weekend's orgy of lawlessness in late July 1836. He was always fair-minded toward Birney and generally supported the rights of people to hold views that might be unpopular with the wider community. Following the attack on Pugh's home and press weeks two earlier, Hammond had published the full text of a public statement by Birney and his antislavery society that described the mob action as an assault on God-given liberties of speech and the press. Now, following the weekend destruction of the *Philanthropist*, Hammond swung into more direct action. By Tuesday morning, he had gathered the signatures of more than three dozen people to organize a public meeting at the courthouse to try to restore calm to the feverish city. In announcing the meeting, the organizers billed themselves as "friends of order, of law and the Constitution," taking care to point out that they had "no connection" with the abolitionists but stood firmly against "the action of a mob."

One of the signers was a future chief justice of the U.S. Supreme Court, Salmon P. Chase, who would warm to the antislavery cause through a budding friendship with Birney. At the moment, the New Hampshire–born Chase was a little-known lawyer and Whig who had moved to the West for good in 1830 at the age of twenty-two. Chase took issue with the tenor of the abolitionists and their "obnoxious" press, but he considered their excesses minor when compared with "the evils produced by the prevalence of the mob spirit." Chase had told an acquaintance before the courthouse meeting that "sooner than see the press put down in that way, I would give ten thousand dollars myself." (The city's highly charged rumor mill churned that comment into something else entirely: Chase was reported to have said he would give $10,000 for an abolitionist press. Concerned that he would be tied too closely to the hated abolitionists, Chase wrote up a statement for the *Gazette* to set the record straight.)

Chase was building his practice in a slow, workmanlike manner. He had previously shown little interest in the slavery issue but knew a number of people involved with the antislavery movement in Cincinnati and considered them "as pure, upright and worthy citizens as Cincinnati contained." He did not yet know Birney, though one of Birney's close collaborators, Isaac Colby, was married to Chase's sister. (That sister was forced to take shelter in Chase's house during the rioting.) The young attorney had been determined not to be labeled as an abolitionist.

But when the controversy over the *Philanthropist* flared in July, Chase took a keener interest in the slavery issue. Chase had attended the earlier Market House meeting on July 23 that had served to rile the anti-Birney forces, but it's unclear if he spoke. When the mob showed up at Birney's door on the night of the rampage, however, Chase stepped forward and used his body to block the entrance to the house, enduring the group's threats until the troublemakers finally accepted that the editor wasn't home. It was the question of press freedom and civil liberties, in general, that drew Chase closer to the fight. "FREEDOM OF THE PRESS AND CONSTITUTIONAL LIBERTY, MUST LIVE OR PERISH TOGETHER," his statement to the newspaper stated.

The sacking of the *Philanthropist* awakened in Chase the same concern that it had in Hammond. As he put it later, "I was opposed at the time to the views of the abolitionists, but I now recognized the slave power as the great enemy of freedom of speech, freedom of the press and freedom of the person." It was Chase who drafted the call for a meeting that Hammond and others signed in an effort to rein in the growing air of mob impunity. Hammond, Chase, and others got together before the August 2 courthouse meeting to ready the agenda and came up with a moderate-sounding statement that danced carefully between the opposing camps. The group conceded that slavery was under the purview of the Southern states alone, protected from outside interference from other states. But it likewise argued that the rights of non-slave-owning states "will never suffer the law and constitution to be trampled in the dust for the purpose of destroying those rights."

The dearest of those rights, Hammond's group argued, was the right of free discussion—the right "of every citizen to write, speak and print upon every subject. . . . If this right shall perish through the violence of a mob, the grave that entombs it must be the sepulchre of American freedom." The statement then laid out a series of resolutions that included one proclaiming that press freedom "MUST BE PRESERVED." The men expressed shame that mobs had been allowed to run amok, and it called for the formation of a citizens' "committee of safety" large enough to "crush any future attempts by mobbish violence, in night time or in day time."

The men trooped to the courthouse—the same place where Birney had stood to confront his critics in January—but were stopped short when they got there. The courtroom was already occupied. Inside, Birney's foes had already gathered. They had beaten Hammond to the punch, taken over the meeting and begun considering their own set of proposals. At the front of the room was Burke, the postmaster who had led the Market House meeting, who'd also been installed as president of this meeting. Judge Burnet, who had led the delegation that sought to get Birney to quit publishing, was named as a vice president. The secretary was Joseph Graham, the man who had authored the threatening handbills against Birney and led the sidewalk rally on the night of the July 30 mob attack.

Their goal on this night was not to work with Hammond's men to find a middle ground but rather to lend legitimacy to the ruinous work of the mob days before. The Burke-led assembly passed a resolution condemning "the Abolition press in this city"—that is, Birney's *Philanthropist*—for "all our recent difficulties." It then approved a separate one that praised Mayor Davies for his "discretion, prudence and energy" in the affair. After that, the group approved a statement endorsing colonization as "the only method of getting clear of the evils of slavery." Then it adjourned, having successfully devoured Hammond's peacemaking session.

* * *

HAMMOND HAD TAKEN PAINS to ensure that he was not identified too closely with Birney's antislavery activists. Although the *Gazette* editor had decried the deeds of the "mobocracy" (a group that, in his estimation, included the *Whig*), he took a tactical step back from that stance and even made a public show of criticizing the abolitionists on the same day as his planned courthouse meeting. In an editorial that morning, Hammond's *Gazette* declared, "The abolitionist movements are wrong in principle, as is every attempt to assert abstract rights against the interests, the feelings, and the present judgments, of a decided majority." In the face of such strong feelings, Birney ought to have "deferred to the wishes" of the community, Hammond wrote. But in the end, Hammond could not condone the illegal acts of "mobocratic violence." He closed the column by vowing that his newspaper would seek to steer a course aimed at keeping the peace without lending a hand to the mobs.

Hammond's outspokenness against mobs would escalate in the days following the ill-fated courthouse session. Now, the editor found himself immersed in a war of words with other local papers amid accusations that he had led his *Gazette* over to the abolitionist side. The *Whig*, in particular, questioned his newspaper's loyalties, saying that the writer of one of its articles was "no doubt an Abolitionist" and that its coverage of the mob violence had been rife with "gross misrepresentations." (For example, the *Whig* accused the *Gazette* of underreporting the size of the crowd that tossed Birney's press into the river, saying it had numbered at least three thousand people.) When it came to the abolitionists, the *Whig* said Hammond was guilty of "encouragement."

Hammond eagerly threw himself into the fray. He suggested, for example, that the organizers of the Market House meeting might be liable for their role in fomenting the attack on the *Philanthropist*. When the *Evening Post* ran an article called "Mind Your Own Business," Hammond unleashed a soaring rebuttal on the obligations of a newspaper editor that sounded remarkably modern. "[I]t is his business, not only to narrate truly, events that may occur, but to trace those events to their causes, be they creditable or discreditable to the actors; and to point out fully and fearlessly the consequences to which they lead, be they for good or evil," he wrote. "An editor stands as a watchman upon a watch-tower, to note the approach of danger, and to give the alarm." If that alarm is ignored and calamity results, Hammond wrote, the editor's job then becomes "to search out the wrong-doers; to present them to the bar of the public; to assign each one his proper share of wrong; to characterize it justly." He was describing accountability.

* * *

BY SPEAKING OUT AGAINST the so-called mobocracy, Hammond, Chase, and the cooler heads of the civil liberties faction lent a boost to the peacekeeping work of the citizen patrols, even as Birney arranged for a new press to continue the *Philanthropist*'s antislavery crusading. And in a sign of building concern over mob justice, Cincinnati's religious press, which normally steered clear of the slavery issue, joined the fracas with strong statements defending freedom of the press. "In this war upon all the decencies and rights of society, silence is connivance," declared the *Journal and Western Luminary.* "It has the wickedness of violence without its courage; and it would be unbecoming our characters as citizens of a free country, as christians and as public journalists, not to speak in terms of strong reprobation."

Farther from home, Birney drew sympathetic treatment from East Coast newspapers, or at least enough to conclude that his point had been made—that most Americans supported a free press. (Those reactions would include the widely circulated letter by the Boston preacher William Ellery Channing that hailed abolitionists for their defense of a free press, which Lovejoy would reprint in the Alton *Observer.*) The controversy over the attack on the *Philanthropist* also drew Salmon Chase deeper into the antislavery cause. Chase would become a well-known antislavery lawyer, serving as Birney's attorney a year later when the editor was charged with harboring a fugitive slave, a biracial woman named Matilda Lawrence who worked in his home. Birney's conviction would be thrown out on appeal by the state Supreme Court.

Birney resumed publishing the *Philanthropist* in September and, although he remained watchful, was left to operate his antislavery newspaper without further attack. This was a significant achievement, but hardly speaks to a Cincinnati transformed. Many of the same political conditions survived. Davies, for example, would be reelected as mayor, demonstrating that residents did not blame him for the mayhem that had engulfed his city. (Davies's political standing would not survive race riots five years later, however.) None of those who took part in the July mobbings faced criminal prosecution, though Achilles Pugh successfully sued four of the men for the destruction of his press, winning a civil judgment of $1,500. But it took three years to do so.

Given all this, it might seem surprising to learn Birney's take on the effects of the violence against his newspaper. He declared those effects to be "most happy." For one, Birney would write in his revived newspaper, there had been widespread condemnation of the mob actions and disapproval of the men who organized the Market House meeting that preceded the July 30 attacks. For another, publicity over the episode had drawn attention to the work of the abolitionists, serving as a kind of recruitment tool for a movement that largely remained at the edge of American society. "The outrage on the *Philanthropist* has given it, and the cause it espoused, a celebrity that it never would, otherwise have obtained," Birney surmised. "It has made abolitionists by the THOUSAND, while the paper by its own unaided efficiency was making them by *tens*." The destruction had accomplished more for the cause of liberty than the abolitionists were capable of on their own, Birney said. He warned, though, that the next threat would likely be against the lives of abolitionists themselves.

To be sure, Birney's rosy-sounding assessment was heavy with what subsequent generations would label as "spin." But to understand his reasoning requires reading the events through the lenses of abolitionists who were seeking to persuade fellow Northerners that the South's quest to safeguard slavery had bred a lawlessness that threatened their own right to speak and write. By this thinking, a ransacked newspaper stood as a potent symbol of the larger struggle over Americans' civil liberties, its gagging as valuable as any of the words it might have printed. While Lovejoy defined his struggle through the prism of morality, Birney was, in a sense, approaching the matter in the language of politics. Defeat thus became success. From destruction, a happy ending.

Such were the "good effects" that Dr. Miles, the Ohio abolitionist, may have had in mind a year later during the meeting at Hurlbut's stone house in Upper Alton. He argued that Lovejoy and the *Observer* should stay and fight, no matter the consequences. There was now successful precedent.

CHAPTER SEVENTEEN

NO RIGHT
TO BE NEUTRAL

B EECHER WASN'T GIVING UP. Even after the humiliation of watching
Linder and his helpers hijack the convention meeting that Beecher
had designed, the Illinois College president had more to say. He believed
there were still good people in Alton who would hear him out. For good or
ill, Beecher now held the reins as the antislavery camp continued to search
for some way to break through the formidable wall that their opponents
had constructed around local opinion. He just needed an audience. So, on
the day after the meeting at Hurlbut's, Beecher agreed to deliver Sunday
sermons at a pair of Presbyterian churches, including the one in Upper
Alton at which Lovejoy served as pastor. His topic would be slavery.

The sermons went smoothly, especially given the unsettled air that had
held since the convention fiasco two days earlier. Beecher made a con-
scious effort to defuse tensions from the pulpit by delivering his message
in, as he put it, "an unexceptionable form." He sought to demonstrate to
the assembled parishioners the virtues of free discussion and the dangers
to everyone in allowing it to be smothered by force. Beecher came away

from the Sunday sermons thinking that his listeners had responded posi-
tively to his words and that the upheaval might be coming to an end. He
even considered leaving town the next day, thinking his work might be done.
But Beecher put his departure on hold after he and Lovejoy were invited
to attend a meeting that had been called for the next day—Monday,
October 30—with a group of citizens to discuss the future of the *Observer*.

The people who attended this meeting inside an Alton store, Alexander
& Co., were neither abolitionists nor their sworn enemies. They were
people with diverse viewpoints but joined by a common belief that the
climate of lawlessness could not go on. In some respects, they represented
the moderate middle that Beecher had described when he prevailed upon
Lovejoy earlier that they should focus the antislavery convention around
free discussion rather than a strong position on slavery. Here, perhaps,
was a group that might serve a calming role—not unlike the one played
by the contingent of cooler heads in Cincinnati during Birney's troubles a
year earlier. It was up to Beecher to win them over, with Lovejoy looking
on from the sideline.

The first point Beecher sought to convey was the wrongness—the
futility, really—of choosing force over argument to confront an idea that
one may see as "erroneous." This was the mob's approach, and to allow
it to use "brute force" to squelch a newspaper was surrendering the very
foundations of civil government and, he added, of religious toleration.
Mob spirit was a contagion that already threatened "every freeman in the
state"—each person had a stake in vanquishing it, including the men
assembled before him now. Beecher hoped to cast this issue as one that
extended far beyond the strategic redoubt known as Alton. "It was not a
local question; and could not be made such," he said.

The meeting then turned to the *Observer*. After spending the previous
several days as largely a spectator to events, it was Lovejoy's turn to
speak. He quickly sought to rebut one of the most potent claims against
him—his now broken "pledge" not to discuss slavery in the newspaper.

Lovejoy allowed that, yes, he had told his original audience in Alton
that he saw little reason to discuss slavery now that he resided in a free
state. But he denied ever promising to keep the topic out of the *Observer*.
What he *had* said during that session, fifteen months earlier, was that no
one could restrict his right to publish, and that he would write about any
topics he thought worth discussing. Some of the men who gathered in the
store now had been present during that earlier meeting and backed up
Lovejoy's account.

Beecher concluded by addressing the responsibilities of the townspeople of Alton in the midst of this telling crisis. The situation was not
yet beyond repair—even "a little energy" shown by the city's elites could
prevent further mayhem, he argued. In fact, Lovejoy's friend Enoch Long
and a few dozen others already had been deputized as special constables
in Upper Alton, though it is not entirely clear by whose authority. They
had begun their patrols during the weekend. (As the abolitionists had met
at Hurlbut's home, Long and his patrol chased away a man on the street
nearby who was "blustering and swaggering and threatening.") If Lovejoy's safety could not be ensured, Beecher ended, he would then advise
the editor to "flee elsewhere." Here, Beecher was answering an earlier
suggestion by Linder's ally John Hogan that Lovejoy should follow the
biblical example of Paul: When persecuted in one city, flee to another.

Beecher returned that night to the church in Upper Alton to preach for
a second time, a continuation of his Sunday talk on slavery. Once again,
Beecher aimed for a calming effect. He said the nation needed a "kind
spirit" in order to be able to discuss ending slavery so that the South did
not panic and react against the work of abolitionists. Beecher said there
did not have to be a clash between the antislavery activists and colonizationists—the two forces arrayed against each other in Alton—as long as
each avoided "false principles of action."

The college president was gamely trying to map a route that might bridge
a gap between the two sides that had only grown wider in recent days.

Despite Beecher's exhortations, that chasm showed no sign of shrinking when it came to the question of Lovejoy's newspaper. His Monday sermon ended peacefully, and Beecher was invited to reprise his message at the Presbyterian church in lower Alton for those who had missed it. Beecher's supporters in the church posted notices around town, a move that Linder's camp saw as brazen in the extreme. Publicly announcing plans to preach abolitionist doctrines—in a house of God, no less—was an affront that could not go unanswered.

* * *

THE TUMULT THAT HAD surrounded Lovejoy for weeks raised the unavoidable question of his personal safety. Lovejoy's home sat at the far eastern end of the city, a long walk that left him exposed as he passed through isolated terrain from his downtown office at the newspaper. At home, Lovejoy and his brothers were sleeping with loaded muskets next to their beds, and his friend Enoch Long had created the force of special constables in Upper Alton whose main purpose seemed to be protecting the abolitionists from mob attack. There were also worrisome signs that Lovejoy was being tracked at his home and in places he went around town.

One evening during this period, Lovejoy, Celia, and the Long couple had gone to the home of a mutual friend for a gathering. Guests looked up to see a man peering in the window. He disappeared, but there was little question among Lovejoy's friends who the man was looking for. That same evening, an intruder appeared crouching outside the Long home, where Lovejoy was a frequent visitor. The Longs' son Hastings, who was still at home, chased the man away by flinging a hammer at him and calling for help from a brother-in-law. Lovejoy's allies began to keep shotguns on hand, always "with plenty of ammunition," one would later recall.

The atmosphere grew so forbidding that Celia Lovejoy had taken to going from her sick bed to the safety of the attic, petrified of the men who prowled outside the Lovejoy home. One evening, Lovejoy returned home and had barely closed the door when chunks of brick smashed through the windows with a terrifying crash. Celia, stricken with fear, was unable to sleep for the rest of the night. At one point in the middle of this turmoil, Beecher and Lovejoy sought Mayor Krum's help. The mayor had been in office a matter of weeks. He agreed to set up a public constabulary force to keep order, but when it was needed, only days later, there would be no such thing.

* * *

ON TUESDAY, OCTOBER 31, Parker, the New Orleans preacher, again led a meeting of the Alton Colonization Society, the group formally arrayed against Lovejoy and the abolitionist camp. It was largely a replay of the society's previous session, with a similar cast of characters. Anyone listening to the gathering would have quickly concluded that Beecher's hope of building a bridge between the two groups—"if each avoided false principles of action"—was a colossal bit of wishful thinking.

Speakers once again delivered remarks that made clear their chief purpose was to target the abolitionists. Parker, who had circulated the pamphlet arguing that the Bible sanctioned slavery, charged that it was "unchristian" of the antislavery activists to enter a community and promote ideas likely to stir up trouble. He said that he felt a personal obligation to avoid topics that would agitate the public. (Parker chose to gloss over the fact that *he* was an outsider to Alton who had zealously stoked the crisis over the *Observer* since his arrival.) The colonization crowd—Hogan, Cyrus Edwards, the Baptist minister John Mason Peck—was jockeying for political position ahead of Beecher's vaunted antislavery sermon the following night. The group's goal was apparent: to banish Lovejoy and his supporters to the inhospitable wilds of the radical outback, where they would be isolated and, with luck, made silent.

The day of Beecher's church sermon—Wednesday, November 1— pulsed with the tension of imminent confrontation. All day before the event, Lovejoy's forces scurried quietly about, preparing for the possibility of an attack against them. Krum knew about the evening sermon but had no plans to attend until Gilman came to his office that afternoon. The businessman was still allied with Lovejoy, despite having pulled away weeks earlier, and he took the chance now to brief the mayor on recent events. Gilman told Krum that a new *Observer* press was ordered and was expected any day. He said the newspaper's supporters had organized into a defense force in case they were targeted but promised to obey the instructions of city authorities. He then invited Krum to come with him.

Gilman led Krum to Amos Roff's store, where Lovejoy, Roff, and a few others waited. Krum learned that the men planned to receive the press whenever it arrived and to store it at Roff's store. They told the mayor that they expected trouble but would defend themselves. Krum looked around and noticed the guns—Lovejoy's men were already armed. Krum said he doubted there would be any violence against them if the press were landed during daylight hours. One of Lovejoy's friends, a hardware merchant named Henry Tanner, spoke up to suggest stockpiling the weapons at Gilman's warehouse. What did Krum think of that idea? The mayor replied carefully. He urged the group to act with "moderation and prudence." Nothing, Krum said, would ignite unrest faster than if they showed up in the streets carrying weapons. If the men were going to stock an armory at Gilman's, they at least should do so quietly. Transfer the guns in a box, the mayor suggested.

At this point, Gilman and Krum caught sight of a steamboat arriving at the downtown dock and went out to see if Lovejoy's new press was on board. It was not. Gilman invited Krum to attend Beecher's sermon that same evening. The mayor wasn't much interested, but Gilman insisted, saying that there might be some difficulty. Gilman then asked Krum what he thought of the idea of taking the guns into the church that night, just in case. Krum replied that he saw little need for that, but Gilman believed that the mayor was underestimating the severity of the situation in his city. "He feared there was more danger than was imagined," Krum would recall.

The mayor proposed instead that the men leave the weapons at Roff's place, near the church. The guns would be safely away from the church, but close enough if they were needed. This struck Lovejoy's defenders as a sensible approach—they decided to store their firearms at a house next to the church, though under the command of one of their own. There was no denying that events in Alton had reached a strange and sorry point: The city's mayor and one of its richest residents were seriously discussing the merits of taking guns into a church for a minister's sermon.

* * *

THE PRESBYTERIAN CHURCH IN downtown Alton was packed by the time Krum arrived that evening for Beecher's sermon. After his earlier hemming and hawing, the mayor had decided to attend after all—thanks in large part to Gilman's anxious urging. Beecher offered a defense of Lovejoy, his words cascading over a room gripped by anticipation. Beecher's talk was proceeding quietly until a rock crashed through a window on the church's west side. Instantly, the church erupted in shouted commands.

"To arms!" yelled one of Lovejoy's allies, possibly Tanner. In moments, the defenders had retrieved their weapons and quickly formed a rank at the front of the church. Inside, Beecher shouted for quiet. He finally managed to calm everyone sufficiently to resume his sermon and finished it without further incident. A crowd gathered as people filed out. Hostile onlookers—some of them just boys—taunted Enoch Long and the other members of the defense force who were deployed in front, calling them "cowards." Two of Beecher's armed defenders were struck by rocks, one in the head and the other in the back, but they did not retaliate. Krum ordered everyone to go home, and in time the crowd retreated into the evening. A mob would later turn up at Lovejoy's house. But when he showed up at the door clutching a shotgun, the men scampered away.

On the far side of the Mississippi, Lovejoy's old nemesis the *Missouri Republican* was monitoring the events around him with increasing bile. On the same day as Beecher's sermon, the newspaper warned the abolitionists that if they continued their campaign to resuscitate the *Observer*—yet again—"the finale will be a result to be regretted." Its editorial ended with what sounded like a suggestion for the anti-Lovejoy mob. "The citizens never will submit to the re-establishment of a paper conducted by the editor of the *Observer* in that city," it said, "and if he wishes martyrdom in the cause, in the shape of a coat of tar and feathers, or a cooling in the Mississippi, he is very likely to attain his desires."

* * *

FROM OPPOSING SIDES OF the skirmishing, Beecher and Hogan took stock of the field of battle. Each sought a way to avert all-out conflict. Beecher broke it down this way: The Alton community was divided into four groups. Two of them—the abolitionists and the mob—stood at opposite poles, probably irreconcilably so. But there were two factions in the middle, each of which generally favored rule of law. One of these middle groups—people we might call civil libertarians—supported Lovejoy's right to publish in spite of abolitionist positions with which they disagreed. (These would be people like Charles Hammond in the Birney crisis in Cincinnati.) The second middle group, Beecher figured, was made up of people who supported law and order but refused to stand up for Lovejoy and his press because they feared that doing so would amount to endorsing the abolitionists' detested doctrines.

These last people might be found among Alton's business elites and perhaps at the meetings of Alton's colonization society. It was this group, Beecher calculated, that would determine the future of the ongoing dispute. If this respectable set could be persuaded to stand for the larger principles of lawfulness and liberty, "the work was done," Beecher figured. The college president felt that he had yet to be able to present his case directly to this audience. He had considered taking his arguments to the colonization society meeting two nights earlier but dropped the idea, figuring he'd be rejected out of hand. Beecher was feeling that he might have come to the end of what he could accomplish in Alton. Maybe it was time to return to his college duties in Jacksonville.

Hogan, the politically keen lawmaker known to his friends as "Honest John," wrestled with his own swelling worry. The standoff over Lovejoy's press—a deadlock that Hogan and his friends Linder and Botkin had no small role in creating—was reaching an alarming temperature and threatened to explode. Beecher happened to be walking down the street with Gilman at the time when they ran into Hogan, who described his worries. Was there any way to alleviate the rising tension while it was still possible? Beecher replied yes, he had already written up terms for a peaceful resolution that would make both sides happy, if reasonable men could hear them out and come to agreement.

Beecher did not explain what those terms were, but the possibility of an end to the turmoil sounded appealing to Hogan, who could see with his own eyes that every attempt so far to get Lovejoy to back down through persuasion, opprobrium, or brute intimidation had come to nothing. And now a new press was on its way. Gilman proposed a meeting of leading Alton citizens—merchants and others—and Hogan concurred. He would call the gathering at his store. What followed were two days of meetings, the most consequential of all that had taken place, or would. It was there,

Lovejoy's brothers would write later, that "the death warrant of our brother was signed, and put into the hands of the mob for its execution."

* * *

THE GATHERING TOOK PLACE in the counting room at Hogan's company in downtown Alton. The star of the first day—Thursday, November 2— was Beecher, who for a week now had been calling all the shots for the abolitionist side. Lovejoy stayed home this day with his stricken wife. Gilman was there, as were Linder, Cyrus Edwards, and some others from the colonization side. The garrulous Hogan led things off by explaining what everyone pretty much knew already—that the city had been convulsed over the question of abolition. Both sides sought common ground, he told the group, and this might be the occasion for accomplishing that end. With that introduction, Hogan yielded the floor to Beecher, who had been at the center of the storm long enough by now to be familiar to many of those gathered.

With all eyes on him, Beecher believed he had two jobs. The first was to persuade the men before him that they were being asked to stand up for law and order—and not for any abolitionists. The second was to get them to see that this matter was too important for anyone to remain on the sidelines. The issues here boiled down to the survival of civil society itself. "They had no right to be neutral on such a question," Beecher thought at the time. By selling these two points, Beecher believed, he would capture the respectable center, relegating the marauding roughnecks of the mob to the far edge of the discussion.

The college president meant it when he told Hogan he had a plan— Beecher now unfurled a set of nine resolutions for the group's consideration. The list should not have surprised anyone who been paying attention to Beecher since the start of the ill-fated antislavery convention seven days earlier. Tops on the list was the right of every citizen to express an opinion—to "freely speak, write, and print on any subject." There should be no legal exceptions to this, except for an "abuse" of the right, and only then through a ruling by a court of law. (Libel would have been considered such an abuse.)

Here, Beecher turned to the concept of the free exchange of ideas, sounding much like a Locke or a Voltaire. "Truth" was arrived at through unfettered discussion, Beecher argued, but any attempt to quell that expression was likely to result in just the kind of "excitement" in which Alton currently stewed. No ideas should be off-limits from such discussion—in fact, unpopular opinions warranted even more protection than others from attempts to censor, Beecher said. And now he turned to the elephant in the room: Lovejoy and his newspaper. The principles he had just enumerated meant that Lovejoy should be allowed to publish, regardless of his views or character. Beecher proposed a final resolution that promised to "protect the press, the property, and the Editor of the Alton *Observer*, and maintain him in the free exercise of his rights, to print and publish whatever he pleases."

It was a masterfully composed argument in support of free speech, with room for Lovejoy's detractors to respect his right to publish without approving of what he printed. Beecher had moved neatly from Enlightenment abstractions to the crisis roiling the coarse streets outside Hogan's office, and with a concrete course of action. He invoked Daniel Webster and the English abolitionist William Wilberforce. He pointed out that Lovejoy and his allies were motivated by religious devotion, not fanaticism. He appealed to the generosity of his audience and to their pragmatic side, noting that a return to peace and quiet would be good for business and help erase the stain of mobism. Beecher told the men that American democracy itself was being tested in Alton.

But as he closed, Beecher knew his argument might be in trouble. Several men who had been involved in the previous disturbances entered the room. They would not be sympathetic to his cause. In any case, Beecher's bottom line could not have been pleasing to his other listeners. For all the lofty ideas he had laid out, the unavoidable message was that Lovejoy should be allowed to continue publishing his unsavory views.

Beecher ended and waited for a reaction. Before him that afternoon sat ministers, men of accomplishment and wealth—gentlemen of property and standing. This was, in Beecher's estimation, a collection of "calm, thoughtful, judicious men." A warm response seemed possible. Instead, Beecher got silence. "Not a single voice was raised" in support of the ideas he had just laid out, Beecher would remember. If anything, the crowd seemed strangely surprised. People acted confused about the purpose of the gathering—wasn't it supposed to be about *compromise*? Others just kept quiet.

Linder rose to speak. There was no use in considering Beecher's resolutions, the attorney general argued. These principles were incorporated in the Bill of Rights, so there was little this group could add by approving them here. Then Linder took a surprising tack: Since some of the men in the room had taken part in or promoted the mob activities against Lovejoy, he said, passing Beecher's resolutions would be the same as to "condemn ourselves." To approve these principles would be admit that they had been "entirely in the wrong." Beecher was aghast. The assembly would not stand in favor of rule of law out of concern for the feelings of those who had violated it?

A motion was made to shelve Beecher's resolutions. But Hogan, eager to salvage the meeting that he had played a role in organizing, proposed instead that they be assigned to a seven-person committee that would include Linder, Edwards, Hogan, Gilman, and a few others. The committee would deliver its response to Beecher's resolution the next day. Yet another meeting had been held, and it, too, had served only to underscore Alton's deep divisions over the issues of slavery and a free press. The city was no closer to a course that might steer it from confrontation. Meanwhile, the so-called neutrals that Beecher had viewed as the key to defusing the crisis didn't seem remotely interested in the job.

The group voted to adjourn until the next day, but first it took one more vote. In case any disturbances broke out before morning, the assembled men agreed, they would do "the utmost of our power" to maintain law and order. Beecher found this a telling action: it suggested that the men who had the power to unleash mayhem or not were in this very room. If Thursday's session had placed Beecher front and center, the next day would return Lovejoy to the stage. It was his last chance to make a case.

CHAPTER EIGHTEEN

A TRAIN OF
MOURNFUL
CONSEQUENCES

T HE AIR AROUND LOVEJOY seemed heavy with significance. He
awoke Friday knowing that all of his crusading in recent months—
not to mention whatever lay ahead—could be decided that very day. The
seven-person committee named the previous afternoon would deliver its
decision on Beecher's sweeping packet of resolutions. Among those, of
course, was whether Lovejoy would be left alone to publish the *Observer*
as he saw fit. Lovejoy had stood back for much of the past week, watching
his friend Beecher try one tactic after another in a quest for peace, only
to be outmaneuvered by the pair's wily opponents, knowing that his very
presence stirred emotions to a fever pitch. The second meeting at Hogan's
would begin at two P.M., giving Lovejoy and his friends a full morning to
consider their options and await what would amount to a trial's closing
argument.

Beecher, taxed from the previous week's skirmishing, holed up in his
room in the Lovejoy home all morning, contemplating the "momentous
interests" that hung in the balance. "A weight was upon my mind," he

would recall. Lovejoy and another friend, Asa Hale, stopped into Beecher's room to look in on the college president. The three spent their visit
in prayer. Beecher looked at Lovejoy, around whom so much turmoil now
swirled, and was seized more than anything by the minister's sense of calm.
Lovejoy's confidence in his cause was so complete, Beecher thought, that
it seemed "child-like." And even though the committee's verdict on the
proposed Beecher solution was now out of their hands, Lovejoy betrayed
only a quiet poise. "He was perfectly cool and collected, and awaited
the result of the report of the committee with great tranquillity of mind,"
Beecher would write.

Lovejoy had been given plenty of time to ponder his own situation. The
editor was displeased by the fact that men of influence—enough influence to
swing the course of events in Alton—had sidestepped the chance to do the
right thing on principle. Instead, they had thrown his fate to "a promiscuous
assembly, many of whom were so deeply committed to the wrong side."

Nonetheless, Lovejoy had come to some decisions. He was well aware
that the ice was cracking beneath his feet. Lovejoy was exposed, and it
was not hard to envision any number of ways he might fall victim to "the
hand of the assassin or the fury of some midnight mob." He recognized
that the people who wished to silence his newspaper might next target his
family in an attempt to chase him from town.

But Lovejoy and his allies doubted that even fleeing would help—he
would likely be followed to a new destination by "friends of mob-law,"
much as he had been hounded in Alton after leaving St. Louis. Staying left
him in peril, but so did leaving as long as Lovejoy insisted on attacking
slavery in print. And resigning as editor might only serve to kill the paper.
Perhaps there was a way to safeguard the new press by storing it for a short
time at the Godfrey & Gilman warehouse. Gilman had already given his
approval to the idea. Having the backing of the city's two most powerful
businessmen would surely offer a strong measure of protection against
mischief, Lovejoy thought.

Beecher could see where Lovejoy was going with this, and he would do little to stop his friend. Lovejoy was choosing "the path of duty," Beecher knew, and was prepared to risk his life to defend the principle of a free press. Lovejoy had reduced it all to a simple, stark question: "Could he as a friend of God and man desert the cause in which he was engaged to save his life?" Even now, however, Beecher believed that once Lovejoy made clear his determination to continue as editor, the opponents would yield. "For I could not believe that they were prepared to perpetuate deliberate murder," Beecher would later write. By afternoon, each man knew his part.

* * *

LINDER HAD SET ANOTHER trap. No sooner had Beecher and Lovejoy assumed their places in Hogan's store than the attorney general took the floor. He had a resolution for the group to consider before moving to the pending business of the previous day. Linder's proposal was this: only residents of Madison County would be allowed to take part in any discussions or voting on the matters before the group. Anyone else was welcome to stay, but as a spectator only. The move was obviously aimed at Beecher, who lived in Jacksonville, which was part of Morgan County. The resolution passed without debate. The nettlesome Beecher was out. Linder had cleanly severed Lovejoy's closest ally and most eloquent advocate—the author of the very resolutions the group was meant to take up now—from any of the discussions. It was clear which way the afternoon would go. Beecher could only sit in "silent sadness" and await the inevitable.

Cyrus Edwards, the Whig senator and gubernatorial candidate, then took the baton. Edwards, who stood an imposing six-foot-four, had chaired the committee considering the Beecher resolutions and now delivered the panel's decisions, following what he called a "deliberate and candid examination." The news was not good. While Beecher's ideas were laudable in their "general spirit," Edwards said, they were no answer to the "fearful excitements" that had grown out of the clash between the two sides over slavery. There was plenty of blame to go around, he said. Foes of the abolitionists had been accused of violating others' civil rights to protect slavery and tagged with "many and most opprobrious epithets, such as pirates, man-stealers, etc.," Edwards said. For its part, Lovejoy's side had been labeled as incendiaries and traitors seeking to stir up slave rebellion, violence, and even a breakup of the Union. The result was an impasse that grew more explosive by the day. "It is not to be disguised," Edwards said, "that parties are now organizing and arming for a conflict, which may terminate in a train of mournful consequences."

But Beecher's terms, which had offered a strong defense of a free press, fell short of solving the emergency because they were too one-sided, Edwards argued, "demanding too much of concession on the one side, without equivalent concession on the other." In place of the Beecher principles, the committee offered its own set of resolutions that tipped the balance unmistakably in the other direction. Both sides would avoid "undue excitements" and employ "moderation" when discussing the rightness of "principles."

Then Edwards addressed the matter of Lovejoy's newspaper. A religious newspaper would be a positive force in the community, if established at "a suitable time" and run by "judicious" owners and editors, Edwards said. But Lovejoy had to go. Although the group conceded that Lovejoy had a legal right to publish, Edwards said it was "indispensible to the peace and harmony of this community" that the editor was "no longer identified with any newspaper establishment in this City." Lovejoy should cut his ties with the *Observer*, as he had once offered to do. "[S]uch a course would highly contribute to the peace and harmony of the place," the committee decided.

Lovejoy, already stripped of his press thanks to the mob's attack in September, was now being told not to bother replacing it. The Hogan group had flipped Beecher's vision on its head—it was Lovejoy who would have to yield everything, Beecher concluded. As he saw it, right would now concede to wrong. "It was not *moderate* discussion which [Lovejoy's] opponents had demanded, but *no* discussion," Beecher would write. "Not that Mr. Lovejoy should print his opinions moderately but that he should not print them at all."

Linder stood up next to urge the larger assembly to approve the measures. Lovejoy's friend Gilman, who had been part of the committee, then rose to dissent from its recommendations. There was much in the package of terms that Gilman opposed—including, no doubt, the gagging of the *Observer*. But Gilman's primary point was that the only way to ensure the rights of all of Alton's citizens would be to enforce the laws that the vigilantes had repeatedly flouted. Only an adherence to the rule of law could prevent other outbreaks of disorder in the future, the businessman argued. Gilman's argument went nowhere.

* * *

A RACKET OF VOICES had swamped Alton during the previous eight days. Botkin's boisterous henchmen at the hijacked convention. Linder's speechifying on a pile of lumber. Parker's fulminating against carpet-bagging abolitionists. The indefatigable Beecher's repeated sermons and bookish appeals to reason. But one voice had been conspicuously missing from the din—Lovejoy's. His moment had come. The sturdily built minister raised his frame and strode calmly to the front of the room. His round face gave away none of the strain that had enveloped him and his family for weeks, nor of the sentiments he was about to reveal. When Lovejoy spoke, his tone was "deep, tender and subdued." He struck a deferential note at first, but soon was working his way up and down a scale of emotions that passed through indignation, sorrow, and defiance, as recreated by Beecher.

"I feel, Mr. Chairman, that this is the most solemn moment of my life," Lovejoy began. The editor said he meant no disrespect, but he was prevented by his conscience from saying the words that he knew the men before him wanted to hear. Lovejoy did not know Edwards, but he expressed surprise that the senator could have placed such a set of resolutions on the table. "Mr. Chairman, I do not admit that it is the business of this assembly to decide whether I shall or shall not publish a newspaper in this city . . . I have a *right* to do it," Lovejoy said. "What I wish to know of you is whether you will protect me in the exercise of this right."

Lovejoy argued that presenting the problem as one of insufficient compromise was specious—there was really only one legitimate side here, not two. The only question was what would prevail, the law or the mob's impulses? "What have I to compromise?" Lovejoy asked. It was true that he had offered to give up control of the *Observer*. But it was one thing to do so voluntarily and quite another to yield to the demand of a mob. "The latter, be assured, I *never* will do," he said.

Lovejoy was aware that he stood alone against larger, more powerful forces. "I am but one and you are many," he told the group. "You can crush me if you will; but I shall die at my post for I cannot and will not forsake it. Why should I flee from Alton? Is this not a free state?" As Lovejoy continued, his remarks gained energy. The editor said it was not the group's job to indulge him with its mercy—he did not need or desire its purported compassion. Lovejoy was making his final appeal to the jury, while at the same time signaling to the panel that he was above whatever verdict it might render. He had broken no laws, deserved no punishment. "Will conduct like this stand the scrutiny of your country? Of posterity? Above all, of the judgment day?" he asked.

His speech now seemed directed to a wider audience than the men seated in Hogan's store. In his seething comments, Lovejoy might easily have been responding to the accumulation of indignities that had been heaped upon him during the previous two years in St. Louis and Alton: the attacks on his presses and his character, the roadside harassment, the siege of his home, the unceasing threats. The utter failure of anyone in a position of authority to intercede on his behalf.

"You may burn me at the stake, as they did McIntosh at St. Louis; or you may tar and feather me, or throw me in the Mississippi, as you have often threatened to do," Lovejoy challenged. "But you cannot disgrace me. I, and I alone, can disgrace myself." Lovejoy's poise broke away in pieces as he ticked off a catalog of woes. He finally yielded to tears while recalling the threats on his life and the heavy toll that the months of ravages had taken on Celia. "I am pursued as a partridge upon the mountain. I am pursued as a felon through your streets," he accused. "And to the guardian power of the law I look in vain for that protection against violence which even the vilest criminal may claim."

Lovejoy's audience, which also included some of his friends and the confounding Krum, was rapt by this figure before them. The hard faces of several were wet with tears—even those of his enemies, Beecher would recall. Lovejoy had laid bare his beliefs, unfurled his final appeal. He concluded on a note that could best be described as a determined resignation. He was going nowhere, but ready to pay the price. "It is because I fear God that I am not afraid of all who oppose me in this city. No, sir, the contest has commenced here and here it must be finished," Lovejoy vowed. "If I fall, my grave shall be made in Alton."

* * *

BEECHER LAY DOWN HIS head and wept. There was no doubt in his mind that Lovejoy had struck his target—the assembled men knew that the editor was right. If the Edwards committee would just say so, Beecher believed, the rest of the group would swing around to defend Lovejoy's right to publish. "It would have carried the whole audience with electric power," Beecher thought. The young physician Benjamin Hart found himself moved enough to make such a statement. Hart, who had turned down a run for mayor, had been part of the Market House delegation in July that sought to dissuade Lovejoy from writing about slavery. But now, following Lovejoy's plaintive appeal, the doctor felt the mood of the crowd shifting in the editor's direction. "I saw this and felt it and was on the point of rising to say something that would turn the tide," Hart would later tell friends. But he was too shy and allowed the moment to pass, missing his chance for good. It was an instant of hesitation for which Hart would say he never forgave himself.

Beecher's hopes rose as the influential Hogan stood to speak. Hogan had played the conciliator since arranging these meetings and had an opportunity now to buy Lovejoy some space to work. Instead, he did the opposite. Hogan, the former minister, argued that what was right was not always the most practical course for a community. Lovejoy may have deserved protection in an abstract sense, Hogan allowed, but that didn't mean it made sense for a place like Alton. Perhaps the Christian thing for Lovejoy to do would be to yield those abstract rights in the interest of peace. The lawmaker then returned to the now familiar canard that Lovejoy had pledged to keep slavery out of the pages of the *Observer*. Graves interjected from the audience to clarify, saying that his friend had never yielded his right to publish as he saw fit.

Linder now came forward to finish the job. In slashing language that made evident there would be no treaty, Linder attacked Lovejoy and the abolitionists as being wholly unconcerned with the community around them. The attorney general said he could see the matter clearly now: The city was under siege by "foreigners." Linder charged that there could be no reasoning with these people, who cared only about "the gratification of their own inclinations" and were too happy to force upon Alton a newspaper it did not want.

Linder then went a step further than the committee had. He proposed not only that the *Observer* not be reestablished in Alton, but that no newspaper like it be allowed to operate there—effectively banning *any* paper that would publish an antislavery viewpoint. Even Edwards was alarmed by this sudden turn, which seemed to go too far. He jumped into the discussion to urge moderation, and persuaded the group to set that proposal aside for the moment.

But following more speeches during which Lovejoy was depicted, among other things, as an "insane person," the assembly ended up revisiting the Linder proposal and approving it, after all. The group also approved a statement from a separate participant that condemned Lovejoy's beliefs as "subversive" but that still deplored "unlawful violence." Krum, who had not spoken during the session, offered the final resolution for the group to consider, and it did not help Lovejoy. "We regret that persons and editors from abroad have seen proper to interest themselves so conspicuously in the discussion and agitation of a question, in which our city is made the principal theatre," the statement said. It amounted to a play on Linder's "foreigners" allegation. The group voted to approve Krum's provision and then adjourned the Friday session, with no further meetings scheduled.

The time for argument and deliberation was done. There would be no middle ground in Alton on which "good men" could find agreement, no camp of cooler heads to champion the principles of civil liberties over the will of the majority. Beecher had an answer, and Lovejoy a plan. Now, all eyes were turned to the Mississippi River, where a steamboat called the *Missouri Fulton* chugged north with its cargo. . . .

* * *

FOR DAYS, THE ALTON dock had been the scene of a tense waiting game. It was an open secret that Lovejoy's press would be arriving from Cincinnati at any moment. The editor's enemies intended to make sure that it never made it into town. They rushed to the dock to check incoming steamboats, making clear their intention to destroy the shipment before

it could be unloaded. At times, the men traded sharp words with disem-
barking passengers who disapproved of their project.

It was a cat-and-mouse game, and Lovejoy's side was playing, too.
Gilman had agreed to harbor the press for a limited time, thinking that
Amos Roff's store was too exposed to possible onslaught. Gilman and the
others knew the mob would be waiting at the dock and arranged instead
to have the press landed quietly at a point called Chippewa, downriver
from town, and then hauled to Alton by horse-drawn wagon. Gilman and
the shipping agent had devised a plan to use signals from shore—a waved
handkerchief in daylight or a candle at night—to tell the captain where
to land the cargo.

On Friday, the same day Lovejoy was making his tearful appeal at
Hogan's store, two of his supporters went to the Chippewa spot to receive
it. But rain that day delayed delivery, and the muddy condition of the roads
made an overland transfer unworkable, anyway. The press would have to
be landed in Alton. On Saturday, Gilman sent a message to the ship that
it should bring the press under cover of early-morning darkness to avoid
possible detection by the mob. The *Missouri Fulton* arrived in St. Louis on
Sunday en route to Alton. Another exchange of messages fixed the exact
delivery time: Lovejoy's press would land at the Alton dock on Tuesday,
November 7, at around three A.M.

Lovejoy and his allies now needed to make sure it survived.

CHAPTER NINETEEN

TIN HORNS
AND TORCHES

T HE WAREHOUSE OF GODFREY, Gilman & Co. looked out over
Alton's downtown like a broad-shouldered sentry, separated
from the Mississippi River by a small street near the city wharf. Built
on ground that sloped abruptly to the river, the one-hundred-foot-long
stone-sided structure stood two stories tall on its northern end nearest
downtown and three floors above ground level on the south end, facing the
river. Because of its location in front of the wharf, the warehouse—which
actually comprised two buildings, placed together side by side—was
convenient for receiving shipments arriving by boat. And its doorway on
the end nearest the river provided a means of moving cargo inside quickly
and with minimal notice—such as a box with a printing press inside.

Gilman had agreed to receive the replacement press "for a short time
only" and to protect it in his warehouse by posting eight to ten armed
men, if necessary. His hope was to place this protective force under the
authority of Alton's civil authorities— Krum, basically—as a way to lend
it legitimacy to act against intruders. Gilman could be excused if he felt

somewhat jittery about the potential risks—the warehouse he shared with Godfrey was already stocked with other goods worth about $30,000. Both businessmen were exposed to considerable potential jeopardy by harboring the press, and Gilman wanted Krum to understand that he intended to protect his property.

Lovejoy had also been wearing a path to Krum's office in search of help. Lovejoy had repeatedly pleaded with Krum to create and command a military force to protect against mob attacks—a move the mayor rejected as outside his authority. But Krum said ordinary residents were legally permitted to organize their own patrols, if they deemed it necessary. Lovejoy then told Krum he would be willing to muster his own force, but under the official authority of the mayor. Again, Krum said no. Krum, the lawyer, explained the legal requirements of creating such a patrol. From Krum's point of view, arranging official protection for Lovejoy's press—even with all the trouble that Alton had already witnessed—wasn't in his mayoral job description.

Following his wrenching speech to the Hogan group, Lovejoy spent the weekend at home with his beleaguered wife, whose state remained brittle. Lovejoy and his two brothers had been joined for a visit by their younger sister Elizabeth, who made the trip west a couple of months earlier. (Their mother, Betsey, originally planned to travel with her, but stayed in Maine after a sudden change in plans.) Edward Beecher also remained at his friend's side as they awaited the arrival of the press.

On Monday, Gilman paid a visit to Krum's office. The press was due to arrive within the next twenty-four hours, and Gilman feared for the loss of his property. He wanted to make sure that he would be justified in using force to protect his warehouse and its contents. Krum explained the law as best he could, though he would later say he was doing so as a private citizen and friend and not in his official role as mayor. Gilman asked Krum to appoint a band of special constables to act as guards, but the mayor demurred. Krum did say, however, that he would put the matter in front of the city's Common Council when it met later that day.

Krum made good on this promise, telling the council that "individual citizens" had told him they felt unsafe. The mayor told the aldermen that he "had much reason to believe that the peace of the city would be disturbed" and asked for authorization to name special constables. But one of the members instead offered a resolution urging that a letter be sent to Lovejoy asking him to surrender the idea of establishing "an abolition press" in Alton. In the end, the council took no action on either idea, leaving Alton duly warned but without the means to confront a mob in any official capacity. By Monday evening, a group of ten to fifteen men armed with a club and pistols hunkered along the banks of the river, looking out for the boat. The men left for drinks after a period of waiting, and then returned to their fruitless vigil before giving up again.

Gilman's plan for landing the press during the wee hours worked perfectly. As three A.M. approached, Gilman and Roff proceeded to Krum's room to warn him that the *Missouri Fulton* was soon to arrive. The mayor dressed quickly and hurried to the dock, where a brilliant, nearly full moon illuminated the scene as the boat glided to a stop at the wharf. Krum watched the deckhands unload the box containing the heavy iron press and hustle it to the Godfrey & Gilman warehouse nearby. Inside, twenty to thirty men, all of them armed, stood guard. Gilman's armed group again offered to place itself in the service of Krum and the city, but the mayor declined, saying that such a force seemed unneeded. At least the press was now safely stowed inside Gilman's vast warehouse.

Lovejoy and Beecher made their way to the warehouse through Alton's empty streets in the pre-dawn darkness, their footsteps echoing off the idled workshops and stores. They helped the others heave the box to the third floor of the warehouse. All felt relief to have collected the press from the dock and gotten it safely stowed. Beecher climbed through an opening to the roof and looked out on the river, now warmed by the glow of dawn. He listened as the early-morning hush gave way to the first sounds of a city wrenching itself awake on an ordinary Tuesday.

After the trials of the previous twelve days, Beecher felt buoyant. The press was in hand. There had been no sign of the feared mob, no violent clash. The crisis was over, he dared to believe. "I looked with exultation on the scenes below," Beecher would remember. "I felt that a bloodless battle had been gained for God and for the truth; and that Alton was redeemed from eternal shame." With such a victory in hand, Beecher decided, it was time to return to his college president's life in Jacksonville. It seemed his work in Alton was complete.

* * *

LOVEJOY, TOO, WAS PLEASED by the turn of events. He and the others decided that only a small force would probably be needed to stand guard in the warehouse—the group could be divided into smaller shifts. For the moment, Lovejoy and Beecher would stay on while the others went home to get some sleep after their all-night watch. Later in the morning, the pair returned to Lovejoy's home for a final prayer together before Beecher's departure. Beecher sought to cheer Celia Lovejoy by expressing his hope that the family's recent troubles were ending and that "more tranquil hours were at hand." With that, Beecher bade the Lovejoys farewell and set out for Jacksonville, some sixty miles away. As he traveled north that day, he caught wind of a report that a mob was planning to strike the Godfrey & Gilman warehouse. Still basking in triumph, Beecher paid the rumor no mind.

The mood was less relaxed in Alton, where word of the press's arrival had gotten out. The sensation of relief that accompanied the successful delivery during the predawn hours gave way to heightened watchfulness and focused preparations as the day wore on. The shelves that normally held guns for sale at Roff's store were now empty, thanks to the arming of the warehouse defense force. One of Lovejoy's defenders, Henry Tanner, who had led Beecher's armed defense at the church, instructed a boy who worked for Roff to quickly prepare a supply of buckshot and to produce some lead balls for the rifles that now made up the team's makeshift arsenal. By nightfall, Platt had run several batches of lead balls for the rifles.

By the end of the day, Gilman and the others had lined up forty-two men in Alton willing to enlist in the corps that would protect the press from attack. Joseph Greeley was among these. Greeley was sitting at the table in his boarding house that evening when he was summoned to the warehouse to join the makeshift militia. Greeley was initially leery. He feared an abolition meeting was in the offing but finally relented after being assured that it was not. Greeley and the others who assembled at the warehouse voted to elect a commander. (There seems to be some dispute over who was elected as captain. By some accounts, the group picked Enoch Long, the church deacon, who many years earlier had served as a soldier in the War of 1812; Greeley, though, said that a different volunteer, W. G. Attwood, was picked). Not all those who agreed to defend Lovejoy were dyed-in-the-wool antislavery activists. One of them was William Harned, a corpulent hotel keeper from Kentucky. He had no love for abolitionists but sided with Lovejoy out of disdain for some of the editor's most vocal tormenters, such as the physicians Thomas Hope and Horace Beall. "What these men hate must be good," was how one witness characterized Harned's views.

By evening, around twenty had agreed to remain at the warehouse with Lovejoy, while the others drifted home. Inside the building, Lovejoy's impromptu team marched and conducted military-style drills to bide the time. Greeley was vaguely aware that the warehouse harbored a printing press that might be the subject of attack, but would later say that no one spelled out the exact purpose of the gathering. The volunteers, spread out across all three floors, thought the evening might prove entertaining. "They expected to have some crackers and cheese, and hear some good stories," Greeley would later testify.

As the defenders mustered, Gilman made yet another trip to Krum's office to warn the mayor that he believed trouble was imminent. (Gilman was so concerned about possible mayhem that he sent his wife and their baby to stay with her father in Upper Alton.) Gilman told Krum that he intended to defend his property against anyone who made a move against it. Krum pooh-poohed Gilman's worries, saying that he had been out in Alton's streets earlier in the day and found the mood quiet. Krum doubted there would be any attack against the press. But that was cold comfort— the mayor seemed the last to know anything. "People seemed to shun me, and were very reluctant to communicate with me at all," Krum would acknowledge later.

Gilman, concerned that his actions be deemed legal, asked the mayor several times what he thought of the armed team that had already taken position inside the warehouse. Krum replied that they had a right to be there to defend Gilman's property and could remain. Krum would later say that his opinion was not intended to be taken as an official approval from the mayor but rather as private advice. Krum told Gilman that in case there was violence that required suppression by an armed force, he would take command of the squad now standing guard at the warehouse. The mayor said it would be up to him to decide whether the use of such a force was justified. Gilman returned to the warehouse, satisfied that use of armed allies to guard his building had met with the approval of the city's mayor. It was clear, though, that Krum had no intention of intervening.

* * *

KRUM MIGHT HAVE WITHDRAWN his rosy assessment of the city's mood if he had passed through the doors of the Tontine, one of a number of "coffee houses" in Alton that plied whiskey by the jug in a downtown pocket not far from the warehouse. By early evening, angry men were growling oaths about the cursed abolitionists and taking swallows of hard drink, distributed by William Carr. Carr had already publicly burnished his credentials as an enemy of Lovejoy and the abolitionists by taking part in Linder's hijacking of the antislavery convention in October, when he managed to be elected secretary by the anti-Lovejoy camp. Some of the men now arrayed along the wall of the Tontine were equally hostile to Lovejoy's newspaper. One of them, David Butler, was overheard "swearing about Abolition and the press; he said he would have the press any how." Suitably fortified, Carr and fifteen to twenty others left the Tontine and set out marching in file through Alton's downtown toward the warehouse, looking to passersby like an army destined for engagement with the enemy.

Word of the impending attack had made it to Gilman in the warehouse before Carr's mob got there. A man named Henry W. West was standing in the doorway of his store when an acquaintance passed and said he'd heard of a plan to burn or blow up the Gilman warehouse if Lovejoy's men did not surrender the press that was known to be inside. West, who happened to be John Hogan's brother-in-law, summoned an Alton lawyer named Edward Keating, and the two men hurried to the warehouse to warn Gilman. West and Keating arrived to find several of the defenders holding guns—Lovejoy, Tanner, and a man named George Walworth among them. Gilman descended to the ground floor from his position upstairs. He sounded surprised to hear of the plan to firebomb the building but told the two visitors that he and his colleagues had decided to defend the warehouse and its contents—to the death, if necessary. Keating and West left.

By now, darkness had settled. Carr's ragged troop from the Tontine was joined by other men who milled restlessly along the river's edge near the warehouse and the state penitentiary next door. The group was keyed up and hungry for confrontation as it grew in number and frenetic energy. One man who trailed the mob to the river was mistaken for an abolitionist and targeted by the men. Furious voices erupted from the group: "Shoot him!" "Throw him into the river!" "Stone him!" The scene grew more chaotic as the ruffians rushed about in the darkness. They eventually left the "abolitionist" alone, consumed with more important aims.

West knew trouble was building. He decided to return to the warehouse. On the way, he ran into the physician Beall, who had been trying to bully Lovejoy and silence the *Observer* for months, most recently as part of Linder's takeover of the Beecher convention. West thought Beall might now be able to persuade the growing mob to disperse, and he asked him to come to the scene to try. But the doctor said no—it was useless to try. West continued to the warehouse.

The scene had grown more chaotic. The men amassed outside the warehouse were blowing tin horns and passing around bottles of liquor. West was back inside the building when the showdown began. A rock thumped off the door, followed by a shower of stones hurled from outside the sturdy warehouse. Gilman called out to the mob from an opening to the attic. It was a shame that the men had come at such an unusual hour to cause trouble, Gilman shouted to the crowd, but he was duty-bound to protect his property. Carr spoke up for the mob. Carr said that they'd come for Lovejoy's press and would have it "at the risk of their lives." Then he pointed a pistol at Gilman, who ducked back inside. More rocks thudded off the door on the ground level and crashed through the few windows on the end of the building. Neither side was backing down. West suggested firing over the men's heads to keep them at bay. Lovejoy warned his men not to "waste" their ammunition.

Before long, rocks gave way to the first report of gunfire—a pistol shot fired from outside the warehouse as the mob surged around it from the river side. Then two more shots, also from the mob. Gilman told West to go notify Krum. By the time West returned, Lovejoy's men inside the warehouse had still not returned fire, but were ready. Several of the men held weapons and muskets and shotguns were lined around the room. West was on the third floor when he heard the shot—this time from inside the building. "Who fired that gun?" someone called out in a scolding tone. It may have been Gilman. "I," came the answer. West had not identified the voice when two or three more shots rang out from the building. By now, rocks were flying through the windows of the warehouse as the situation deteriorated.

Krum heard the gunfire as he made his way to the warehouse, at around nine or ten P.M. One of those shots had struck and wounded a man named Lyman Bishop, who'd been among the crowd outside the warehouse. Comrades grabbed Bishop, one on each arm and leg, and carried him splayed to Hart's medical office, where he later would be pronounced dead. Krum arrived to see that blood had now been spilled. He moved into the crowd and asked what they intended to do. The answer came quickly: to seize the press. Someone suggested that Krum impart the mob's demand to those inside the warehouse. The mayor moved through the mob and Gilman opened the door to let him in.

Amid the candles' flickering, Krum could see that Gilman, Lovejoy, Enoch Long, and Thaddeus Hurlbut held weapons. Long asked if the defense squad was justified in using force to repel the mob. Krum answered yes: "I thought they had a right to do as they were doing." He conveyed a message from the mob: the press would be theirs, or else. As he exited, Krum warned the men outside that they were breaking the law and, in case that was not in itself persuasive, that they would be fired upon by those inside if they failed to disperse. For his trouble, Alton's mayor was told to "get out of the way and go home." Adding to insult, Krum was struck by pellets of birdshot as he spoke to the mob. Several in the crowd held weapons. Among the armed men was Dr. Beall and his friend James Jennings, the physician who also had been part of the roadside tar-and-feather mob a few months earlier.

* * *

THE SHOOTING OF BISHOP at first quieted the mob, and then stoked it to greater fury. The group had swelled to some two hundred people, and more had guns. Amid the boozy shouting came the crash of rocks through the windows. The two sides were now trading volleys of gunfire. Lovejoy's friend Reuben Gerry, who in September had sheltered an earlier press in his own warehouse before the mob seized it, now stood in the attic on one side of the Gilman building, hurling jugs and other stoneware onto the crowd. The diminutive Tanner poked his rifle out the window, taking a bead on a gunman below who threatened to shoot Gerry.

The skirmish was spinning out of control. A half mile away, the wife of Lovejoy's trusted friend Frederick Graves had made her way into the Presbyterian church and was ringing its bell in an effort to draw the attention of authorities. Mrs. Graves would sound the bell for two hours that night, but there was no militia to stop the violence, in spite of the previous warnings. Krum said it was now too late to organize Alton citizens into a force to save the besieged warehouse. One of the men inside the warehouse would later observe: "The thought never entered our minds that the mob was as bad as it turned out to be."

The flummoxed Krum managed to summon the Alton municipal court judge, William Martin, who proved no match for the mayhem. Martin tried in vain to recruit others to help him stop the violence but "did not use his authority as a peace officer because he was satisfied it would do no good." A justice of the peace, Sherman Robbins, proved equally impotent. When Robbins told a member of the mob to go home, the man responded with a threat instead. He ordered Robbins to leave if he didn't want to get hurt—"the press would be had at all events." In a separate encounter, Krum confronted a man who had raced onto the scene in bare feet and shirt sleeves on a chilly evening. The man, Solomon Morgan, apparently had been drinking heavily and was shouting and acting "crazy," according to one description. When Krum stopped him, Morgan asked the mayor "how he would like to have every damned nigger going home with his daughter." (Krum was unmarried.) Morgan had previously threatened to kill the misidentified "abolitionist" if he did not join the mob.

Soon, cries went up from the crowd. "Fire the building!" "Burn 'em out!" "Shoot every damned abolitionist as he leaves!" It was not long before someone had placed a ladder against the windowless west side of the stone warehouse to gain access to its wooden roof. An armed member of the mob named James Rock appeared with what looked like a keg of gunpowder. By now, an attacker had reached the roof with a burning wad of tar and was attempting to torch it. The arson development suddenly opened a new and frightening front in the escalating confrontation. Because there were no windows on the side of the building where Rock and the others had placed the ladder, Lovejoy's defenders were helpless to stop the torching from their positions inside the warehouse. The only way to push back the fire starters was to dart outside and fire at the ladder—in full view of the armed men in the crowd.

* * *

INSIDE THE IMMENSE WAREHOUSE, Lovejoy and his friends pondered their deteriorating position. What had once looked like an evening of crackers and cheese and good cheer had, in the span of a few hours, unraveled into life-threatening bedlam. The gathering of Lovejoy's allies was fast resembling a last stand inside a burning fort. For all their careful laying-in of weapons and ammunition, the men in Gilman's warehouse were besieged. They now knew there would be no rescue by the Alton authorities. The liquor-soaked mob outside had grown noisier and more determined as the evening wore on. The attackers had set part of the roof on fire and were trying to ignite more.

Lovejoy and the men who surrounded him in the clamor of the moment had endured much together since his arrival in Alton to start a new life the previous year. Most were men of the church—people like the deacon Long, fellow Sunday school volunteer Roff, the ever-reliable Hurlbut, and the generous Gilman—whose moral beliefs led them to the twin causes that Lovejoy had braided into one: liberty for the slave and for the press. Together they had prayed with Lovejoy and stood by him, risking their own standing in Alton, in confronting some excruciating decisions amid growing community hostility.

Now these men collectively faced a situation that carried terrifying urgency. They were fully surrounded by an armed force much larger than their own. They could surrender to the mob and walk out alive, abandoning the press to certain destruction at the hands of lawless men. Or they could stand firm in the warehouse and face the growing possibility of being consumed by fire or shot to death trying to escape. Gilman earlier had told Krum that his defenders were prepared to protect the warehouse—and the press inside—even if it meant jeopardizing their lives. It was apparent now that they were doing just that.

The fire was the greatest immediate threat. A decision was made that someone go outside and shoot the fire starter off the ladder. That would solve the peril of the spread of fire. Five of the warehouse defenders burst out and fired shots in the direction of the ladder and the crowd around it, wounding several people. A teenaged boy named Okey was among those struck by birdshot as he ascended the ladder with a wad of burning material. Okey would later claim that it was Dr. Hope who had instructed him to climb the ladder. Within the mob outside, someone had the idea to target the ground-floor door from which members of Lovejoy's group had emerged to take shots in the direction of the ladder. Two or more gunmen from the mob—the exact number is not clear—took up positions behind a pile of lumber near the warehouse door. If anyone exited that door again, the gunmen would be ready.

The mob had renewed its efforts to torch the roof, which proved a stubborn burn—Lovejoy's group would have to stage another sortie aimed at the arsonists using the ladder. Lovejoy and his storekeeper friend, Royal Weller, agreed to go, with one or two others prepared to follow.

The door opened. The men waiting patiently behind the wood pile drew a bead. Lovejoy went first, with Weller behind. A volley of shots exploded from behind the lumber. There was no time to react. Lead balls—five of them—tore into Lovejoy's body before he'd taken so much as a step. Badly wounded, the editor spun back inside the warehouse and hauled himself up a flight of stairs to the second-floor counting room. "Oh, God, I am shot," Lovejoy managed, his arms clutching his chest. "I am shot." He then collapsed dead before his comrades, with wounds to his chest, abdomen, and left arm. Weller suffered a nonlethal wound below the knee. Roff, the stove dealer, also took a step outside and was immediately fired upon. He was struck once in the ankle.

Adding to the calamity, members of the mob were preparing to set off an explosive charge along the western side of the flaming building by wedging a keg of gunpowder between the wall and an abandoned steam boiler that had been discarded nearby. Gilman and the others were now eager to end the encirclement without further carnage. William Harned, the rotund Kentuckian, called out to the mob from upstairs to report that Lovejoy was dead. West ran upriver away from the building to scout an escape route for those still in the warehouse. He then went to the door on the north end and shouted to the crowd that Lovejoy was dead.

West and Keating came to the door and offered a truce from the mob: Gilman and the rest should run for safety. The attackers had promised not to shoot. "For God's sake, leave the building and let them in, or all the property will be destroyed," West urged. All but a few of the warehouse men hid their weapons and fled toward the river. They encountered a hail of gunfire despite the mob's promise. None were hurt. Robbins, the justice of the peace, would say later that it was likely the men would have burned to death if they had remained in the building.

West climbed the ladder to extinguish the roof fire, resorting to using his hat as a water bucket. (Hope filled it from the river.) West was first to enter the now abandoned warehouse and eventually made his way to the counting room, where Lovejoy lay dead on a cot. (Beall, no longer carrying a gun, also went to the site of the body.) Hurlbut remained with Lovejoy's body. Weller stayed behind, too, sitting on a chair and washing his own bloodied leg. When Hope, a physician, offered to remove the lead ball from the wound, Weller refused, saying he would sooner die than accept help from a member of the mob. Around the warehouse, candles continued burning. Other members of the mob were soon inside, and it was not long before they had located the heavy iron press on the top floor. They tossed it out from a window onto the stones below.

Before long, anyone could hear the sound of pounding on the wharf nearby. The mob had wrestled its prey to the edge of the Mississippi and now was engaged in what it came to do. The vigilantes were calm, focused on their errand. Dr. Beall was there, exhorting the others. "Now boys, we must stick together," Beall said. "If anyone is arrested we must come to the rescue." The pounding continued, followed by the splash of objects tossed in the water. The group looked "happy" in its task, a witness would describe later. It was after midnight, nearly twenty-four hours since the press had arrived by boat at this same spot. Under the glow of an ample November moon, Elijah Lovejoy's printing press splintered to bits beneath the hammer blows of the mob's men. They tossed the chunks into the Mississippi and were done with Lovejoy for good.

CHAPTER TWENTY

A MARTYR IN THE CAUSE

A FEW FRIENDS STAYED in the warehouse with Lovejoy's body until morning and then moved it by horse-drawn hearse to his home, where brothers Owen and John had stood guard during the night's rioting. Celia and the couple's son, Edward, had taken shelter in a friend's home in Upper Alton and remained there. As the wagon carrying Lovejoy's body passed through Alton's streets on the way to the Lovejoy home, his foes greeted it with derisive comments and jeers. One mocked the solemnity of the moment by exclaiming, "If I only had a fife, I'd play the dead march for him." That speaker was identified as the physician Beall, who had been so visible an armed presence within the mob.

Celia collapsed when she learned of her husband's death, "trembling as if an arrow had pierced her heart." Overcome with grief, she was unable to attend the burial the following day. Henry Tanner, one of the men who had been with Lovejoy during the warehouse battle, and others slogged through the mud of a rainstorm to reach the burial site. Lovejoy's friends decided that a spartan service, without speeches, was the best way to avoid stirring their enemies to graveside mischief. "It was a rainy, depressing day," Tanner would write later. "We chafed in an angry mood as we thought of the silence then forced upon us!" Lovejoy's old minister friend Thomas Lippincott delivered a few prayers but no remarks. The burial ceremony ended quickly, "There had been no inquest over his body, no flowers upon his coffin," Tanner recalled. "Mob-law not only reigned but was insultingly triumphant."

Lovejoy was buried on November 9. It was his thirty-fifth birthday.

News of the killing coursed its way to Maine and to Lovejoy's mother, Betsey. She would have been in Alton if she had stuck with her plans to travel west with Elizabeth. Now she scrambled to learn the fates of her three surviving children there, her words tumbling in a frantic, unpunctuated cascade. "My dear children Owen Elizabeth and John are you yet alive Don't my dear children harbor any vengeful feelings toward the murderers of your dear brother but humble yourselves under the mighty hand of God," she wrote. At the bottom of the page, Betsey's panicked queries poured forth again: "Owen my son are you yet alive Elizabeth do write John where are you your mother is——." Her sentence trailed off. In the margin, the distraught mother scribbled a separate burst of words expressing wonderment that she could even hold a pen.

The immediate public reaction to Lovejoy's slaying in the Alton area hovered somewhere between a smug I-told-you-so and outright silence. The *Missouri Republican*, which had long disparaged Lovejoy as an irritant, announced the news of the riot in an article that claimed he had been the person who fatally shot Bishop, the man felled amid the mob. (Bishop's shooter was never identified.) Lovejoy was killed, the newspaper reported, while he was shooting repeatedly at a man on the ladder—a version at variance with other accounts. The *Republican* had little trouble laying blame for the tragedy at the feet of the abolitionists. "Every one must regret this unfortunate occurrence but the guilt of the transaction must ever rest with those who madly and obstinately persisted in the attempt to establish an abolition press there," the *Republican* pronounced. "[P]ublic opinion will hold them responsible for the fatal consequences."

For its part, the Alton *Telegraph* didn't even bother running its own story—it reprinted a piece from another Alton newspaper, the *Spectator*, a self-protective summary of the incident by Mayor Krum that pinned blame on no one. The *Spectator* itself was otherwise silent, and even lamented a week later that it faced a dearth of news with which to fill its columns. "The times are so dull that they afford no news," the *Spectator* whined. "We have examined all our papers for something new and have not been able to discover anything." The *Telegraph* took a more forthright tack: The paper said it preferred not to stir up "exciting feelings that should be allowed to subside." It would have nothing more to say.

Lovejoy would, however. A letter found after his death offers a glimpse into his mental state during the final, tumultuous weeks that ended with the mob attack. The letter had been delivered to the editor two years earlier, when some of Lovejoy's supporters in St. Louis were urging him to "pass over in silence" anything having to do with slavery. For some reason, Lovejoy had recently added a notation, dated October 24—two days before the start of the antislavery convention in Alton. "I did not yield to the wishes here expressed, and in consequence have been persecuted ever since," Lovejoy scribbled on the letter. "But I have kept a good conscience in the matter, and that more than repays me for all that I have suffered or will suffer. I have sworn eternal opposition to Slavery, and, by the blessing of God, I will never go back."

* * *

ON DECEMBER 8, BARELY a month after Lovejoy's death, hundreds of people crowded into Faneuil Hall in Boston to protest the Alton mob's action and show support for free speech. The meeting was a sign of how widely Lovejoy's killing would soon ripple. The mob attack may have produced shrugs in Alton and St. Louis, but it evoked horror across the North and even stoked condemnation in some quarters of the South. Although mob attacks were nothing new—even against newspapers, as the *Philanthropist* case had demonstrated—the killing of an editor in a free state was something else entirely. It suggested to many people in the North how far slavery's defenders were willing to go in order to squelch debate over human bondage in the United States. The fight against slavery and the struggle to safeguard Americans' freedom to express their opinions were wedded as never before.

The idea for the Boston protest meeting came from William Ellery Channing, the Unitarian minister and abolitionism skeptic, who was joined by one hundred citizens of prominence in seeking to use the meeting place for a free-speech rally. Faneuil Hall was a public meeting space owned by the city of Boston that had hosted any number of political get-togethers. But the city's mayor and common council rejected Channing's request, fearing that any resolutions passed at the meeting would not accurately reflect majority opinion in Boston on a potentially explosive issue—a topic Boston's fathers preferred not to touch. Channing fought back, however, by mobilizing public dismay over the idea that the city would deny its residents the chance to freely gather to, as he put it, "express their utter and uncompromising reprobation of the violence which has been offered to the freedom of speech and the press." Other influential voices soon joined Channing, and the city leaders gave in. They required, though, that the meeting take place during daytime hours.

It was a packed affair. Some local businesses closed their accounting operations to allow workers to attend the session, and the crowd was divided roughly evenly into thirds: abolitionists and those in favor of free discussion, their bitter opponents, and a separate group of residents who "swayed to and fro by every speaker." Channing sponsored several resolutions favoring the right of citizens to freely air opinions, including those unpopular with the majority. The proposed resolutions staked out a clear disapproval of the vigilante tactics that had been used to silence Lovejoy. Channing spoke briefly but eloquently, according to an attendee, and the overall mood in the noisy hall was "decorous, in perfect harmony and sympathy with the great cause of human freedom."

The session took a decidedly bitter turn when the state's attorney general James T. Austin rose to speak. Austin let loose with a vitriolic denunciation of Lovejoy, depicting the minister-editor as a man who had once stubbornly sought to promote slave rebellion while living in Missouri, even in the face of repeated community appeals to stop. Austin compared Lovejoy's actions in defense of slaves to a person who liberates wild animals into the city. "The people of Missouri had as much reason to be afraid of their slaves, as we should have of the wild beasts of the menagerie," Austin said. "They had the same dread of Lovejoy that we should have of this supposed instigator, if we really believed the bars would be broken, and the caravan let loose to prowl about our streets."

Austin argued that Lovejoy deserved no sympathy or approval from the assembly because he had "excited the passions of men, by conduct unwise, impolitic, rash, extravagant and unchristian; and the consequence of his conduct was such as might have been anticipated." Lovejoy had died, the attorney general declared, "as a fool dieth." Austin seemed to lend his support to the Alton mob by comparing its actions to those of the long-ago Boston patriots who, driven by self-preservation, had marched from the very same hall in which he now stood to go and toss British tea into Boston Harbor. "If the press becomes an incendiary to put the passions of mankind in a blaze, who but its conductors are to blame, if it perishes in the conflagration it has made?" Austin asked. "And what better are we ever to expect, than that an Abolition press will be destroyed, if it is established in a slave state or on the borders of it? We execrate the mob, but we cannot wonder at its outrage."

With his sneering assessment, Austin had tossed a rhetorical match into the cauldron of divided opinion before him. Loud applause and whoops of support came from many in the crowd who shared his view of American abolitionists as reckless extremists. (This, in the city that two years earlier had watched a mob capture and parade William Lloyd Garrison through its streets, tethered by a rope.) But Austin's address, fiery as it was, would turn out to be only the second-most memorable speech the standing crowd in Faneuil Hall would hear that day.

Amid the din that suddenly rocked the hall, a young man pressed his way forward through the crowd and hopped onto the speaker's platform with a shout. The speaker chastised Austin for comparing the "drunken murderers of Lovejoy" with the "patriot fathers" of the Boston Tea Party. "To draw the conduct of our ancestors into a precedent for mobs, for a right to resist laws we ourselves have enacted, is an insult to their memory," he said. "Sir, when I heard the gentleman lay down principles which place the murderers of Alton side by side with Otis and Hancock, with Quincy and Adams, I thought those pictured lips"—he stopped to gesture toward portraits of these men ringing the great hall—"would have broken into voice to rebuke the recreant American, the slanderer of the dead."

The meeting room exploded in a geyser of cheers and angry booing. *Recreant American*! *Slanderer of the dead*! "Take that back!" came shouts of protest from Austin's side. "Go on! Go on!" others countered, offering encouragement. Still other members of the audience looked at each other and whispered: "Who is this young man?" The speaker was Wendell Phillips, a Harvard-educated lawyer who had edged his way into abolitionism in defiance of his upper-crust breeding through his ties with Garrison and marriage to Ann Greene, a Garrisonian activist in her own right. His decision to speak up during the Faneuil Hall meeting—accounts vary on whether or not he had planned to speak—marked a coming-out of sorts for Phillips, who had just turned twenty-six. Seen as a rising star in the local antislavery movement, he had spoken in modest-sized meetings, but this was the first time he had gone before a large audience.

Dressed in a long frock coat and small cape, Phillips furiously attacked Austin's depiction of Lovejoy as a provocateur, asking how Lovejoy could have crossed into a free state but somehow still remain subject to the dictates of a slave state. "The czar might as well claim to control the deliberations of Faneuil Hall, as the laws of Missouri demand reverence, or the shadow of obedience, from an inhabitant of Illinois," he said. To blame Lovejoy for not bending to the will of the community in choosing what to print lent the fickle mob more power than any despot, Phillips argued. "Welcome the despotism of the Sultan, where one knows what he may publish and what he may not, rather than the tyranny of this many-headed monster, the mob, where we know not what we may do or say, till some fellow-citizen has tried it, and paid for the lesson with his life."

To portray Lovejoy as "imprudent," as Phillips charged that Austin had done, made no sense, either. "Imprudent to defend the liberty of the press! Why? Because the defence was unsuccessful?" Phillips asked. "Does success gild crime into patriotism, and want of it change heroic self-devotion into imprudence?" Phillips gave the crowd a jolt when he returned to the topic of American independence and asked if the physician Joseph Warren had been "imprudent" when he was killed leading patriot forces during the Battle of Bunker Hill. Would anyone, Phillips asked, have said that Warren had "died as a fool dieth"? The audience answered the young abolitionist with thunderous applause.

Phillips would produce more cheering as he went and closed on a note that likely would have gratified the younger version of Lovejoy, who had always viewed his move to the West as a mission to secure the values of his native New England along the rollicking frontier. Lovejoy knew he faced a crucial battle after suffering the loss of three presses and having been forced to flee from Missouri to Illinois, Phillips said. "The people there, children of our older States, seem to have forgotten the blood-tried principles of their fathers the moment they lost sight of our New England hills," he intoned. "Something was to be done to show them the priceless value of the freedom of the press, to bring back and set right their wandering and confused ideas."

Abolition-minded attendees wept later as they replayed the events of the day and what they saw as a dramatic victory for the forces of free speech. Vaulted into the public view through his improvised Lovejoy speech, Phillips would emerge as one of the abolitionist movement's most eloquent advocates during the decades to follow. Whether or not Phillips intended to address the Faneuil Hall gathering that day, even many years later his "Freedom Speech" would be listed among the classics of American oratory.

Phillips had successfully captured the outrage and alarm that many others in the North were expressing over the slaying of an editor—and man of the cloth, at that—simply for the words he had chosen to write. Religious and lay newspapers throughout New England and elsewhere across the North decried Lovejoy's killing as an affront to democracy itself, and they declared him a martyr to any number of related causes. Phillips labeled him a "martyr in defence of a free press." To the *Vermont Watchman*, Lovejoy was a "martyr in the cause of freedom." The *Maine Wesleyan Journal* called him the "martyr in the cause of Abolitionism." The *Belfast Journal*, published not far from Lovejoy's hometown of Albion, named him a "martyr in the cause of liberty of speech and the press."

Channing, always a strong defender of unpopular opinion, once predicted the stirring effect that the slaying of an abolitionist would have on the antislavery movement. Channing had written that a "murdered Abolitionist would do more for the violent destruction of slavery than a thousand societies. His name would be sainted. The day of his death would be set apart for solemn, heart-stirring commemoration." While Channing's projection proved to be wildly exaggerated in Lovejoy's case, the editor's killing provided a potent rallying cry in the cause of free speech. Sympathetic newspapers, such as Garrison's *Liberator*, marked the tragedy by painting their front pages with thick black borders. "Not only has an editor been murdered for publishing his opinions, but the press throughout the country has had an outrage committed on it, and the rights which every editor possesses have been rudely and ruthlessly violated," thundered New Hampshire's *Herald of Freeman.* "The right of discussing the subject of Slavery is now the very Thermopylae of American freedom. Let this right be surrendered and what comes next?" asked the *Boston Recorder.* Antislavery groups across the North passed resolutions protesting the mob's violent actions and proclaiming Lovejoy an American hero.

Although reaction in Illinois was mostly muted, scores of newspapers elsewhere in the North seized on the tragedy as a damning example of mobs run amok. They used fierce language to indict Alton and its leaders for failing to defend Lovejoy and his band of supporters in the exercise of their First Amendment rights. "Let its name be written in the catalogue of all that is execrable—let the emigrant avoid it as he values his liberty," the *Vermont Caledonian* spat, condemning Alton as "this Sodom of the West." The *Record* in Lynn, Massachusetts, wrote Alton off as a city "where freedom is disowned," a place suitable for the exile of the basest of criminals. "What freeman—who but a savage, or a cold-hearted murderer would now go to Alton?" the newspaper wrote. "Meanness, infamy, and guilt are attached to the very name." From Cincinnati, Charles Hammond made good on his proclaimed view that editors should assign blame where it is warranted. His *Gazette* issued a harsh judgment on Krum's handling of the affair, saying that the actions taken by the mayor "appear to have been well calculated to encourage the violence they were directed to suppress."

Amid the lionizing and justified indignation, however, one aspect of the Alton affair proved unsettling: In carrying out their defense of an antislavery press, the editor and his freedom-loving colleagues had made use of lethal weapons. Indeed, Austin had sought to use this fact during his acrimonious Faneuil Hall speech to paint Lovejoy and his men as little better than the mob. "I have as little sympathy for a minister of the gospel who is found, gun in hand, fighting in a broil with a mob, as I have for one who leaves his pulpit to mingle in the debates of a popular assembly," Austin had said. "In either situation he is *marvellously out of place.*"

Even high-profile abolitionists were aghast that Lovejoy had veered from their movement's stated doctrine of nonresistance to fight back against the attackers. Garrison would declare that while Lovejoy may have died a martyr, he did not qualify as "a Christian martyr." Channing warned abolitionists of a "dangerous precedent" if they did not in a unified voice condemn Lovejoy's apparent violation of the so-called peace principle. Angelina Grimké, the well-known antislavery lecturer and wife of the Lane veteran Theodore Weld, said she was shocked at news of the episode "not because an abolitionist had fallen the victim of popular fury, but because he did not fall the *unresisting* victim of that fury." Grimké even held Celia Lovejoy at fault for having beaten back the men who invaded her family home in St. Charles, saying the action offered a bad example. "If we want to see an example of true moral greatness in woman, under the most appalling circumstances," Grimké offered, "let us look at Mary standing by the cross of her beloved son, in perfect silence, in holy resignation."

Lovejoy's posthumous defenders argued that he was justified in using force to defend himself and his press, if unwise in defying a siege imposed by a far stronger foe. "It is said, he died with murderous weapons in his hands, and with the blood of a fellow being on them," Beecher would argue. "This is false. He died in defense of justice, and of the law, and of right: and with the instrument of justice in his hands." For at least part of the evening, Gilman and the rest had believed they were acting under the authority of the civil authorities, though Krum later denied that. It is possible that Lovejoy and his allies believed their initial show of resistance might alone chase the mob away—a strategy that, had it worked, "would no doubt have been generally commended," said the Reverend Silas McKeen, who delivered a sermon in Lovejoy's memory in Maine at the request of the slain editor's family. McKeen said that any folly on Lovejoy's part was instead testament to the "most disgraced" state of law and justice in Alton. "Charging Mr. Lovejoy with imprudence in seeking to defend his press and life, is one of the severest reflections which can be cast on the authorities and people of Alton," McKeen said in his December 31 eulogy.

And what of justice in Alton? Who would be held responsible for the lethal mayhem of November 7? Who would be punished? And for what crimes? Even as McKeen was speaking to Lovejoy's grieving kin in Maine, the authorities back in Alton were preparing to answer those very questions. The result was a strange pair of dueling trials held several weeks later, in January 1838, that could charitably be described as a troubling exercise in criminal justice. The near farcical proceedings would see the return of Linder—as both prosecutor *and* defense lawyer—and a separate Lovejoy nemesis serving as a jury foreman. It is safe to say that the proceedings would not have stood up to scrutiny by contemporary legal standards.

A grand jury, in fact, did find people to charge with crimes. The first, surprisingly, was the warehouse owner, Winthrop Gilman, who was indicted on a riot charge, along with eleven other Lovejoy supporters, including Weller, Long, Tanner, Roff, and Hurlbut. A second set of accusations, also for the crime of riot, was leveled at eleven members of the mob, including the physician Beall, the accused fire starter James Rock, and William Carr, who had poured drinks at the Tontine and later was seen flashing a pistol at Gilman. The back-to-back trials were hardly the stuff of a courtroom procedural. Everyone knew who had taken part in the chaotic events—the real question was whether, in either case, the acts had added up to rioting.

But two facts stood out. The first was that no one would be charged with Lovejoy's death, beyond the crime of "riot," which carried a maximum punishment of six months in jail or a $200 fine. Officially, Lovejoy's killer or killers would never be identified. The second unusual aspect of the trials were the roles played by Lovejoy's well-known opponents. The most remarkable turn was by Linder, who got himself named as a prosecutor in the case against Gilman, then abruptly switched sides to serve as a defense lawyer for the accused members of the mob. Alexander Botkin, the florid merchant who had helped engineer the takeover of the state antislavery convention by packing it with his and Linder's men, would serve as a jury foreman in the trial of the mob men.

Gilman was allowed to be tried separately from the other warehouse defenders and was first to face trial when court proceedings opened on January 16. He offered a self-defense case and argued he was part of a civil militia that had been blessed by Mayor Krum as the city's top law-enforcement official. (Krum continued to deny that he had ever granted the Gilman group such authority.) One of Gilman's lawyers, a respected former state prosecutor named Alfred Cowles, leavened the defense with a press-freedom argument, saying that the mob's violent siege was an unlawful assault on constitutionally protected speech. "This interference with liberty of the press is one that American citizens will not brook," Cowles said.

Linder, ever the political animal, used the Gilman trial as a chance to score points against abolitionism, and sounded at times as if he were addressing the deceased Lovejoy. In a lengthy, hostile harangue, Linder recounted boastfully how his "Western boys" had so outmaneuvered the activists at the antislavery convention that it "blew up in smoke." He mocked Lovejoy's "peace-loving men" for taking guns into a church meeting and for their repeated efforts to form a militia. The attorney general saved his bitterest remarks for what he said were the abolitionists' efforts to use the *Observer* to shove their doctrines down Alton's throat. "A printing press! A press brought here to teach rebellion and insurrection to the slave; to excite servile war; to preach murder in the name of religion," Linder told the jury. "I might depict to you the African, his passions excited by the doctrines intended to have been propagated by that press. As well might you find yourself in the fangs of a wild beast."

Linder said the abolitionists had made a dupe of the wealthy Gilman. The trial lasted a day, and the jury took only fifteen minutes to acquit Gilman. Linder quickly dropped the case against the other warehouse defenders.

Linder had better luck when he swapped hats two days later to serve as defense lawyer for the men accused in the mob attack. (Cowles, one of Gilman's defense lawyers, also traded roles, this time acting as prosecutor.) The case also lasted a day, with many of the same elements brought into evidence—the gathered crowd, the shots exchanged, the fire ignited, the press destroyed. In an unusual move, the judge hearing the case, William Martin, offered his own testimony on what he saw at the warehouse that night. Botkin, the jury foreman, also was called as a witness. The outcome would be the same as in the Gilman trial. It was the job of Botkin, back in the jury box, to announce the verdict: not guilty. The deeds of November 7 had shocked much of the country, but they did not meet the legal requirements to prove a charge of riot in Alton, Illinois.

In a strict sense, no one would be punished for Lovejoy's death or the destruction of his press, nor for the firebombing of Gilman's warehouse. But that's not fully true. Alton's reputation would be badly stained as a result of the mob's killing of Lovejoy, and it is fair to say that it never achieved the role of an important Western hub that its promoters once envisioned. Aggravated by the economic downturn, a kind of civic torpor followed the ugly chapter of mob violence against Lovejoy. The once bustling port slowly atrophied, and even the sturdy Godfrey, Gilman & Co. would end up folding. The economic crisis of 1837 delivered a hard blow to the city, one commentator wrote, "but the 'Lovejoy Riots' dealt it a well-nigh fatal one."

Many of the players in the Lovejoy saga would end up leaving town. Gilman eventually abandoned Alton for New York, where he became a successful banker. Tanner also returned to the East Coast. Lovejoy's loyal associate editor, Thaddeus Hurlbut, revived the *Observer* for several months in 1838, but traces of the newspaper vanished in April, after which it was moved to Cincinnati. Owen Lovejoy sought financial help from the Eastern abolitionists to keep the paper going in Illinois, but that bid was unsuccessful. Nonetheless, the state's abolitionists would find a new outlet when they persuaded the warhorse editor Benjamin Lundy to shift his itinerant *Genius of Universal Emancipation* to the town of Hennepin. Lundy published the paper there for about a year and a half before his death in 1839 of "bilious fever." Hurlbut later became pastor of the same Presbyterian church in Upper Alton where Lovejoy had presided at the time of his death.

Hogan and Krum each relocated to St. Louis, where Hogan would win a seat in Congress and Krum would eventually be elected as mayor. (As a circuit court judge in St. Louis in 1846, Krum would be the first jurist to receive a court case involving the disputed rights of a Black man named Dred Scott.) For Linder, the taint of the Lovejoy affair and earlier scrapes, notably his shooting of a fellow senator in the barber shop and reported drunkenness, soon torpedoed a once-promising political career. Linder was out of the attorney general's post less than two months after the Alton riot, according to a letter from Alton at the time. Cyrus Edwards also ended up narrowly losing his gubernatorial race in 1838. Several figures—the judge William Martin, Linder's law partner Edward Keating, and anti-Lovejoy physician Thomas M. Hope—would serve terms as Alton mayor in the following decades.

Celia Lovejoy would endure an itinerant life of poverty and illness. She was pregnant when her husband was slain, but the child apparently did not survive infancy. She eventually married Royal Weller, the friend who had accompanied Lovejoy out the warehouse door into a hail of gun-fire. The marriage didn't last. Celia would move to Cincinnati, where her failed attempt to run a boarding house left her in such straits that local abolitionists sent an appeal nationwide for donations to help the widow, who was "sick and afflicted, destitute and forsaken." Her own mother, a slaveholder, forever blamed the damnable abolitionists for Celia's abject condition. Celia Lovejoy died in 1870 at age fifty-seven—in Tanner's words, a "broken-down, prematurely old person" with "scarce a trace of her early beauty." Edward Lovejoy would later write that his mother "drank deeply of the bitter cup of adversity." The younger Lovejoy would move west and become a lawyer and judge before finding his own way into the newspaper business as editor of a weekly in Northern California. There, during the years after the Civil War, Lovejoy lent his newspaper's support to the dominant Republican Party and espoused generally liberal positions on issues such as granting women the vote.

Beecher may have departed from Alton in the nick of time: In the aftermath of Lovejoy's killing, the editor's friends claimed to have learned of a plan to assassinate Beecher. Edward Beecher would continue as president of Illinois College until he left to take a preaching post at the Salem Street Church in Boston in 1844. Beecher scrambled after Lovejoy's death to write an account—a firsthand work that has helped writers like me piece together the story of that fateful period. Beecher's *Narrative of Riots at Alton*, published the following year, goes beyond chronicling Lovejoy's thinking and actions. It is a powerful defense of free inquiry—"probably the most eloquent" such text ever written in the United States, one scholar has asserted. Beecher would return to Illinois in 1855 to preach and help usher slaves to freedom through the Underground Railroad. By then, much of the country was talking about a different Beecher, his sister Harriet, and her own contribution to the growing slavery discussion, *Uncle Tom's Cabin*.

* * *

JAMES BIRNEY'S OWN ANTISLAVERY journey would carry him far beyond Cincinnati. Following the restoration of the *Philanthropist* in the fall of 1836, Birney's role in the American Anti-Slavery Society would intensify. A year later, he relocated with his family once again—this time to New York to serve the society as a corresponding secretary, a top post. The *Philanthropist* announced Birney's move to New York in September 1837, explaining that his "efforts will be more influential there than here in behalf of abolition." The newspaper did not mention that a big part of the reason Birney was being recruited by the society's leaders—people like the Tappans and Theodore Weld—was to keep the peace in the antislavery movement, where tensions were growing between the traditional leadership and its more radical Garrisonian wing over a number of issues, including the role of women and the efficacy of political action.

As the rift within the Anti-Slavery Society widened (eventually leading to a formal split), Birney joined traditionalists in embracing a view that slavery could be fought through the ballot box by running antislavery candidates—an approach Garrison rejected as pointless and morally suspect. Adherents of the more conservative breakaway branch created the Liberty Party—the nation's first political party devoted to ending slavery. It chose Birney to run in the 1840 presidential election. Members of the new party, whose backers included Edward Beecher and Owen Lovejoy, knew they had no chance of winning—they were out to make a point about the bankruptcy of the two major parties when it came to ending slavery.

Birney captured a minuscule 7,400 votes out of 2.4 million cast nation-wide that year, a reflection of the abolitionist movement's fringe status and the divisions that kept many activists from showing up to vote for him. Birney would do somewhat better in 1844, garnering 62,000 votes out of 2.6 million. (A bit of trivia: Birney may have siphoned enough votes in New York from the Whig candidate, Henry Clay, to swing the state's thirty-six electoral votes—and thus the national election—to the pro-expansion Democrat, James K. Polk.) Birney would be the last candidate to run under the banner of the Liberty Party, but the slavery issue was now lodged in the nation's party dynamics. In Cincinnati, the *Philanthropist* would continue issuing its antislavery message under Birney's former assistant, Gamaliel Bailey Jr. The newspaper halted publication in 1843—seven years after the mobs tried unsuccessfully to silence it.

EPILOGUE

❧

L OVEJOY'S DEATH PROVIDED AN energizing jolt to the antislavery
movement and acted as a catalyst for growing sentiment in the
North—and not just among abolitionists—that Southern attempts to
quash dissent on slavery imperiled their own civil liberties. This had
been Birney's view of things, of course. The killing of a newspaper editor
helped abolitionists broaden their still narrow cause into one of rescuing
the country from a host of dangerous predators, including mob justice
and the systematic suppression of speech, that mocked the very promise
of American democracy.

The old warrior John Quincy Adams interpreted Lovejoy's death as a
national wake-up call—"a shock as of an earthquake throughout this continent, which will be felt in the most distant regions of the earth." Lincoln,
at the time still an Illinois lawmaker, used the episode to warn about the
threat to civil discourse represented by a "mob law"—so evident during
the 1830s—that permitted crowds to "throw printing presses into rivers"
and "shoot editors." Ralph Waldo Emerson added his voice, declaring that
"the brave Lovejoy gave his breast to the bullets of a mob, for the rights of
free speech and opinion, and died when it was better not to live."

John Brown, who later would lead the raid on Harper's Ferry, was so
affected by the news of Lovejoy's killing that he pledged then to "conse-
crate my life to the destruction of slavery." Lovejoy's brother Owen made
good on a similar graveside vow to fight against slavery—first as a Congregational minister and activist in the Underground Railroad and later

as an abolitionist congressman from Illinois. In Congress, Owen Lovejoy would be one of President Lincoln's staunchest allies and a ferocious critic of slavery in the House of Representatives. (When a colleague from Virginia warned Lovejoy during a raucous floor debate that he would be hanged "as high as Haman" if he ever ventured into the South, Lovejoy replied with devastating brevity: "I have no doubt of it.") Lovejoy would remain in Congress until his death in 1864, a year before the end of the Civil War and ratification of the Thirteenth Amendment, which abolished slavery. His brother's friend Edward Beecher would conduct his funeral.

* * *

ELIJAH LOVEJOY'S STRUGGLE AND eventual martyrdom certainly lent force to abolitionism across the country and provided its birth spark in Illinois. "The nation was asleep: and nothing but an earthquake shock could arouse her to life," Beecher would say. Lovejoy's greatest legacy, however, was in giving his life in the defense of a free press. He labored during a time when the idea of press liberty lay in a murky zone somewhere between the untested promises of the Bill of Rights and the protections that would later be enshrined in the law. (These safeguards came thanks to passage of the Fourteenth Amendment after the Civil War and a number of helpful Supreme Court rulings during the twentieth century that significantly expanded prerogatives for journalists.) People like Lovejoy and Birney operated in a rough-and-tumble world where the freedom to publish was usually understood to carry an obligation not to go too far, but American courts had yet to make clear where those lines lay. Publishing in the face of community opposition was an act of faith and demanded courage implicitly.

Modern readers might assume that First Amendment protections written by the nation's founders left the press with an unrestrained ability to publish as it saw fit. But the real world of the early 1800s was more complicated than that. Although the Bill of Rights barred Congress from passing any laws "abridging" freedom of the press, it was left to the states to protect the press—or not to—as they wished. Only with the ratification of the monumentally important Fourteenth Amendment in 1868 were states barred from curtailing the "privileges or immunities" of U.S. citizens, meaning that the protections spelled out in the Constitution would apply equally across all states. (It was not until the 1900s that the Supreme Court would reliably apply the amendment's provisions at the state and local level, however.) In terms of press liberty, then, Lovejoy occupied a moment during which ordinary Americans believed fervently in their right to speak and publish—for proof, one has only to read the knock-down, drag-out political tussles that played out in the era's newspapers—even though they lacked the kind of legal rulings that would guide subsequent generations of journalists.

The young nation had appeared to falter in its First Amendment promise of a free press when John Adams and his Federalist backers in Congress passed the aforementioned Sedition Act, which was used to charge, jail, and fine a number of editors and other critics with the crime of "seditious libel," a vague and sweeping concept borrowed from English common law. Luckily for the future of a robust American press, though, the sedition law and its frightening repercussions didn't last beyond Adams's single term in office.

. With the demise of the Sedition Act, American editors enjoyed a remarkable degree of freedom to comment on public affairs and to crank out the no-holds-barred partisan commentary that, as we have seen, defined much of what filled newspapers during Lovejoy's lifetime. But journalists were at the mercy of laws governing the press and criminal libel in their individual states. This was driven home by a decisive Supreme Court ruling in a case called *Barron v. Baltimore*, in 1833. The court decision held that the Bill of Rights did not apply to state and local governments, essentially leaving citizens subject to whatever laws or constitutional protections their individual states had enacted on press and other liberties. (It was just such an approach that the Fourteenth Amendment would be designed to repair.) For editors such as Lovejoy and Birney, the *Barron* ruling meant that the federal courts offered little practical protection for their writings. And, in fact, there were no landmark press-freedom cases before or during the period when they were facing violent opposition.

Complicating matters, the censorship these editors faced came not from any government entity, but rather from private people acting on their own authority, often in mobs. Although the downfall of the Sedition Act underscored a belief that suppression by the government was antithetical to free expression, the policing of citizens' speech by community members was a real, but murkier matter. To whom could Lovejoy or Birney appeal when a threatening handbill appeared, or when a mob bashed their presses into oblivion? Who would safeguard the liberty of the press that they believed had been granted as the natural right of free men long before the first day of nationhood? Who would define the meaning of freedom of the press as it was promised in the First Amendment?

The answer, it turned out, was the American people. At a time when the young nation was still groping toward an understanding of just how "free" its press would be, Lovejoy and his newspaper colleagues helped pave the way toward a more modern view that the press *should* be free to write about the issues of the day, even slavery. They did this by tapping into what the legal scholar Michael Kent Curtis calls the "popular free speech tradition"— the public consensus that American freedom of expression encompasses unfettered commentary about public issues, even when those viewpoints are reviled. Curtis places Lovejoy and other abolitionists at a turning-point moment in the formation of a modern view of press rights, when the people's conception of press liberty proved as consequential as any court decision.

It has been said that abolitionism produced the country's first real struggle over press freedom. Americans in the North, even those who held no fondness for abolitionism, recoiled at the notion of censorship and rejected the South's attempts to export its model of suppression—in essence, a new form of sedition law—to their own states. Lovejoy and Birney awakened many Americans, who were already inclined to favor a robust press, to the ways in which attempts to quash the written word menaced the democracy they cherished. The summary killing of a newspaper editor was occasion to fear for the republican ideal itself. Attempts to gag discussion on slavery would be added to the disquieting narrative of a tyrannical "slave power" bending the country to its will.

The crisis surrounding speech during those years also allows us to consider some what-if questions that have lasting relevance for a country yet to come to terms with its profound legacy of slavery. The imposition of a broad and, in some cases, state-sanctioned censorship regime around slavery not only subverted American expression, it meant the country was unable to engage in a peaceful, wide-ranging debate about its most fundamental flaw. In building an intellectual Great Wall behind which the South could nurse self-serving narratives of its own invention, did slavery's defenders cost the country an opportunity to deal with its demons honestly? In their determination to stifle speech in the 1830s, did they increase the odds of war later? It may seem naive to ask such questions. But it is safe to say that any reckoning with slavery must address as well the efforts to smother the words of people like Lovejoy. There is also a hefty dollop of irony here: The South's insistence on silence on slavery only begot more of the noise it didn't want. The Lovejoys and Birneys and Adamses in Congress reacted to censorship with louder trumpets, sounded from a higher platform. The overreach of the would-be censors handed Northerners who had little interest in abolitionism a reason to care, and many did just that. After Lovejoy's death, abolitionism was no longer seen as the exclusive preserve of radicals and dangerous hotheads.

* * *

CENTRAL TO THE LARGER story of press freedom in America was the courage that Lovejoy showed—acting on principle and so often all alone—in the face of hectoring foes and an absence of government support. He and Birney were not the first American journalists to face violence—one has only to consider the way patriot mobs harassed printers of pro-British material during the drive for independence. Nor would they be the last. Other newspaper editors, including Cassius Marcellus Clay in Kentucky, would be mobbed during the years of continued censorship before the Civil War, a period that saw the world of newspapers divide into camps—"fanatics" and "fire-eaters"—according to their views on slavery. A century later, dozens of reporters covering the American civil rights movement were set upon and beaten by white mobs across the South.

A line can be traced that connects Lovejoy's crusade with a more robust notion of a free press that has sprouted in the modern era, thanks to Supreme Court rulings such as *Near v. Minnesota* and *New York Times Co. v. Sullivan*. It may be an uneven, zigzagging line, interrupted by breaks and crossouts, but it is there. Lovejoy could be hard-headed and sanctimonious, his words lashing and relentless. He could have left well enough alone. Instead, Lovejoy reminds us that a free press is not just a clause in the Bill of Rights but a cause that has been cultivated and defended by generations of its practitioners, too many of whom have died in its exercise. Lovejoy was the first of them to fall. In fighting his battle, Lovejoy triumphed for the rest. His victory would not be measured in the number of slaves freed or sins redeemed, but rather in the simple, audacious fact of published words, delivered to life by a press and the sacred kiss of ink on paper.

POSTSCRIPT

❧

A MONG THE MOST BIZARRE aspects of the Alton trials was that, despite numerous witnesses called over two days of testimony, there was no real effort to identify who fired the shots that killed Lovejoy (or, for that matter, the man in the mob, Bishop). There is no sign of any official attempt at investigation. Whether the grand jury considered the matter of the shooter before producing its rioting indictments is unknown.

So who killed Lovejoy?

The answer is: it depends on whom you believe. The doctors Beall and Hope *both* claimed to be the ones to have fired the fatal shots, according to unverifiable accounts of their contemporaries. Others believed that James Rock, the fire starter, was the gunman. A separate version holds that a third physician, James Jennings of Virginia, was the shooter, but that "he didn't like to talk about it." Given the chaotic conditions that prevailed on the night of the riot, it is conceivable that several or all of these men had the opportunity to fire when Lovejoy emerged from the warehouse. Lovejoy was hit multiple times, but no attempt was made by authorities to link his wounds with any weapon, as far as anyone knows. The identity of Lovejoy's killer (or killers) would remain a matter of lore—a cause for speculation or boasting.

Beall, the Maryland doctor who was part of the roadside tar-and-feather mob and other attempts to muzzle the *Observer*, reportedly made his way to Texas to serve with the Texas Rangers. By one account, Beall was killed by Comanche fighters, but details of his post-Alton life remain murky.

(Another account holds that Beall, as a regimental surgeon, was killed by one of his own men.) Jennings, who'd also been part of the tar-and-feather group, fled Alton after the riot and left a cold trail. A report later circulated that Jennings died in a knife fight in Vicksburg, Mississippi, but this is also unsubstantiated. Rock, after years of criminal activities, landed in a Missouri prison after attempting to murder a woman, according to a version written by George Thompson, an Illinois abolitionist who served time there for trying to lead slaves to freedom. Rock admitted to Thompson that he had ignited the warehouse fire and said only that a "young doctor" fired the deadly shot.

Hope, who tended to be noisy in his views and forever remained an outspoken defender of slavery, would eventually rise to prominence in Alton. A few years after the Lovejoy killing, he was named U.S. Marshall for the region. A successful businessman, Hope became Alton's mayor during the 1850s and was a Democratic candidate for governor after the Civil War. After his death in 1885, he was buried in Alton Cemetery. Visitors today can find Hope's burial spot there. It sits about one hundred yards from the oak-shaded grave of Elijah P. Lovejoy.

ACKNOWLEDGMENTS

❧

WORK ON THIS BOOK spanned continents. I began early readings while living in China, deepened my research during summer stays in the United States, and put the words down in my latest home in the United Arab Emirates. During those years, I called upon friends, colleagues, and a small army of librarians across the United States to help me collect materials that were at times half a world away from my grasp. Friends trooped to libraries on my behalf, while archivists shipped documents or gave their time when I showed up to plumb collections in places from Maine to Ohio to Illinois.

I could not have found the breadth of sources used to tell this story without Devaki Vadakepat Menon, my unflappable research helper. Her resourcefulness was a marvel to watch, and her patience easily outlasted my machine-gun bursts of requests. A measure of her generous heart is how quickly she embraced Lovejoy, even while I was still taking his measure.

I owe special thanks to Kent Avery and Mark Magnier for venturing into libraries in Maine and Michigan to collect needed materials, and to other generous friends for taste-testing my draft manuscript: Matt Knight, Demetra Giatas, and Colette Plum. Colette's meticulous notes helped me produce a more rigorous and readable book. Gerry Boyle, one of my earliest role models as a rookie reporter, encouraged me to pursue this project years later as we pedaled the back roads of central Maine, not far from Lovejoy's hometown in Albion.

Todd Shuster and Justin Brouckaert, of Aevitas Creative Management, helped me imagine Lovejoy's story as a narrative, and went above and beyond the call of an agent's duty to find a home for it when prospects looked dicey. Many thanks, as well, to Justin for valuable feedback on the draft manuscript.

Jessica Case at Pegasus Books saw the power of Lovejoy's story from the start, and remained true to that vision with every astute edit she made to the manuscript. I'm deeply grateful for her desire to pull Lovejoy from history's shadows.

My deep respect for librarians swelled to adoration during this project. Those at the Collection of Elijah Parish Lovejoy Materials, Colby College Special Collections & Archives, in Waterville, Maine, provided my first peek at Lovejoy's correspondence and writings about him. A digitized trove of Lovejoy family letters at the Southwest Collection/Special Collections Library at Texas Tech University in Lubbock, Texas, helped me peer into Elijah Lovejoy's evolving thinking and tell his story with more texture than I could have managed otherwise. Mickey deVisé, of the Cincinnati History Library and Archives at the Cincinnati Museum Center, threw herself headlong into the search for materials about James Birney and others during my time there, then good-naturedly fielded a blizzard of long-distance questions for months after I left.

I am grateful to the librarians at the Abraham Lincoln Presidential Library and Museum in Springfield, Illinois, for providing key documents and helping me get through reels of 180-year-old newspapers on microfilm, and to Kevin George of the State Historical Society of Missouri for shipping still more newspapers on microfilm to me in Maine. It was a treat to scroll through those antique papers for days at a time in a cozy nook at the Norway Public Library in Maine, where I had borrowed my first books as a young reader many years earlier. Librarians at the Louisa H. Bowen University Archives & Special Collections at Southern Illinois University Edwardsville and the Amistad Research Center at Tulane University in New Orleans scanned and shipped me letters and other materials, while the JKM Trust Library in Chicago provided copies of handwritten minutes from church meetings in the 1830s. Yale University's Divinity Library in New Haven helped me gain access to Charles Beecher's unpublished manuscript, while the Massachusetts Historical Society in Boston kindly made available Lovejoy correspondence.

I am a journalist, and do not pretend to be a historian or academician. I gained much from the work of a handful of those who, many years before me, bothered to examine Lovejoy's life—in particular the scholar Merton L. Dillon, whose 1960s-era biography was thorough and compelling. The blazes left by Dillon helped keep me on course when the trail grew faint. In Alton, local history experts Lacy Spraggins McDonald and Don Huber bent over backwards to help me gather details of Lovejoy's life and death on the Mississippi so that I could see the place as he might have. Lacy's comments on the Alton history portions of my draft spared me embarrassment.

To my mom, Sylvia, whose voice carried the first stories I would hear, my eternal thanks for caring about all the ones I would tell—even from places you wished I hadn't gone. Thanks, also, to Faye Taylor, mother-in-law extraordinaire, who cheered me on heartily and patiently endured parcels of musty old volumes until I could collect them.

I owe my deepest debt to Monique, my collaborator in everything that matters, whose towering smarts, limitless faith, and Zen-like calm saw me through this adventure, as with so many others before it. And thank you, my dearest Selma, for sharing your love of story and a good character, and for never complaining that a dead man had commandeered my attention. Now you can read what all the fuss was about.

BIBLIOGRAPHY

Abzug, Robert H. *Cosmos Crumbling: American Reform and the Religious Imag-ination*. New York: Oxford University Press, 1994.

————. *Passionate Liberator: Theodore Dwight Weld and the Dilemma of Reform*. New York: Oxford University Press, 1980.

Adams, Alice Dana. *The Neglected Period of Anti-Slavery in America (1808–1831)*. Gloucester, MA: Peter Smith, 1964.

"The Alton Tragedy," *The Advocate of Peace (1837–1845)* 2, no. 7 (August 1838).

American Anti-Slavery Society. "The Narrative of Amos Dresser," published online, https://www.loc.gov/resource/rbaapc.08010/?sp=1.

Appomattox. *The Letter of Appomattox to the People of Virginia*. Richmond: Thomas W. White, 1832.

Aptheker, Herbert. "The Negro in the Abolitionist Movement." *Science & Society* 5, no. 2 (spring 1941): 148–172.

Austin, James T. *Speech Delivered in Faneuil Hall*. Boston: John H. Eastburn, 1837.

Barnes, Gilbert Hobbs. *The Antislavery Impulse 1830–1844*. New York: Harcourt, Brace and World, 1933.

Bay, W.V.N. *Reminiscences of the Bench and Bar of Missouri*. St. Louis: F.H. Thomas and Company, 1878.

Beecher, Charles. "Life of Edward Beecher," unpublished manuscript, microfilm at Yale University Divinity School Library, film Ms27, Yale Divinity School Library, Yale University.

Beecher, Edward. *Narrative of Riots at Alton: in Connection with the Death of Rev. Elijah P. Lovejoy*. Alton, IL: George Holton, 1838.

Bernard, Burton C. "Remarks at Unveiling of Memorial of Celia Ann Lovejoy at Alton City Cemetery." Speech, Alton, Illinois, November 9, 1987. Burton C. Bernard Collection, Louisa H. Bowen University Archives & Special Collections, Southern Illinois University, Edwardsville, IL.

Beveridge, Albert J. *Abraham Lincoln, 1809–1858, Volume I*. Boston: Houghton Mifflin Company, 1928.

"Biographical Sketch of Rev. Thos. Lippincott." *The Presbytery Reporter* 8, no. 3 (January 1870; whole no. 159): 37–70.

Birney, James Gillespie. *Letter on Colonization, Addressed to the Rev. Thornton J. Mills, Corrseponding Secretary of the Kentucky Colonization Society*. New York: American Anti-Slavery Society, 1838.

Birney, William. *James G. Birney and His Times: The Genesis of the Republican Party with Some Account of Abolition Movements in the South Before 1828*. New York: Negro Universities Press, 1868, 1969.

Bowen, A.L., Thaddeus Hurlbut, J.M. Buchanan, and W.C. Quigley. "Anti-Slavery Convention Held in Alton, Illinois, October 26–28, 1837." *Journal of the Illinois State Historical Society* (1908–1934) 20, no. 3 (October 1927): 329–356.

Bradley, Roma Linder. "Usher F. Linder: Orator from Coles." Master's thesis, Indiana University, 1963.

Brewer, William M. "John Russwurm," *Journal of Negro History*. 13, no. 4 (October 1928): 413–422.

Brown, Joseph. "Early Reminiscences of Alton," Lecture, Opera House, Alton, Illinois, February 21, 1896.

Brown, William W. *Narrative of William W. Brown, A Fugitive Slave. Written by Himself*.

Digitized edition. Chapel Hill: University of North Carolina at Chapel Hill, 2001.

Channing, William Ellery. *Slavery*. Project Gutenberg http://www.gutenberg.org/files/44736/44736-h/44736-h.htm#ebook.

Chrystal, William G. "The *Wabuska Mangler* as Martyr's Seed." *Nevada Historical Society Quarterly* 37, no. 1 (Spring 1994): 18–34.

Copeland, David. "Religion and Colonial Newspapers." In *Media and Religion in American History*, 54–67. Edited by Wm. David Sloan. Northport, AL: Vision Press, 2000.

Curtis, Michael Kent. "The Curious History of Attempts to Suppress Antislavery Speech, Press, and Petititon in 1835–37." *Northwestern University Law Review* 89, no. 3 (1995): 785–870.

———. *Free Speech, "The People's Darling Privilege": Struggle for Freedom of Expression in American History*. Durham, NC: Duke University Press, 2000.

———. "Teaching Free Speech from an Incomplete Fossil Record." *Akron Law Review* 34, no. 1, article 8 (2001): 1–35.

Davis, David Brion. *Inhuman Bondage: The Rise and Fall of Slavery in the New World*. New York: Oxford University Press, 2006.

Davis, Geo. T. M. *Autobiography of the Late Col. Geo. T. M. Davis*. New York: Published by His Legal Representatives, 1891.

Dickerson, Donna Lee. *The Course of Tolerance: Freedom of the Press in Nineteenth-Century America*. New York: Greenwood Press, 1990.

Digital Public Library of America. "The Panic of 1837," Primary Source Sets, accessed April 8, 2020. https://dp.la/primary-source-sets/the-panic-of-1837.

Dillon, Merton L. *The Abolitionists: The Growth of a Dissenting Minority*. New York: W. W. Norton and Company, 1979.

———. *Elijah P. Lovejoy, Abolitionist Editor*. Urbana, IL: University of Illinois Press, 1961.

Dimmock, Thomas. "Lovejoy: An Address." Speech, Church of the Unity, St. Louis, Missouri, March 14, 1888.

Duerk, John A. "Elijah Lovejoy: Anti-Catholic Abolitionist." *Journal of the Illinois State Historical Society* (1998–) 108, no. 2 (Summer 2015): 103–121.

Dumond, Dwight L., ed. *Letters of James Gillespie Birney 1831–1857, Volume I*. Gloucester, MA: Peter Smith, 1966.

Easterly, Reverend Frederick John. *The Life of Rt. Rev. Joseph Rosati, C.M., First Bishop of St. Louis, 1789–1843*. Washington, DC: Catholic University of America Press, 1942.

Eaton, Clement. "A Dangerous Pamphlet in the Old South." *Journal of Southern History* 2, no. 3 (August 1936): 323–334.

———. *The Freedom-of-Thought Struggle in the Old South*. New York: Harper Torchbooks, 1964.

Feldberg, Michael. *The Turbulent Era: Riot and Disorder in Jacksonian America*. New York: Oxford University Press, 1980.

Fladeland, Betty. *James Gillespie Birney: Slaveholder to Abolitionist*. Ithaca, NY: Cornell University Press, 1955.

Ford, Thomas. *A History of Illinois, from Its Commencement as a State in 1818 to 1847*. Volume I. Chicago: S.C. Griggs & Co., 1854.

Ford, Gov. Thomas. *A History of Illinois, from Its Commencement as a State in 1818 to 1847, Volume II*. Chicago: Lakeside Press, 1946.

Garrison, William Lloyd. *Thoughts on African Colonization: Or an Impartial Exhibition of the Doctrines, Principles, and Purposes of the American Colonization Society*. Boston: Garrison and Knapp, 1832.

Gill, John. *Tide without Turning: Elijah P. Lovejoy and Freedom of the Press*. Boston: Starr King Press, 1958.

Goodman, Paul. *Of One Blood: Abolitionism and the Origins of Racial Equality*. Berkeley, CA: University of California Press, 1998.

Greve, Charles Theodore. *Centennial History of Cincinnati and Representative Citizens. Vol. I*. Chicago: Biographical Publishing Company, 1904.

Grimsted, David. *American Mobbing, 1828–1861: Toward Civil War*. New York: Oxford University Press, 1998.

———. "Rioting in Its Jacksonian Setting." American Historical Review, 77, no. 2 (April, 1972): 361-397.

Hamilton, Thomas. *Men and Manners in America, Vol. II*. Edinburgh: William Blackwood, 1833.

Hamlin, Griffith A. *Monticello: The Biography of a College*. Fulton, MO: William Woods College, 1976.

Harris, N. Dwight. *The History of Negro Servitude in Illinois, and of the Slavery Agitation in That State, 1719–1864*. Chicago: A.C. McClurg & Co., 1904.

Hart, Albert Bushnell. *Salmon Portland Chase*. Boston: Houghton Mifflin, 1890.

Harvard Business School. "1837: The Hard Times." Historical Collections, accessed April 8, 2020. https://www.library.hbs.edu/hc/crises/1837.html.

Hermann, Janet S. "The McIntosh Affair." *Bulletin of the Missouri Historical Society* 26, no. 2 (January 1970): 123–143.

History of Madison County, Illinois, with Biographical Sketches of Many Prominent Men and Pioneers. Edwardsville, IL: W.R. Brink & Co., 1882.

Hodes, Frederick A. *Rising on the River: St. Louis 1822 to 1850, Explosive Growth from Town to City*. Tooele, UT: Patrice Press, 2009.

Hoffman, Judy. *God's Portion: Godfrey, Illinois 1817–1865*. Nashville: Cold Tree Press, 2005.

Holmes, J. Welfred. "Some Antislavery Editors at Work: Lundy, Bailey, Douglass." *CLA Journal* 7, no. 1 (September 1963): 48–55.

Illinois Anti-Slavery Society. *Proceedings of the Ill. Anti-Slavery Convention Held at Upper Alton*. Alton, IL: Parks and Breath, 1838.

John, Richard R. *Spreading the News: The American Postal System from Franklin to Morse*. Cambridge, MA: Harvard University Press, 1995.

Journal of the Senate of the 10th General Assembly of the State of Illinois. Vandalia, IL: William Walters, 1836.

Journal of the Upper Alton Lyceum. Scanned pages posted by Fold3 by Ancestry, accessed August 16, 2020, https://www.fold3.com/page/1395-elijah-parish-lovejoy-18021837/stories.

Kerber, Linda K. "Abolitionists and Amalgamators: The New York City Race Riots of 1834." *New York History* 48, no. 1 (January 1967): 28–39.

Kielbowicz, Richard B. "The Law and Mob Law in Attacks on Antislavery Newspapers, 1833–1860." *Law and History Review* 24, no. 3 (Fall 2006): 559–600.

Krum, John. "To the Public." *Human Rights* 3, no. 6 (December 1837).

Lehman, Christopher P. *Slavery in the Upper Mississippi Valley, 1787–1865: A History of Human Bondage in Illinois, Iowa, Minnesota, and Wisconsin*. Jefferson, NC: McFarland & Co., 2011.

Leonard, Thomas C. *News for All: America's Coming-of-Age with the Press*. New York, Oxford: Oxford University Press, 1995.

Lincoln, William S. *Alton Trials: of Winthrop Gilman et al.* New York: J.F. Trow, 1838.

Linder, Usher F. *Remniscences of the Early Bench and Bar of Illinois*. Chicago: Chicago Legal News Company, 1879.

Lovejoy, Joseph C., and Owen Lovejoy. *Memoir of the Rev Elijah P Lovejoy; Who Was Murdered in Defence of the Liberty of the Press, at Alton, Illinois, Nov. 7, 1837*. New York: John S. Taylor, 1838.

Lyons, John F. "The Attitude of Presbyterians in Ohio, Indiana, and Illinois toward Slavery, 1825–1861." *Journal of the Presbyterian Historical Society* (1901–1930) 11, no. 2 (June 1921): 69–82.

Magdol, Edward. *Owen Lovejoy: Abolitionist in Congress*. New Brunswick, NJ: Rutgers University Press, 1967.

Marsh, Roswell. "Biography [of] the Life of Charles Hammond of Cincinnati, Ohio." Historical & Philosophical Society of Ohio. Printed at Steubenville Herald Office, 1863.

Martin, Asa Earl. "Pioneer Anti-Slavery Press." *Mississippi Valley Historical Review* 2, no. 4 (March 1916): 509–528.

Martineau, Harriet. *The Martyr Age of the United States of America, with an Appeal on Behalf of the Oberlin Institute in Aid of the Abolition of Slavery*. Newcastle upon Tyne, England: Finlay and Charlton, 1840.

Mayer, Henry. *All on Fire: William Lloyd Garrison and the Abolition of Slavery*. New York: W.W. Norton, 1998.

McCandless, Perry. *A History of Missouri, Volume II, 1820 to 1860*. Columbia, MO: University of Missouri Press, 2000.

McNamara, Peter. "Sedition Act of 1798." *The First Amendment Encyclopedia*, presented by the John Siegenthaler Chair of Excellence in First Amendment Studies, Middle Tennessee State University. https://mtsu.edu/first-amendment/article/1238/sedition-act-of-1798.

Meinke, Scott R. "Slavery, Partisanship, and Procedure in the U.S. House: The Gag Rule, 1836–1845." *Legislative Studies Quarterly* 32, no. 1 (February 2007): 33–57.

Merideth, Robert. *The Politics of the Universe: Edward Beecher, Abolition, and Orthodoxy*. Nashville: Vanderbilt University Press, 1963, 1968.

Miller, William Lee. *Arguing about Slavery: The Great Battle in the United States Congress*. New York: Alfred A. Knopf, 1996.

Moorhead, James H. "The 'Restless Spirit of Radicalism': Old School Fears and the Schism of 1837." *Journal of Presbyterian History*, 78: 1 (Spring 2000): 19–33.

Nelson, Harold L., ed. *Freedom of the Press from Hamilton to the Warren Court*. New York: Bobbs-Merrill Co., 1967.

Nerone, John. *Violence against the Press: Policing the Public Sphere in U.S. History*. New York: Oxford University Press, 1994.

Nord, David Paul. *Faith in Reading: Religious Publishing and the Birth of the Mass Media in America*. New York: Oxford University Press, 2004.

Norton, W.T., ed. *Centennial History of Madison County, Illinois, and Its People, 1812–1912, Volume I*. Chicago: Lewis Publishing Company, 1912.

Noyes, Mrs. Charles P., ed. *A Family History in Letters and Documents, 1667–1837, Volume II*. St. Paul, MN: 1919.

Nye, Russell B. *Fettered Freedom: Civil Liberties and the Slavery Controversy*. East Lansing, MI: Michigan State College Press, 1949.

Ohio Anti-Slavery Society. *Narrative of the Late Riotous Proceeding against the Liberty of the Press in Cincinnati: With Remarks and Historical Notices, Relating to Emancipation: Addressed to the People of Ohio* (1836).

"A Partial Transcription of Inward Slave Manifests." Slave Data Collection, accessed June 23, 2020, https://www.afrigeneas.com/slavedata/.

Pease, Theodore Calvin. *The Frontier State 1818–1848*. Chicago: A.C. Clurg & Co., 1922.

Peck, J.M. *A Gazetteer of Illinois, in Three Parts, Containing a General View of the State, a General View of Each County, and a Particular Description of Each Town, Settlement, Stream, Prairie, Bottom, Bluff, etc.—Alphabetically Arranged*. Jacksonville, IL: R. Goudy, 1834.

Pendleton, Othniel A., Jr. "Slavery and the Evangelical Churches." *Journal of the Presbyterian Historical Society* (1943–1961) 25, no. 3 (September 1947): 153–174.

Phillips, Wendell. *Freedom Speech of Wendell Phillips, Faneuil Hall, December 8, 1837, with Descriptive Letters from Eye Witnesses*. Boston: Wendell Phillips Hall Association, 1891.

Presbyterian Church in the U.S.A. Synods, Illinois, and Presbyterian Church in the U.S.A. (New School) Synods, Illinois. *Minutes, Vol. 1*. JKM Library Trust, Chicago.

"Princeton Seminary and Slavery." Princeton Theological Seminary, accessed July 6, 2020, https://slavery.ptsem.edu/.

Rammelkamp, Charles, ed. "Thomas Lippincott, A Pioneer of 1818 and His Diary." Internet Archive, accessed August 16, 2020, https://archive.org/stream/jstor-40187004/40187004_djvu.txt, 237–255.

Ratner, Lorman A., and Dwight L. Teeter Jr. *Fanatics and Fire-Eaters: Newspapers and the Coming of the Civil War*. Urbana, IL: University of Illinois Press, 2004.

Records of the American Catholic Historical Society of Philadelphia 62, no. 3 (September 1951).

Reid, Harvey. *Biographical Sketch of Enoch Long, an Illinois Pioneer*. Chicago: Fergus Printing Company, 1884.

Richards, Leonard L. *"Gentlemen of Property and Standing"*: *Anti-Abolition Mobs in Jacksonian America*. New York: Oxford University Press, 1970.

———. *The Slave Power: The Free North and Southern Domination 1780–1860*. Baton Rouge, LA: Louisiana State University Press, 2000.

Richardson, William A., Jr. "Dr. David Nelson and His Times." *Journal of the Illinois State Historical Society* 13 (1920–1921): 433–463.

Root, Erik S. "The Virginia Slavery Debate of 1831–1832." In *Encyclopedia Virginia*, April 3, 2018, accessed July 12, 2020, https://www.encyclopedia-virginia.org/Virginia_Slavery_Debate_of_1831–1832_The.

Ruchames, Louis. "Wendell Phillips' Lovejoy Address." *New England Quarterly* 47, no. 1 (March 1974): 108–117.

Rugoff, Milton. *The Beechers: An American Family in the Nineteenth Century*. New York: Harper & Row, Publishers, 1981.

Simon, Paul. *Freedom's Champion—Elijah Lovejoy*. Carbondale: Southern Illinois University Press, 1994.

Sloan, Wm. David, ed. *Media and Religion in American History*. Northport, AL: Vision Press, 2000.

———. *The Media in America: A History*. Seventh Edition. Northport, AL: Vision Press, 2008.

Smith, Albert. "Memorial Sermon on the Death of Capt. Benjamin Godfrey, Founder of Monticello Seminary, Godfrey, Madison Co., Illinois." *The Echo*, no. 17 (Midsummer 1902): 3–16.

Staiger, Bruce C. "Abolitionism and the Presbyterian Schism of 1837–1838." *Mississippi Valley Historical Review* 36, no. 3 (December 1949): 391–414.

Stewart, James Brewer. *Holy Warriors: The Abolitionists and American Slavery*. New York: Hill and Wang, 1976.

Tanner, Henry. *History of the Rise and Progress of the Alton Riots, Culminating in the Death of Rev. Elijah P. Lovejoy, Nov. 7, 1837*. Buffalo, NY: Printing House of James D. Warren, 1878.

———. *The Martyrdom of Lovejoy. An Account of the Life, Trials, and Perils of Rev. Elijah P. Lovejoy*. Chicago: Fergs Printing Company, 1881.

Thompson, George. *Prison Life and Reflections: Or Narrative of the Arrest, Trial, Conviction, Imprisonment, Treatment, Observations, Reflections, and Deliverance of Work, Burr and Thompson*. Oberlin, OH: James Fitch, 1847.

Tocqueville, Alexis de. *Democracy in America, Volume II*. Project Gutenberg ebook, last updated February 7, 2013. https://www.gutenberg.org/files/816/816-h/816-h.htm#.

Trexler, Harrison Anthony. *Slavery in Missouri 1804–1865*. Dissertation, Johns Hopkins University, 1914. Baltimore: Johns Hopkins Press, 1914.

Tyler, Alice Felt. *Freedom's Ferment: Phases of American Social History from the Colonial Period to the Outbreak of the Civil War*. New York: Harper Torchbooks, 1944.

Walters, Ronald G. *American Reformers, 1815–1860*. New York: Hill and Wang, 1978.

Weisenburger, Francis P. "Charles Hammond, the First Great Journalist of the Old Northwest." *Ohio Archaeological and Historical Quarterly* 43, no. 4 (October 1934): 338–427. https://resources.ohiohistory.org/ohj/browse/displaypages.php?display%5b%5d=0043&display%5b%5d=337&display%5b%5d=427.

Whittlesey, M.K. "Elijah P. Lovejoy." *Magazine of Western History* (1884–1891) 6 (July 1887): 228–233.

Wiebe, Robert H. *The Segmented Society: An Introduction to the Meaning of America*. New York: Oxford University Press, 1975.

Wirls, Daniel. "'The Only Mode of Avoiding Everlasting Debate': The Overlooked Senate Gag Rule for Antislavery Petitions." *Journal of the Early Republic* 27, no. 1 (Spring 2007): 115–138.

Wohlgemuth, E. Jay. "A Forgotten Leader." Ms. 731, Literary Club Papers, Cincinnati History Library and Archives at Cincinnati Museum Center.

Wyatt-Brown, Bertram. *Lewis Tappan and the Evangelical War against Slavery*. Baton Rouge, LA: Louisiana State University Press, 1969.

Wyly-Jones, Susan. "The 1835 Anti-Abolition Meetings in the South: A New Look at the Controversy over the Abolition Postal Campaign." *Civil War History* 47, no. 4 (December 2001): 289–309.

NOTES

p. 3   **her mother's home:** John E. Lovejoy to Elizabeth Lovejoy, July 26, 1836, Folder 7, Box 2, Elijah P. Lovejoy Papers, 1804–1891 and undated, Southwest Collection/Special Collections Library, Texas Tech University, accessed July 25, 2020, https://swco.ttu.edu/location/Manuscripts /lovejoy/Lovejoy_Elijah_Guide.html.

p. 4   **"a few miscreants":** Elijah P. Lovejoy to Joseph C. Lovejoy, July 30, 1836, in Lovejoy and Lovejoy, *Memoir*, 181.

p. 5   **hiring out their slaves:** *St. Louis Observer*, July 21, 1836.

p. 6   **"first symptoms of riot and disorder":** Alton *Telegraph*, May 11, 1836.

p. 7   **"fellowship with the abolitionists":** Lovejoy and Lovejoy, *Memoir*, 221.

p. 8   **"a solemn pledge":** Dillon, *Elijah P. Lovejoy, Abolitionist Editor*, 93.

p. 9   **"I was no Abolitionist":** Elijah P. Lovejoy to Joseph C. Lovejoy, July 30, 1836, in Lovejoy and Lovejoy, *Memoir*, 182.

p. 11   **"disgusted with the West":** John E. Lovejoy to Elizabeth Lovejoy, July 26, 1836.

p. 15   **a number of hymns to boot:** Lovejoy and Lovejoy, *Memoir*, 18.

p. 15   **Betsey lined up:** Elizabeth Lovejoy, undated autobiography, Folder 1, Box 4, Elijah P. Lovejoy Papers, accessed July 25, 2020, https://swco.ttu .edu/location/Manuscripts/lovejoy/Lovejoy_Elijah_Guide.html.

p. 16   **"friendless, hopeless, and forlorn":** Lovejoy and Lovejoy, *Memoir*, 22.

p. 17   **"shocking profanity and intemperance":** Elijah P. Lovejoy to Elizabeth Lovejoy, Sept 20, 1824, Folder 13, Box 1, Elijah P. Lovejoy Papers, accessed July 25, 2020, https://swco.ttu.edu/location /Manuscripts/lovejoy/Lovejoy_Elijah_Guide.html.

p. 19   **"his changeable longings":** Alexis de Tocqueville, *Democracy in America*, Volume II, Project Gutenberg ebook, book 2, section 2, chapter 13: "Causes of the Restless Spirit of Americans in the Midst of Their Prosperity," accessed July 3, 2020, https://www.gutenberg.org /files/816/816-h/816-h.htm#link2HCH0034.

p. 20   **"to travel on foot":** Lovejoy Diary, 1827, Collection of Elijah Parish Lovejoy Materials, Colby College Special Collections & Archives, Waterville, Maine.

p. 22   **prospects in the tiny settlement:** Dillon, *Elijah P. Lovejoy*, 11.

p. 22   **seven days and seventeen hours:** Hodes, *Rising on the River*, 43.

p. 23   **eight hundred steamboat landings:** Hodes, *Rising on the River*, 42.

p. 23   **outbreaks of deadly cholera:** McCandless, *A History of Missouri*, 219.

p. 24   **His weight was up:** Lovejoy and Lovejoy, *Memoir*, 32.

p. 26   **"an adulterer and murderer for our President":** Elijah P. Lovejoy to Daniel and Elizabeth Lovejoy, March 15, 1829, Folder 18, Box 1, Elijah P. Lovejoy Papers, accessed July 4, 2020, https://swco.ttu.edu /location/Manuscripts/lovejoy/Lovejoy_Elijah_Guide.html.

p. 26   **"without the moral precepts":** *St. Louis Times*, February 18, 1832.

p. 27   **The *Beacon* later returned fire:** Quoted in Dillon, *Elijah P. Lovejoy*, 17.

p. 27   **"a first rate NEGRO MAN":** Quoted in Simon, *Freedom's Champion*, 14.

p. 27   **"what little learning I obtained":** William W. Brown, *Narrative of William W. Brown*, electronic edition, 27, accessed August 5, 2020, https://docsouth.unc.edu/fpn/brownw/brown.html#BroNarr26.

p. 30   **Godfrey had paid:** Hamlin, *Monticello: The Biography of a College*, 23.

p. 30   **a tenth of his income:** Noyes, *A Family History*, 611.

p. 31   **"Temperance goes well":** Noyes, *A Family History*, 614.

p. 31   **"but one house occupied":** Norton, *Centennial History of Madison County*, 470.

p. 31   **So foul was the odor:** "Biographical Sketch of Rev. Thos. Lippincott," 49.

p. 31   **a stalwart of the Presbyterian church:** "Biographical Sketch of Rev. Thos. Lippincott," 60–61.

p. 32   **twelve hundred slaves and indentured Black people:** Richards, *The Slave Power*, 73.

p. 32   **Kidnappers in Illinois profited:** Lehman, *Slavery in the Upper Mississippi Valley*, 33.

p. 32   **took up the fight:** "Biographical Sketch of Rev. Thos. Lippincott," 57.

p. 32   **about seventeen hundred votes:** Lehman, *Slavery in the Upper Mississippi Valley*, 34.

p. 32   **two short-lived monthly newspapers:** Rammelkamp, "Thomas Lippincott," 255.

p. 33   **traversing the Atlantic:** Hamlin, *Monticello*, 22.

p. 33   **lost everything in the wreck:** Smith, "Memorial Sermon," 5.

p. 34   **deal with God:** Hoffman, *God's Portion*, 61–62.

p. 34   **a Godfrey-skippered vessel:** "A Partial Transcription of Inward Slave Manifests," Rolls 1, 2, and 3, Slave Data Collection, accessed June 23, 2020, http://www.afrigeneas.com/slavedata/.

p. 34   **Many more such records:** "A Partial Transcription of Inward Slave Manifests," Introduction, accessed June 23, 2020, https://www.afrigeneas.com/slavedata/manifests.html.

p. 35   **"it would make a novel":** Smith, "Memorial Sermon," 4.

p. 35   **"Godfrey was a changed man":** Hoffman, *God's Portion*, 62.

p. 35   **raised in the wilds:** The details of Long's early life and his arrival on the frontier is taken from Reid, *Biographical Sketch of Enoch Long*, chaps. 4 and 5.

p. 36   **"his standing in society":** Reid, *Biographical Sketch of Enoch Long*, 63.

p. 36   **"not been engaged in a duel":** Quoted in Reid, *Biographical Sketch of Enoch Long*, 65.

p. 36   **a site of worship:** Norton, *Centennial History of Madison County*, 339.

p. 37   **"on the side of morality":** Reid, *Biographical Sketch of Enoch Long*, 58.

p. 39   **launching a frontier newspaper:** McCandless, *A History of Missouri*, 179.

p. 40   **"my path through this life":** Elijah P. Lovejoy to Elizabeth Lovejoy, August 31, 1836, Lovejoy and Lovejoy, *Memoir*, 184.

p. 41   **"she is very beautiful":** Elijah P. Lovejoy to Elizabeth Lovejoy, March 10, 1835, Lovejoy and Lovejoy, *Memoir*, 133–134.

p. 42   **"ought to be supported":** Elijah P. Lovejoy to Elizabeth Lovejoy, August 31, 1836, Lovejoy and Lovejoy, *Memoir*, 187.

p. 43   **fifty businessmen:** Hoffman, *God's Portion*, 20.

p. 43   **"the emigrant from the East":** *History of Madison County*, 91.

p. 44   **"a most despicable opinion":** Ford, *A History of Illinois*, vol. II, 90.

p. 44   **"cultural and social extremes":** Hoffman, *God's Portion*, prologue, page not numbered.

p. 45   **the cost of parcels:** *History of Madison County*, 382.

p. 46   **"make it quite problematical":** Peck, *A Gazetteer of Illinois*, 175.

p. 47   **secular news and "general intelligence":** Alton *Observer*, September 8, 1836.

p. 49   **ministers read the news:** Sloan, *The Media in America*, 72.

p. 50   **"newspapers penetrate":** Hamilton, *Men and Manners in America*, 73–74.

p. 50   **"Nothing but a newspaper":** Tocqueville, *Democracy in America*, volume 2, book 2, section 2, chapter 6, "Of the Relation Between Newspapers and Public Associations," accessed July 3, 2020, https://www.gutenberg.org/files/816/816-h/816-h.htm#link2HCH0027.

p. 51   **fought two rival editors:** Nerone, *Violence against the Press*, 73.

p. 52   **"non-payment of subscriptions":** Leonard, *News for All*, 37.

p. 54   **"the common ties of brotherhood":** Hamilton, *Men and Manners in America*, 74–75.

p. 55   **towering heaps of newspapers:** John, *Spreading the News*, 38–39.

p. 60   **"overflowing with new comers":** Alton *Observer*, November 3, 1836.

p. 61   **"the admiration of every beholder":** Alton *Observer*, December 15, 1836.

p. 61   **well-to-do Upper Alton:** Hoffman, *God's Portion*, 88.

p. 62   **"The tide of liberty":** *New England Spectator* and *Pittsburgh Times*, excerpted in Alton *Observer*, October 27, 1836.

p. 62   **list of signers:** Alton *Observer*, November 3, 1836.

p. 63   **"more numerous and aggravated":** Elijah P. Lovejoy to Daniel and Elizabeth Lovejoy, January 24, 1832, Lovejoy and Lovejoy, *Memoir*, 40.

p. 64   **several had employed slave labor:** "Princeton Seminary and Slavery," accessed July 6, 2020, https://slavery.ptsem.edu/the-report/seminary-founders/.

p. 65   **the millennialist promise:** Walters, *American Reformers*, 26–27.

p. 66   **the notion of activism:** Stewart, *Holy Warriors*, 37.

p. 66   **forerunner of the mass media:** Nord, *Faith in Reading*, 82.

p. 66   **guardians of New England Calvinism:** Wyatt-Brown, *Lewis Tappan*, 49.

p. 67   **"benevolent empire":** Wyatt-Brown, *Lewis Tappan*, 50.

p. 67   **one million Bibles:** Nord, *Faith in Reading*, 86.

p. 67   **three thousand auxiliaries:** Walters, *American Reformers*, 32.

p. 68   **a form of local news:** David Copeland, "Religion and Colonial Newspapers," 59.

p. 68   **"calling me to the West":** Elijah P. Lovejoy to Owen Lovejoy, August 26, 1832, in Lovejoy and Lovejoy, *Memoir*, 66.

p. 68   **Lovejoy was back in St. Louis:** The role of Gamble is cited in Simon, *Freedom's Champion*, 23.

p. 72   **the Arkansas vigilantes:** Alton *Observer*, December 15, 1836.

p. 73   **"made the blood curdle":** St. Louis *Observer*, May 5, 1836, reprinted in Lovejoy and Lovejoy, *Memoir*, 168–174.

p. 73   **slow death before a large crowd:** Hermann, "The McIntosh Affair," 125–127.

p. 74   **"the crowd retired quietly":** *Missouri Republican*, April 30, 1836.

p. 74   **McIntosh's bones:** *Missouri Republican*, May 3, 1836.

p. 74   **drew sharp condemnation:** Hermann, "The McIntosh Affair," 130.

p. 76   **Henry Clay and Francis Scott Key:** "Princeton Seminary and Slavery," accessed July 6, 2020, https://slavery.ptsem.edu/the-report/colonization-movement/.

p. 76 **to avoid sectional strife:** Staiger, "Abolitionism and the Presbyterian Schism," 396.

p. 77 **"garbled and falsified":** Elijah P. Lovejoy to Elizabeth Lovejoy, April 1, 1833, Folder 4, Box 2, Elijah P. Lovejoy Papers, accessed July 6, 2020, https://swco.ttu.edu/location/Manuscripts/lovejoy/Lovejoy_Elijah_Guide.html.

p. 77 **"a curse, politically and morally":** St. Louis *Observer*, June 1834, in Lovejoy and Lovejoy, *Memoir*, 118–119.

p. 78 **"injurious to the community":** St. Louis *Observer*, April 16, 1835, in Lovejoy and Lovejoy, *Memoir*, 123.

p. 80 **"the very first principles of liberty":** St. Louis Observer, May 21, 1835, in Lovejoy and Lovejoy, *Memoir*, 130.

p. 81 **Beecher was clearly moved:** Dillon, *Elijah P. Lovejoy*, 62.

p. 81 **"unjustifiable" methods:** St. Louis *Observer*, October 22, 1835.

p. 81 **"time that someone teach them":** Edward Beecher to Elijah P. Lovejoy, December 20, 1835, Folder 6, Box 2, Elijah P. Lovejoy Papers, accessed July 20, 2020, https://swco.ttu.edu/location/Manuscripts/lovejoy/Lovejoy_Elijah_Guide.html.

p. 81 **declaration of principles:** Mayer, *All on Fire*, 174.

p. 83 **more than 250,000 Americans:** Walters, *American Reformers*, 80.

p. 83 **"a foul-mouthed fellow":** Elijah P. Lovejoy to Joseph Lovejoy, November 21, 1834, Folder 5, Box 2, Elijah P. Lovejoy Papers, accessed July 8, 2020, https://swco.ttu.edu/location/Manuscripts/lovejoy/Lovejoy_Elijah_Guide.html.

p. 84 **little with which to disagree:** St. Louis *Observer*, October 1, 1835.

p. 85 **act "with great caution":** Samuel Hart to Elijah P. Lovejoy, September 8, 1835, Folder 6, Box 2, Elijah P. Lovejoy Papers, accessed July 20, 2020, https://swco.ttu.edu/location/Manuscripts/lovejoy/Lovejoy_Elijah_Guide.html.

p. 85 **"I claim the right":** St. Louis *Observer*, November 5, 1835, in Lovejoy and Lovejoy, *Memoir*, 141.

p. 86 **The prudent course now:** "To the Rev. E. P. Lovejoy," October 5, 1835, in Lovejoy and Lovejoy, *Memoir*, 137.

p. 86 **"mad schemes of the Abolitionists":** St. Louis *Observer*, October 22, 1835, in Lovejoy and Lovejoy, *Memoir*, 136.

p. 86 **conservatives were swayed:** Elijah P. Lovejoy to "My Dear Brother," January [no date], 1836, Folder 7, Box 2, Elijah P. Lovejoy Papers, accessed July 25, 2020, https://swco.ttu.edu/location/Manuscripts/lovejoy/Lovejoy_Elijah_Guide.html.

p. 87 **took turns whipping the men:** *Missouri Republican*, October 22, 1835; Lovejoy and Lovejoy, *Memoir*, 137.

p. 87 **"reckless and wicked interference":** *Missouri Republican*, October 20, 1835.

p. 87 **lying in wait:** Elijah P. Lovejoy to "My Dear Brother," January 1836.

p. 87 **one of the friends rode:** Lovejoy to "My Dear Brother," January 1836.

p. 89 **"sanctioned by the sacred Scriptures":** Lovejoy and Lovejoy, *Memoir*, 138–139.

p. 89 **"to defend, fearlessly":** St. Louis *Observer*, November 5, 1835, in Lovejoy and Lovejoy, *Memoir*, 140.

p. 91 **"ashamed of their doings":** Elijah P. Lovejoy to Elizabeth Lovejoy, November 23, 1835, Folder 6, Box 2, Elijah P. Lovejoy Papers, accessed July 20, 2020, https://swco.ttu.edu/location/Manuscripts/lovejoy/Lovejoy _Elijah_Guide.html.

p. 91 **"I gave up":** Elijah P. Lovejoy to "My Dear Brother," January 1836, reprinted in Lovejoy and Lovejoy, *Memoir*, 164.

p. 91 **"I have much to endure":** Elijah P. Lovejoy to Absalom Peters, February 22, 1836, American Home Missionary Society records, 1816–1907, Amistad Research Center, Tulane University, New Orleans, LA.

p. 92 **"philosophical and safe":** Charles Beecher, "The Life of Edward Beecher," 128.

p. 92 **"not an abolitionist":** Elijah P. Lovejoy to Joseph Lovejoy, November 2, 1835, in Lovejoy and Lovejoy, *Memoir*, 157.

p. 93 **He found bitter irony:** Elijah P. Lovejoy to Elizabeth Lovejoy, November 23, 1835, Folder 6, Box 2, Elijah P. Lovejoy Papers, accessed July 20, 2020, https://swco.ttu.edu/location/Manuscripts/lovejoy/Lovejoy _Elijah_Guide.html.

p. 93 **Lovejoy wrote approvingly:** Elijah P. Lovejoy to Edwin F. Hatfield, January 21, 1836, Grenville H. Norcross autograph collection, 1489– 1937, Massachusetts Historical Society.

p. 93 **by every moral person:** Barnes, *The Antislavery Impulse*, 103.

p. 96 **walked with a limp:** Bay, *Reminiscences of the Bench and Bar*, 440.

p. 96 **sworn in as a lawyer:** *Vermont Patriot and State Gazette*, January 10, 1831.

p. 96 **Congress quickly passed a law:** Nelson, *Freedom of the Press*, 140.

p. 96 **"Irony, sarcasm, and wit":** Bay, *Reminiscences of the Bench and Bar*, 441.

p. 96 **"most unfit":** *Missouri Republican*, September 12, 1835.

p. 97 **"unworthy of a judge":** "Judge Lawless' Charges to the Grand Jury," *Missouri Republican*, May 26, 1836.

p. 100 **147 riots in 1835:** Grimsted, *American Mobbing*, 4.

p. 101 **A separate mob:** Wyatt-Brown, *Lewis Tappan*, 116–19.

p. 101   **dead or alive:** Richards, *"Gentlemen of Property and Standing,"* 16–17.

p. 101   **Aggressors grabbed at Garrison:** Mayer, *All on Fire*, 204–205.

p. 102   **heads plunked on poles:** Grimsted, *American Mobbing*, 139, 170.

p. 102   **"I knelt to receive the punishment":** American Anti-Slavery Society, "The Narrative of Amos Dresser," 12–14, accessed July 10, 2020, https://www.loc.gov/resource/rbaapc.08010/?sp=1.

p. 102   **seven gallons of alcoholic beverages:** Abzug, *Cosmos Crumbling* 82; National Institute on Alcohol Abuse and Alcoholism, "Apparent Per Capita Alcohol Consumption: National, State and Regional Trends, 1977–2016," Surveillance Report #110, accessed July 10, 2020, https ://pubs.niaaa.nih.gov/publications/surveillance110/CONS16.htm.

p. 103   **"crazy-headed blockheads":** Quoted in Richards, *"Gentlemen of Property and Standing,"* 10.

p. 103   **a threat to be eradicated:** Wiebe, *The Segmented Society*, 51–52, 83–85. See also Grimsted, "Rioting in Its Jacksonian Setting," 368–370.

p. 103   **nuisance abatement:** See Kielbowicz, "The Law and Mob Law."

p. 104   **a letter protesting:** St. Louis *Observer*, July 14, 1836.

p. 104   **hid for days:** Richardson, "Dr. David Nelson," 443–44.

p. 106   **"a foreigner":** St. Louis *Observer*, July 21, 1836.

p. 106   **miracles and vestments:** *Records of the American Catholic Historical Society*, 173.

p. 106   **"fire is cold and ice is hot":** Lovejoy and Lovejoy, *Memoir*, 104.

p. 107   **seventy-five thousand Roman Catholics:** Tyler, Freedom's *Ferment*, 360–61.

p. 107   **convent life in general:** *Records of the American Catholic Historical Society*, 177.

p. 108   **three thousand of its five thousand inhabitants:** Easterly, *The Life of Rt. Rev. Joseph Rosati*, 128.

p. 108   **a noisy violation:** St. Louis *Observer*, October 30, 1834.

p. 108   **"forger and slanderer":** *Records of the American Catholic Historical Society*, 174.

p. 108   **his attacks on Catholicism:** St. Louis *Observer*, November 5, 1835.

p. 109   **viewed abolitionists as extremists:** See Duerk, "Elijah Lovejoy: Anti-Catholic Abolitionist."

p. 109   **beating drums and calling for recruits:** St. Louis *Observer*, extra edition, August 10, 1836.

p. 109   **heaved into the water:** John Lovejoy to Elizabeth Lovejoy, July 26, 1836, Folder 7. Box 2, Elijah P. Lovejoy Papers, accessed July 25, 2020, https://swco.ttu.edu/location/Manuscripts/lovejoy/Lovejoy_Elijah_Guide.html.

p. 111   **forty thousand Black people:** To arrive at this mid-decade estimate, I interpolated a conservative figure based upon census statistics for 1830 and 1840. The slave population in Missouri was about 25,000 in 1830 and nearly 58,000 in 1840. See Trexler, *Slavery in Missouri*, 10.

p. 111   **"educated in the midst of Slavery":** St. Louis *Observer*, April 16, 1835, in Lovejoy and Lovejoy, *Memoir*, 125.

p. 113   **the constitution-writing convention:** Fladeland, *James Gillespie Birney*, 5–6.

p. 113   **the aunt who raised Birney:** Details on Birney's early life in William Birney, *James G. Birney and His Times*, chaps. 1–4.

p. 114   **family largesse:** Fladeland, *James Gillespie Birney*, 11.

p. 114   **"turn slave-catcher?":** William Birney, *James G. Birney and His Times*, 34.

p. 115   **number of Birney's slaves:** Fladeland, *James Gillespie Birney*, 19.

p. 115   **"the generality of planters":** William Birney, *James G. Birney and His Times*, Appendix D, 424.

p. 115   **mayor of Hunstville:** William Birney, *James G. Birney and His Times*, 52.

p. 115   **the sale of liquor:** Fladeland, *James Gillespie Birney*, 33.

p. 116   **Southerners dominated:** Goodman, *Of One Blood*, 15.

p. 116   **the ACS agent:** William Birney, *James G. Birney and His Times*, 112.

p. 117   **slave states to the north:** William Birney, *James G. Birney and His Times*, 128–129.

p. 117   **"much frightened at the proposition":** William Birney, *James G. Birney and His Times*, 120n.

p. 117   **Northern Black people:** Aptheker, "The Negro in the Abolitionist Movement," 158–159.

p. 117   **effectively killed colonization:** Mayer, *All on Fire*, 142.

p. 117   **"a thorough indifference":** James Gillespie Birney, *Letter on Colonization*, 34.

p. 118   **dozens of local colonization societies:** Fladeland, *James Gillespie Birney*, 75–76.

p. 118   **the 1833 vote to emancipate:** William Birney, *James G. Birney and His Times*, 134–35.

p. 119   **"curdled my blood":** Quoted in Barnes, *The Antislavery Impulse*, 66–67.

p. 119   **Rioters burned houses:** Richards, *Gentlemen of Property and Standing*, 34; Feldberg, *The Turbulent Era*, 38.

p. 120   **Many left for good:** Greve, *Centennial History of Cincinnati*, 593.

p. 120   **"it was at *their* tables":** Weld quoted in Abzug, *Passionate Liberator*, 95

p. 121 **"evangelists of abolitionism"**: Barnes, *The Antislavery Impulse*, 78.

p. 121 **"slumber soft and peaceful"**: James G. Birney to Gerrit Smith, November 14, 1834, in Dumond, *Letters of James Gillespie Birney*, 150.

p. 121 **"inconsistent with the Great Truth"**: Quoted in Fladeland, *James Gillespie Birney*, 83.

p. 122 **he paid back wages**: William Birney, *James G. Birney and His Times*, 139.

p. 122 **"to a comfortless grave!"**: James Gillespie Birney, *Letter on Colonization*, 19.

p. 122 **Birney's former colleagues**: Theodore D. Weld to Birney, August 7, 1834, in Dumond, *Letters of James Gillespie Birney*, 128.

p. 123 **shunned even by his friends**: William Birney, *James G. Birney and His Times*, 146; Fladeland, *James Gillespie Birney*, 90.

p. 123 **in hostile territory**: Wyatt-Brown, *Lewis Tappan*, 133–34.

p. 123 **"happy and contented" life**: F.T. Taylor and others to James G. Birney, July 12, 1835, in Dumond, *Letters of James Gillespie Birney*, 199–200.

p. 124 **"too long a shot"**: Quoted in the *Philanthropist*, January 8, 1836.

p. 125 **a "rebuke which is . . . so richly merited"**: *Journal of the Senate*, 196–198.

p. 126 **One of those dissenters**: Beveridge, *Abraham Lincoln*, vol. 1, 194.

p. 126 **"sufferers for the liberty of thought"**: Alton *Observer*, January 5, 1837.

p. 127 **"withold any further publication"**: Alton *Observer*, February 2, 1837.

p. 127 **a 61-to-0 vote**: Trexler, *Slavery in Missouri*, 134.

p. 128 **"The Drunkard's Grave"**: Alton *Observer*, January 19, 1837.

p. 128 **"like an 'oasis'"**: Joseph Brown, "Early Reminiscences of Alton," 5.

p. 129 **members were fined**: My main source on the organization of the Upper Alton Lyceum and its slavery debate is a set of excerpts from the *Journal of the Upper Alton Lyceum*, scanned pages of which are posted online by Fold3 by Ancestry, accessed July 15, 2020, https://www.fold3.com/page/1395-elijah-parish-lovejoy-18021837/stories.

p. 129 **He quit the group**: Dillon, *Elijah P. Lovejoy*, 103.

p. 130 **"an enormous injustice"**: Alton *Observer*, February 2, 1837.

p. 130 **"inconsistent with the law of God"**: Lyons, "The Attitude of Presbyterians," 71–72.

p. 130 **even some Northern Presbyterians**: Staiger, "Abolitionism and the Presbyterian Schism," 395–396.

p. 131 **scholars argue**: See Staiger, 414; Moorhead, "'Restless Spirit of Radicalism,'" 28–29.

328 NOTES

p. 131   the "Curse of Ham": See David Brion Davis, *Inhuman Bondage*, chap. 3.

p. 132   "heinous sin against God": Presbyterian Church in the U.S.A. (New School) Synods, Illinois, *Minutes*, vol. 1, 84–85; Alton *Observer*, December 15, 1836.

p. 132   Garrison and others: Pendleton, "Slavery and the Evangelical Churches," 160.

p. 133   "never did I hear the pastor": Alton *Observer*, February 9, 1837.

p. 134   "from a man to a brute": Alton *Observer*, February 9, 1837.

p. 135   "SET HIM FREE": Alton *Observer*, March 16, 1837, in Lovejoy and Lovejoy, *Memoir*, 206.

p. 135   "out of my Sunshine": Abraham Byrd to Lovejoy, January 26, 1837, copy and typed transcription, Elijah Parish Lovejoy Materials.

p. 136   475-mile rail link: Greve, *Centennial History of Cincinnati*, 590.

p. 136   several dozen slave-owning families: Wohlgemuth, "A Forgotten Leader," 2–3.

p. 136   a visit to Cincinnati: William Birney, *James G. Birney and His Times*, 205.

p. 137   "madness and folly": James G. Birney to Gerrit Smith, November 11, 1835, in Dumond, *Letters of James Gillespie Birney*, 259; William Birney, *James G. Birney and His Times*, 207.

p. 137   forty muskets: William Birney, *James G. Birney and His Times*, 208, 217.

p. 137   "defend his wife and children": William Birney, *James G. Birney and His Times*, 217.

p. 138   the mob vanished: Material on Hammond's life comes mainly from Marsh, "Biography [of] the Life of Charles Hammond."

p. 138   "the aim was sure": Weisenburger, "Charles Hammond," 415, accessed Juy 30, 2020, https://resources.ohiohistory.org/ohj/browse/displaypages.

p. 139   Birney assured residents: James G. Birney to Charles Hammond, November 14, 1835, in Dumond, *Letters of James Gillespie Birney*, 263–273.

p. 140   "a waste of time": James G. Birney to Lewis Tappan, November 28, 1835, in Dumond, *Letters of James Gillespie Birney*, 277.

p. 140   "pestiferous breath": Quoted in *Philanthropist*, January 1, 1836.

p. 141   "honest and benevolent man": *Philanthropist*, January 8, 1836.

p. 141   "My griefs are mine alone": *Philanthropist*, January 29, 1836.

p. 142   the South Carolina legislature: *Philanthropist*, January 8, 1836.

p. 142   "your voice may be raised": *Philanthropist*, January 1, 1836.

p. 143   **"upon 'incendiary missiles'"**: William Birney, *James G. Birney and His Times*, 211.

p. 143   **locked themselves inside:** Detailed accounts of the events of January 22 are contained in William Birney, *James G. Birney and His Times*, chap. 21, and *Philanthropist*, January 29, 1836.

p. 147   **"the mayor of this city":** *Philanthropist*, February 12, 1836.

p. 150   **once freely published:** Adams, *The Neglected Period of Anti-Slavery*, 42.

p. 150   **Osborn's own views:** Martin, "Pioneer Anti-Slavery Press," 512.

p. 151   **"monsters in human flesh":** Quoted in Martin, "Pioneer Anti-Slavery Press," 517.

p. 151   **"mischievous in its tendency":** Quoted in Martin, "Pioneer Anti-Slavery Press," 519.

p. 151   **without wide readership:** Adams, *Neglected Period of Anti-Slavery*, 45.

p. 152   **possible alternatives to Liberia:** Tyler, *Freedom's Ferment*, 483; Martin, "Pioneer Anti-Slavery Press," 524–525.

p. 152   **traveled with the freed people:** Mayer, *All on Fire*, 52.

p. 152   **"this foul blot":** Martin, "Pioneer Anti-Slavery Press," 522.

p. 152   **hailed Lundy's *Genius*:** Mayer, *All on Fire*, 53.

p. 153   **home to about five thousand slaves:** Mayer, *All on Fire*, 80.

p. 153   **beaten badly:** Holmes, "Some Antislavery Editors," 49.

p. 153   **offered $100 to free Garrison:** The story of the prosecution is told in Mayer, *All on Fire*, chap. 5.

p. 154   **first Black antislavery newspaper:** Brewer, "John Russwurm," 413–414.

p. 154   **racist diatribes:** Brewer, "John Russwurm," 414.

p. 154   **lasted only two years:** Aptheker, "The Negro in the Abolitionist Movement," 156.

p. 154   **Black readers in the North:** Aptheker, "The Negro in the Abolitionist Movement," 165.

p. 156   **Others backed gradual emancipation:** Root, "The Virginia Slavery Debate of 1831–1832https://www.encyclopediavirginia.org/Virginia_Slavery_Debate_of_1831–1832_The."

p. 157   **"the silence of fifty years":** Both quoted in Eaton, *The Freedom-of-Thought Struggle*, 167.

p. 158   **"It must be so":** Eaton, *The Freedom-of-Thought Struggle*, 169–170.

p. 158   **discovered sixty copies:** Eaton, "A Dangerous Pamphlet in the Old South," 327.

p. 158   **distribution of the *Appeal*:** Eaton, "A Dangerous Pamphlet in the Old South," 329.

p. 159   **calling for individual actions:** Appomattox, *The Letter of Appomattox to the People of Virginia*, 28–30.

p. 159 **to produce "conspiracy or insurrection":** Curtis, *Free Speech*, 136–137.

p. 159 **similar versions of laws:** Eaton, *The Freedom-of-Thought Struggle*, 124–128; Nye, *Fettered Freedom*, 123–124.

p. 160 **an 1804 law:** Trexler, *Slavery in Missouri*, 202; Nye, *Fettered Freedom*, 124n.

p. 160 **North failed to act:** Eaton, *The Freedom-of-Thought Struggle*, 198–199.

p. 160 **demanding the extradition:** Wyatt-Brown, *Lewis Tappan*, 156.

p. 161 **175,000 separate pieces:** John, *Spreading the News*, 261.

p. 161 **burned the antislavery journals:** John, *Spreading the News*, 258.

p. 162 **"justified in that step":** Quoted in Richards, *Gentlemen of Property and Standing*, 74.

p. 163 **"every two-bit postmaster":** Quoted in Dickerson, *The Course of Tolerance*, 89.

p. 163 **states were free to do so:** Dickerson, *The Course of Tolerance*, 101.

p. 163 **destruction under state laws:** Dickerson, *The Course of Tolerance*, 104; John, *Spreading the News*, 274–275.

p. 163 **Birney discovered:** William Birney, *James G. Birney and His Times*, 184–185.

p. 164 **a "positive good":** Wyly-Jones, "The 1835 Anti-Abolition Meetings," 307.

p. 164 **"the darkest ages":** St. Louis *Observer*, December 31, 1835.

p. 164 **"less absurd than wicked":** St. Louis *Observer*, March 17, 1836.

p. 165 **"Follow the farmer":** Barnes, *The Antislavery Impulse*, 136.

p. 165 **women's signatures:** Barnes, *The Antislavery Impulse*, 143; Miller, *Arguing about Slavery*, 110.

p. 166 **to reprise the strategy:** Miller, *Arguing about Slavery*, 107; Barnes, *The Antislavery Impulse*, chap. 11.

p. 166 **Fairfield noted:** Miller, *Arguing about Slavery*, 28.

p. 167 **this tabling stratagem:** Miller, *Arguing about Slavery*, 144–145.

p. 167 **"arrest discussion of slavery":** Quoted in Richards, *The Slave Power*, 32.

p. 168 **A separate gag:** Wirls, "'The Only Mode of Avoiding Everlasting Debate,'" 123–124.

p. 168 **dwindling votes:** Meinke, "Slavery, Partisanship, and Procedure," 44.

p. 170 **the Panic of 1837:** "1837: The Hard Times," Historical Collections, Harvard Business School, accessed April 8, 2020, https://www.library .hbs.edu/hc/crises/1837.html; Digital Public Library of America, https ://dp.la/primary-source-sets/the-panic-of-1837"The Panic of 1837."

p. 170 **$1 million in bad loans:** Ford, *A History of Illinois*, 177–178.

p. 171 **leave him penniless:** Reid, *Biographical Sketch of Enoch Long*, 72–73.

p. 171 **"gone a whoring":** Alton *Observer*, May 25, 1837.

p. 173   **a worried friend wrote:** I. Russell to Elijah P. Lovejoy, April 29, 1837.

p. 173   **marry a Black woman:** Lovejoy and Lovejoy, *Memoir*, 212.

p. 173   **light up their windows:** Kerber, "Abolitionists and Amalgamators," 33.

p. 174   **"pure gloss of an African complexion":** Reprinted in Lovejoy and Lovejoy, *Memoir*, 200–201.

p. 174   **the whisper campaign:** Lovejoy and Lovejoy, *Memoir*, 212.

p. 174   **"gaining favor daily":** Elijah P. Lovejoy to Joseph Lovejoy, April 14, 1837, Folder 8, Box 2, Elijah P. Lovejoy Papers, accessed July 22, 2020, https ://swco.ttu.edu/location/Manuscripts/lovejoy/Lovejoy_Elijah_Guide.html.

p. 176   **"excite public indignation":** Lovejoy and Lovejoy, *Memoir*, 214.

p. 177   **terrible for the city's image:** *Missouri Republican*, August 25, 1837.

p. 178   **"odious doctrines":** *Missouri Republican*, July 17, 1837.

p. 179   **a former butcher:** Linder, *Reminiscences*, 74.

p. 179   **it wasn't his work:** Gill, *Tide without Turning*, 118.

p. 180   **"unwise agitation":** B.K. Hart and others to Elijah P. Lovejoy, July 24, 1837, in Lovejoy and Lovejoy, *Memoir*, 226; Norton, *Centennial History of Madison County*, 471.

p. 181   **"the downfall of our free institutions":** Alton *Observer*, July 20, 1837.

p. 182   **"this I cannot admit":** Elijah P. Lovejoy to B.K. Hart and others, July 26, 1837, in Lovejoy and Lovejoy, *Memoir*, 227–229.

p. 183   **ruin of the white man:** Linder, *Reminiscences*, 19.

p. 183   **"country more striking and bold":** Quoted in Bradley, "Usher F. Linder: Orator from Coles," 10.

p. 184   **Linder eked out a living:** Details on Linder's early life in Bradley, "Usher F. Linder: Orator from Coles," 1–7.

p. 184   **"almost irresistible":** Beveridge, *Abraham Lincoln*, vol. 1, 180.

p. 184   **"one of the most picturesque figures":** Beveridge, *Abraham Lincoln*, vol. 1, 180.

p. 184   **the attorney general's post:** *Missouri Republican*, February 15, 1837.

p. 185   **an instrument of slave insurrection:** Lincoln, *Alton Trials*, 77.

p. 185   **potential electoral benefits:** Harris, *The History of Negro Servitude in Illinois*, 62.

p. 185   **neck-deep in intrigue:** Linder, *Reminiscences*, 260.

p. 185   **proposed 1824 convention:** Norton, *Centennial History of Madison County*, 54.

p. 185   **the State Bank of Illinois:** Ford, *A History of Illinois*, 176.

p. 185   **"like a bombshell":** Linder, *Reminiscences*, 261.

p. 185   **Linder wrote a letter of apology:** *Missouri Republican*, February 15, 1837.

p. 186   **reputation for drinking:** *Missouri Republican*, February 15, 1837.

p. 186   **no hard evidence:** The hypothesis that Linder ghost-wrote the Botkin resolution is advanced by Lovejoy biographer John Gill, who claims that their wording matches Linder's writing style. But Gill, whose mostly well-researched book takes a number of generous narrative liberties for dramatic effect, does not offer any side-by-side comparisons to support his assertion. See Gill, *Tide without Turning*, 232, 13n.

p. 186   **"Now is the time":** Alton *Observer*, August 17, 1837.

p. 187   **attacks on clergymen:** Mayer, *All on Fire*, 235; Dillon, *The Abolitionists*, 117.

p. 187   **"converting mistakes into crimes":** Alton *Observer*, August 17, 1837.

p. 188   **"teach him by practice":** *Missouri Republican*, July 17, 1837.

p. 188   **"Something must be done":** Lovejoy and Lovejoy, *Memoir*, 230. Joseph and Owen Lovejoy, the two brothers who compiled the posthumous "memoir," attribute this quotation to the *Missouri Republican* of August 17, 1837. But the issue from that day does not contain this passage, based on my search. It is possible that the Lovejoys, whose record of years of press coverage otherwise proved highly reliable, were incorrect about the date or the newspaper. The language of the quotation makes clear that it was from Missouri, however.

p. 189   **agreed to let him go:** Elijah P. Lovejoy to Elizabeth Lovejoy, September 5, 1837, in Lovejoy and Lovejoy, *Memoir*, 232–234.

p. 189   **"they expressed their amazement":** Geo. T. M. Davis, *Autobiography*, 62. Davis describes, but does not name, the physicians who made the late-night visit. But a Davis friend, Thomas Dimmock, later said that the doctors were Beall and Jennings. See Dimmock, "Lovejoy: An Address," 8.

p. 190   **a spasm of destruction:** Lovejoy and Lovejoy, *Memoir*, 231; *Missouri Republican*, August 24 and 25, 1837.

p. 190   **"justified the harsh measures":** *Missouri Republican*, August 24, 1837.

p. 190   **"condemned by but few":** *Missouri Republican*, August 25, 1837.

p. 190   **"terminates the existence of a print":** Quoted in Simon, *Freedom's Champion*, 87.

p. 191   **it, too, would face attack:** Simon, *Freedom's Champion*, 88.

p. 191   **Another candidate:** Alton *Telegraph*, August 31, 1837. A notation at the bottom of the notice mentions that it was meant for insertion in the Alton *Spectator* as well.

p. 191   **Halderman, the physician:** Norton, *Centennial History of Madison County*, 471; Alton *Telegraph*, August 30, 1837.

p. 192   **a well-regulated police force:** Alton *Telegraph*, September 20, 1837.

p. 192   **"been mobbed down":** Elijah P. Lovejoy to Elizabeth Lovejoy, September 5, 1837, in Lovejoy and Lovejoy, *Memoir*, 232.

p. 193   **"mobism will triumph":** Lovejoy and Lovejoy, *Memoir*, 245–246.

p. 193   **"not much of an abolitionist":** Letter from A. [surname unclear] to Elijah P. Lovejoy, September 6, 1837, Folder 8, Box 2, Elijah P. Lovejoy Papers, accessed July 22, 2020, https://swco.ttu.edu/location/Manuscripts/lovejoy/Lovejoy_Elijah_Guide.html.

p. 193   **a separate donation:** John Rankin to Elijah P. Lovejoy, September 11, 1837, Folder 8, Box 2, Elijah P. Lovejoy Papers, accessed July 22, 2020, https://swco.ttu.edu/location/Manuscripts/lovejoy/Lovejoy_Elijah_Guide.html.

p. 194   **"a dreadful opposition to encounter":** Lovejoy to Gerrit Smith, September 4, 1837, copy of typed transcription, Elijah Parish Lovejoy Materials.

p. 195   **"rights secured to us":** Winthrop S. Gilman statement, "To our fellow citizens of the State of Illinois," September 7, 1837.

p. 195   **mailing copies of the statement:** Elijah P. Lovejoy to Erastus Wright, September 8, 1837, Abraham Lincoln Presidential Library & Museum, Springfield, IL.

p. 195   **a sudden change of heart:** Dillon believes that Gilman changed his mind "overnight," but there is no evidence of this. It seems quite possible that Gilman agreed to write the declaration even though he thought Lovejoy should no longer run the newspaper.

p. 196   **"most cheerfully" step down:** "To the Friends of the Redeemer," September 11, 1837, in Lovejoy and Lovejoy, *Memoir*, 248–250.

p. 196   **had yet to be paid:** "Statement of the Observer's Affairs," September 11, 1837, Abraham Lincoln Presidential Library & Museum.

p. 197   **"trying to kill your brother":** Lovejoy and Lovejoy, *Memoir*, 250.

p. 197   **support among Alton's elites:** See Dillon, *Elijah P. Lovejoy*, 122. Dillon maintains that this "indecision" essentially signaled to Lovejoy's foes that they were free to use violence against him. Gill refers to this civic abdication as the "defection of the neutrals."

p. 197   **The biblical argument:** Lovejoy and Lovejoy, *Memoir*, 247.

p. 200   **sombreros and hanging beards:** William Birney, *James G. Birney and His Times*, 257.

p. 200   **a pack of men:** James G. Birney to Lewis Tappan, April 29, 1836, in Dumond, *Letters of James Gillespie Birney*, 319.

p. 200   **"guilt of the instigators and abettors":** James G. Birney to the Anti-Slavery Record, April 29, 1836, in Dumond, *Letters of James Gillespie Birney*, 320, 3n.

p. 201   **An ally in Kentucky:** John Jones to James G. Birney, April 30, 1836, in Dumond, *Letters of James Gillespie Birney*, 322.

p. 201   **a "servile parasite":** William Birney, *James G. Birney and His Times*, 248.

p. 201   **"freedom for the *white*":** James G. Birney to Gerrit Smith, September 13, 1835, in Dumond, *Letters of James Gillespie Birney*, 243.

p. 202   **a familiar face:** William Birney, *James G. Birney and His Times*, 240.

p. 202   **not a single local newspaper:** William Birney, *James G. Birney and His Times*, 241.

p. 202   **subscriptions had risen:** Ohio Anti-Slavery Society Executive Committee, *Narrative of the Late Riotous Proceeding*, 12.

p. 202   **so impressed by Birney's work:** Benjamin Lundy to James G. Birney, March 27, 1836, in Dumond, *Letters of James Gillespie Birney*, 312–15.

p. 203   **not a single peace officer:** Ohio Anti-Slavery Society, *Narrative*, 12; Birney, 241.

p. 204   **members of the Southern planting class:** Ohio Anti-Slavery Society, *Narrative*, 14.

p. 205   **Birney's brother-in-law:** Fladeland, *James Gillespie Birney*, 137.

p. 205   **The Franklin House owner:** *Philanthropist*, July 22, 1836.

p. 205   **took note of the boarder revolt:** Ohio Anti-Slavery Society, *Narrative*, 17.

p. 206   **"A band of lawless men":** *Philanthropist*, July 22, 1836.

p. 206   **"enemies of America":** Cincinnati *Whig*, July 19, 1836.

p. 206   **"the position of the assassin":** Excerpts quoted in Ohio Anti-Slavery Society, *Narrative*, 20–22.

p. 207   **"do not trade with that man":** Quoted in Ohio Anti-Slavery Society, *Narrative*, 22.

p. 207   **"not more than 1,000":** Ohio Anti-Slavery Society, *Narrative*, 23.

p. 208   **the Philanthropist must cease:** Cincinnati *Gazette*, July 25, 1836.

p. 208   **He replied to the committee:** Cincinnati *Gazette*, August 1, 1836.

p. 208   **"this excitement cannot be kept down":** Ohio Anti-Slavery Society, *Narrative*, 30.

p. 209   **not the *Philanthropist*'s tone:** Ohio Anti-Slavery Society, *Narrative*, 32–35.

p. 209   **Responsibility lay with city authorities:** Ohio Anti-Slavery Society, *Narrative*, 36–37.

p. 210   **"utmost abhorrence":** Cincinnati *Whig*, August 1, 1836.

p. 210   **"vengeance of the multitude":** Quoted in Ohio Anti-Slavery Society, *Narrative*, 39.

p. 210   **tar and feather:** Birney Cincinnati *Gazette*, August 2 and 3, 1836.

p. 211   **"men receiving orders":** Ohio Anti-Slavery Society, *Narrative*, 39; William Birney, *James G. Birney and His Times*, 246.

p. 211   **a pile of wreckage:** Cincinnati *Gazette*, August 2, 1836.

p. 212   **The teen waited:** William Birney, *James G. Birney and His Times*, 246–247.

p. 212   **mangled body of the press:** Cincinnati *Gazette*, August 2, 1836.

p. 212   **burned down five tenements:** Cincinnati *Republican*, April 13, 1836; Greve, *Centennial History of Cincinnati*, 597.

p. 212   **as Davies finished his remarks:** Ohio Anti-Slavery Society, *Narrative*, 40.

p. 213   **"instantly seized and lynched":** James G. Birney to Lewis Tappan, August 10, 1836, in Dumond, *Letters of James Gillespie Birney*, 349.

p. 215   **"There goes the abolition press":** Lovejoy and Lovejoy, *Memoir*, 250–251.

p. 216   **began cracking it open:** Alton *Telegraph*, September 27, 1837.

p. 216   **"quiet and gentlemanly mob":** Alton *Telegraph*, September 27, 1837; Lovejoy and Lovejoy, *Memoir*, 251.

p. 216   **"However worthy of censure":** Alton *Telegraph*, September 27, 1837.

p. 217   **"he will not continue":** Quoted in Simon, *Freedom's Champion*, 92.

p. 217   **"a crisis in Illinois":** Excerpt in the *Liberator*, November 3, 1837.

p. 217   **slipped him a note:** The account of the St. Charles assault is drawn from Lovejoy's own description of events in a letter to the abolitionist editor Joshua Leavitt, reprinted in Lovejoy and Lovejoy, *Memoir*, 251–260.

p. 220   **not allowed to preach:** Letter from "A Christian," published in the *Philanthropist*, September 8, 1837.

p. 220   **"they hate Abolitionism":** Elijah P. Lovejoy to Joshua Leavitt, October 3, 1837, in Lovejoy and Lovejoy, *Memoir*, 258–260.

p. 221   **Another name stood out:** Alton *Telegraph*, November 1, 1837.

p. 222   **"unchristian and abusive epithets":** Alton *Telegraph*, November 1, 1837.

p. 222   **Parker and Edwards delivered speeches:** *Western Pioneer*, October 26, 1837.

p. 222   **Peck, the Baptist preacher:** Lovejoy and Lovejoy, *Memoir*, 263.

p. 222   **"a very few restless spirits":** *Western Pioneer*, October 26, 1837.

p. 223   **"no cowardice in him":** Elijah P. Lovejoy to Joshua Leavitt, in Lovejoy and Lovejoy, *Memoir*, 259.

p. 223   **"an old bear":** Minutes of the Presbyterian Church in the U.S.A. (New School) Synods, Illinois, vol. 1, JKM Library Trust, Chicago, IL, 90; James M. Buchanan to James G. Birney, August 18, 1837, in Dumond, *Letters of James Gillespie Birney*, 416–417.

p. 223 **the growing regional divide:** For more detailed analyses of the role of the slavery issue in the church schism, see Staiger, "Abolitionism and the Protestant Schism"; Lyons, "The Attitude of Presbyterians"; and Moorhead, "The 'Restless Spirit' of Radicalism.'"

p. 224 **entered Yale at age fifteen:** Charles Beecher, "The Life of Edward Beecher," 17–18.

p. 224 **his sermons weren't of much use:** Rugoff, *The Beechers*, 89–90; Merideth, *The Politics of the Universe*, 62–63.

p. 224 **"prolonged nervous strain":** Merideth, *The Politics of the Universe*, 59.

p. 224 **eager to name him:** Merideth, *The Politics of the Universe*, 75–76.

p. 225 **"a horridly ugly little village":** Merideth, *The Politics of the Universe*, 80–81.

p. 225 **"decidedly hostile":** Edward Beecher, *Narrative of Riots at Alton*, 22.

p. 225 **"I say go on":** Edward Beecher to Elijah P. Lovejoy, December 20, 1835, Folder 6, Box 2, Elijah P. Lovejoy Papers, accessed July 20, 2020, https://swco.ttu.edu/location/Manuscripts/lovejoy/Lovejoy_Elijah_Guide.html.

p. 226 **reduce the possibility of violence:** Edward Beecher, *Narrative*, 24–25.

p. 227 **two starkly competing visions:** Alton *Telegraph*, October 18, 1837.

p. 231 **shook his fist in Lovejoy's face:** Edward Beecher, *Narrative*, 29–30; Tanner, *The Martyrdom of Lovejoy*, 219–20; Lovejoy and Lovejoy, *Memoir*, 265.

p. 231 **Linder's barrage took aim:** Tanner, *Martyrdom*, 220.

p. 232 **erupted in noisy cheering:** Illinois Anti-Slavery Society, "Proceedings of the Ill. Anti-Slavery Convention Held at Upper Alton," 7–8; Tanner, *Martyrdom*, 221.

p. 232 **"all our men are joining":** Lovejoy and Lovejoy, *Memoir*, 266; Tanner, *Martyrdom*, 220–221.

p. 233 **They quietly scattered:** Edward Beecher, *Narrative*, 34.

p. 234 **home of Thaddeus Hurlbut:** Elijah P. Lovejoy to James G. Birney, *Philanthropist*, November 28, 1837.

p. 234 **a group of special constables:** Edward Beecher, *Narrative*, 36.

p. 235 **favored moving it to Quincy:** Winthrop S. Gilman statement, November 9, 1837, transcription in Collection of Elijah Parish Lovejoy Materials.

p. 235 **"I can as yet see anything encouraging":** David Nelson to Absalom Peters, June 13, 1837, Abraham Lincoln Presidential Library & Museum.

p. 236 **"one medium double press":** Bowen et al., "Anti-Slavery Convention," 330.

p. 236 **a redemptive ending:** Edward Beecher, *Narrative*, 45.

p. 237   **Hammond had published:** Cincinnati *Gazette*, July 20, 1836.

p. 238   **Chase wrote up a statement:** Cincinnati *Gazette*, August 4, 1836.

p. 238   **"pure, upright and worthy citizens":** Hart, *Salmon Portland Chase*, 49.

p. 239   **"the great enemy":** Hart, *Salmon Portland Chase*, 49.

p. 240   **included the *Whig*:** Cincinnati *Whig*, August 17, 1836.

p. 240   **a course aimed at keeping the peace:** Cincinnati *Gazette*, August 2, 1836.

p. 241   **guilty of "encouragement":** Excerpted in Cincinnati *Gazette*, August 5, 1836; Cincinnati *Whig*, August 17, 1836.

p. 241   **might be liable:** Cincinnati *Whig*, August 16, 1836.

p. 241   **"search out the wrong-doers":** Cincinnati *Gazette*, August 6, 1836.

p. 242   **"terms of strong reprobation":** Cincinnati *Journal and Western Luminary*, August 4, 1836.

p. 242   **his point had been made:** William Birney, *James G. Birney and His Times*, 254.

p. 242   **residents did not blame him:** The scholar John Nerone argues compellingly that the leaders of the anti-abolitionist actions came out ahead in the end, having proven Cincinnati's reliability to Southern slave states and escaping blame for the disorder.

p. 243   **"abolitionists by the THOUSAND":** *Philanthropist*, September 23, 1836.

p. 245   **effort to defuse tensions:** Edward Beecher, *Narrative*, 45.

p. 246   **"not a local question":** Edward Beecher, *Narrative*, 46–47.

p. 247   **backed up Lovejoy's account:** Edward Beecher, *Narrative*, 47.

p. 247   **"blustering and swaggering":** Tanner, *Martyrdom*, 222.

p. 247   **biblical example of Paul:** Edward Beecher, *Narrative*, 48–49; Reid, *Biographical Sketch of Enoch Long*, 87–89; Tanner, *Martyrdom*, 222; Tanner, *History of the Rise and Progress of the Alton Riots*, 6.

p. 248   **posted notices around town:** Lincoln, *Alton Trials*, 73.

p. 248   **passed through isolated terrain:** Edward Beecher, *Narrative*, 67.

p. 248   **flinging a hammer at him:** Reid, *Biographical Sketch of Enoch Long*, 91.

p. 248   **"plenty of ammunition":** Reid, *Biographical Sketch of Enoch Long*, 91.

p. 249   **stricken with fear:** Lovejoy and Lovejoy, *Memoir*, 280; Edward Beecher, *Narrative*, 90.

p. 249   **a public constabulary force:** Edward Beecher, *Narrative*, 49; Dillon, *Elijah P. Lovejoy*, 147.

p. 249   **a personal obligation:** Lovejoy and Lovejoy, *Memoir*, 267.

p. 250   **invited Krum to come:** The account of Krum's actions on November 1 come from his subsequent court testimony in Lincoln, *Alton Trials*, 35–39.

p. 251   **decided to store their firearms:** Tanner, *History*, 8.

p. 252 **Two of Beecher's armed defenders:** Krum testimony in Lincoln, *Alton Trials*, 37; Gilman statement, November 9, 1837.

p. 252 **"if he wishes martyrdom":** *Missouri Republican*, November 1, 1837.

p. 253 **abolitionists' detested doctrines:** Edward Beecher, *Narrative*, 50–51.

p. 253 **his college duties:** Edward Beecher, *Narrative*, 51–52.

p. 254 **"the death warrant":** Lovejoy and Lovejoy, *Memoir*, 268.

p. 254 **"no right to be neutral":** Edward Beecher, *Narrative*, 52.

p. 255 **"protect the press":** Official Minutes of the Meeting Held at Alton, in Tanner, *Martyrdom*, Appendix, 194–97.

p. 255 **American democracy itself:** Edward Beecher, *Narrative*, 54–60.

p. 256 **Others just kept quiet:** Edward Beecher, *Narrative*, 60.

p. 256 **assembly would not stand:** Edward Beecher, *Narrative*, 60–61.

p. 260 **"committed to the wrong side":** Edward Beecher, *Narrative*, 65.

p. 260 **"some midnight mob":** Edward Beecher, *Narrativen*, 67.

p. 260 **a strong measure of protection:** Edward Beecher, *Narrative*, 66.

p. 261 **"deliberate murder":** Edward Beecher, *Narrative*, 67–68.

p. 261 **"silent sadness":** Edward Beecher, *Narrative*, 70.

p. 262 **"a train of mournful consequences":** Official Minutes, Tanner, *Martyrdom*, 198.

p. 262 **"undue excitements":** Official Minutes, Tanner, *Martyrdom*, 200.

p. 262 **"contribute to the peace":** Official Minutes, Tanner, *Martyrdom*, 201.

p. 263 **"he should not print them at all":** Edward Beecher, *Narrative*, 76.

p. 263 **adherence to the rule of law:** Official Minutes, Tanner, *Martyrdom*, 201.

p. 263 **"deep, tender and subdued":** Edward Beecher, *Narrative*, 85.

p. 265 **"I look in vain":** Edward Beecher, *Narrative*, 89–90.

p. 265 **"my grave":** Edward Beecher, *Narrative*, 91.

p. 266 **an instant of hesitation:** Quoted in Dimmock, "Lovejoy: An Address," 9–10.

p. 266 **"their own inclinations":** Lovejoy and Lovejoy, *Memoir*, 276.

p. 267 **the Linder proposal:** Edward Beecher, *Narrative*, 95.

p. 267 **"editors from abroad":** Official Minutes, Tanner, *Martyrdom*, 204.

p. 268 **rushed to the dock:** Gilman statement, November 9, 1837.

p. 269 **eight to ten armed men:** Gilman statement, November 9, 1837.

p. 270 **goods worth about $30,000:** Winthrop S. Gilman to Chandler R. Gilman, November 8, 1837, in Noyes, *A Family History*, 660.

p. 270 **sudden change in plans:** Elizabeth Lovejoy to John Lovejoy, September 25, 1837, Folder 8, Box 2, Elijah P. Lovejoy Papers, accessed July 22, 2020, https://swco.ttu.edu/location/Manuscripts/lovejoy/Lovejoy_Elijah_Guide.html.

p. 270 **Gilman paid a visit:** Krum testimony, in Lincoln, *Alton Trials*, 39–40.

p. 271   **one of the members:** Lincoln, *Alton Trials*, 32.

p. 271   **their fruitless vigil:** Testimony of Edward Keating, in Lincoln, *Alton Trials*, 13.

p. 272   **"Alton was redeemed":** Edward Beecher, *Narrative*, 100–101.

p. 272   **paid the rumor no mind:** Edward Beecher, *Narrative*, 103.

p. 273   **lead balls for the rifles:** Platt testimony, in Lincoln, *Alton Trials*, 20–21.

p. 273   **"What these men hate":** Samuel Willard, in Tanner, *Martyrdom*, appendix C, 217.

p. 274   **his wife and their baby:** Tanner, *Martyrdom*, 154.

p. 274   **use of such a force:** Krum testimony, in Lincoln, *Alton Trials*, 41.

p. 275   **"swearing about Abolition":** Greeley testimony, in Lincoln, *Alton Trials*, 112.

p. 275   **Keating and West left:** Testimony of Henry W. West, in Lincoln, *Alton Trials*, 15; Testimony of Edward Keating, in Lincoln, *Alton Trials*, 9–10.

p. 275   **"Shoot him!":** Testimony of Webb C. Quigley, in Lincoln, *Alton Trials*, 115.

p. 276   **blowing tin horns:** Tanner, *Martyrdom*, 155.

p. 276   **pointed a pistol:** Willard, in Tanner, *Martyrdom*, 224; Gilman statement, November 9, 1837.

p. 276   **Lovejoy warned:** West testimony, in Lincoln, *Alton Trials*, 17.

p. 277   **more shots rang out:** West testimony, in Lincoln, *Alton Trials*, 16.

p. 277   **"they had a right":** Krum testimony, in Lincoln, *Alton Trials*, 44.

p. 277   **"get out of the way":** Krum testimony, in Lincoln, *Alton Trials*, 46.

p. 277   **tar-and-feather mob:** West testimony, in Lincoln, *Alton Trials*, 96.

p. 278   **now too late:** Gilman statement, November 9, 1837.

p. 278   **"it would do no good":** Testimony by William Martin, in Lincoln, *Alton Trials*, 118.

p. 278   **"the press would be had":** Testimony by Sherman Robbins, in Lincoln, *Alton Trials*, 108.

p. 279   **"Fire the building!":** Lovejoy and Lovejoy, *Memoir*, 290.

p. 279   **helpless to stop the torching:** Gilman statement, November 9, 1837.

p. 280   **Five of the warehouse defenders:** Gilman statement, November 9, 1837.

p. 280   **it was Dr. Hope:** Willard account, in Tanner, *Martyrdom*, 227.

p. 281   **Badly wounded:** Description of Lovejoy's shooting in Lovejoy and Lovejoy, *Memoir*, 290–291.

p. 281   **a keg of gunpowder:** Reid, *Enoch Long*, 100.

p. 281   **"leave the building":** Lovejoy and Lovejoy, *Memoir*, 291.

p. 281   **would have burned:** Robbins testimony, in Lincoln, *Alton Trials*, 109.

p. 282   **the site of the body:** West testimony, in Lincoln, *Alton Trials*, 96.

p. 282   **he would sooner die:** Lovejoy and Lovejoy, *Memoir*, 292.

p. 282   **tossed it out:** Robbins testimony, in Lincoln, *Alton Trials*, 109.

p. 282   **the sound of pounding:** Krum, "To the Public."

p. 282   **"happy" in its task:** Krum testimony, in Lincoln, *Alton Trials*, 100; Greeley testimony, 23.

p. 282   **the physician:** Beall Willard, in Tanner, *Martyrdom*, 228.

p. 284   **"in an angry mood":** Tanner, *Martyrdom*, 152.

p. 284   **"My dear children":** Elizabeth Lovejoy to Owen, Elizabeth and John Lovejoy, undated letter, Folder 8, Box 2, Elijah P. Lovejoy Papers, accessed July 22, 2020, https://swco.ttu.edu/location/Manuscripts /lovejoy/Lovejoy_Elijah_Guide.html.

p. 285   **"the fatal consequences":** *Missouri Republican*, November 10, 1837.

p. 285   **"times are so dull":** Norton, *Centennial History of Madison County*, 192.

p. 285   **"exciting feelings":** Alton *Telegraph*, November 15, 1837.

p. 285   **"a good conscience":** Reprinted in Lovejoy and Lovejoy, *Memoir*, 138.

p. 286   **"utter and uncompromising reprobation":** William Ellery Channing letter to citizens of Boston, November 27, 1837, quoted in Curtis, *Free Speech*, 245.

p. 286   **the crowd was divided:** Martineau, *The Martyr Age*, 40.

p. 287   **"perfect harmony and sympathy":** Artemus Bowers Muzzey, "The Birth Speech of Wendell Phillips," in Phillips, *Freedom Speech of Wendell Phillips*, 5.

p. 287   **"same dread of Lovejoy":** Austin, *Speech Delivered in Faneuil Hall*, 8.

p. 287   **"as a fool dieth":** Austin, *Speech Delivered in Faneuil Hall*, 9.

p. 287   **"we cannot wonder":** Austin, *Speech Delivered in Faneuil Hall*, 12–13.

p. 288   **"the recreant American":** Phillips, *Freedom Speech*, 9.

p. 288   **The meeting room exploded:** Muzzey, "The Birth Speech of Wendell Phillips," 5–6.

p. 288   **planned to speak:** Ruchames, "Wendell Phillips' Lovejoy Address," 108–17.

p. 289   **"The czar might as well":** Phillips, *Freedom Speech*, 10.

p. 289   **"this many-headed monster":** Phillips, *Freedom Speech*, 14.

p. 289   **thunderous applause:** Phillips, *Freedom Speech*, 14.

p. 290   **"Something was to be done":** Phillips, *Freedom Speech*, 16.

p. 290   **attendees wept later:** Martineau, *The Martyr Age*, 40.

p. 290   **classics of American oratory:** Phillips, *Freedom Speech*, introduction.

p. 290   **a "murdered Abolitionist":** Channing, *Slavery*, 161.http://www .gutenberg.org/files/44736/44736-h/44736-h.htm#Page_161.

p. 291   **reaction in Illinois:** Harris, *The History of Negro Servitude in Illinois*, 97.

p. 291   **actions taken by the mayor:** For various newspaper reactions, see Lovejoy and Lovejoy, *Memoir*, 322–337; Tanner, *Martyrdom*, 163.

p. 292   **"marvellously out of place"**: Austin, *Speech Delivered in Faneuil Hall*, 10.

p. 292   **"a Christian martyr"**: Mayer, *All on Fire*, 237.

p. 292   **a "dangerous precedent"**: Quoted in "The Alton Tragedy," *The Advocate of Peace*, 65.

p. 292   **"in holy resignation"**: "The Alton Tragedy," 63–64.

p. 292   **"in defense of justice"**: Edward Beecher, *Narrative*, 136.

p. 293   **his December 31 eulogy**: Lovejoy and Lovejoy, *Memoir*, 300–14.

p. 294   **"This interference"**: Lincoln, *Alton Trials*, 68.

p. 294   **his "Western boys"**: Lincoln, *Alton Trials*, 72–77.

p. 295   **"a well-nigh fatal one"**: Willard, in Tanner, *Martyrdom*, 231.

p. 296   **keep the paper going**: Magdol, *Owen Lovejoy*, 28.

p. 296   **Lundy published the paper**: Pease, *The Frontier State*, 370–71.

p. 296   **the same Presbyterian church**: Bowen et al., "Anti-Slavery Convention," 335.

p. 296   **Linder was out**: *Liberator*, December 22, 1837.

p. 296   **life of poverty and illness**: Ohio State Convention of Abolitionists, "Letter of Appeal," March 1, 1841, Abraham Lincoln Presidential Library & Museum; Tanner, *Martyrdom*, 90; Edward Lovejoy is quoted in Bernard, "Remarks at Unveiling of Memorial of Celia Ann Lovejoy at Alton City Cemetery."

p. 297   **the younger Lovejoy**: Chrystal, "The *Wabuska Mangler* as Martyr's Seed," 23–26.

p. 297   **the Salem Street Church**: Rugoff, *The Beechers*, 200.

p. 297   **"the most eloquent"**: Dillon, *Elijah P. Lovejoy*, 181.

p. 300   **"nothing but an earthquake"**: Edward Beecher, *Narrative*, 135.

p. 301   **borrowed from English common law**: McNamara, "Sedition Act of 1798," https://mtsu.edu/first-amendment/article/1238/sedition-act-of-1798.

p. 302   **policing of citizens' speech**: See Nelson, *Freedom of the Press*, xxii, and Dickerson, *The Course of Tolerance*, xii–xiii. Dickerson writes that most Americans believed majority opinion should prevail in cases where expression was deemed obnoxious, and that the idea that the First Amendment implied a government duty to protect minority opinion was "novel and uncomfortable."

p. 302   **the people's conception**: Curtis, *Free Speech*, 1–21, 250–260, 416–417; see also Curtis, "The Curious History" and "Teaching Free Speech."

p. 303   **new form of sedition law**: Ratner and Tweeter, *Fanatics and Fire-Eaters*, 24.

p. 304   **patriot mobs**: See Nerone, *Violence against the Press*, 37–45.

p. 304   **"fanatics" and "fire-eaters":** See Ratner and Tweeter, *Fanatics and Fire-Eaters*.

p. 304   **civil rights movement:** Leonard, *News for All*, 80–81.

p. 305   **doctors Beall and Hope:** Willard, in Tanner, *Martyrdom*, 231.

p. 305   **"he didn't like to talk":** Interview with John W. Harned, *Greenville Advocate*, November 4, 1897, Abraham Lincoln Presidential Library & Museum; Joseph Brown, "Early Reminiscences of Alton," 8.

p. 306   **killed by one of his own:** See Dimmock, "Lovejoy," 14; Whittlesey, "Elijah P. Lovejoy"; Simon, *Freedom's Champion*, 140–141.

p. 306   **a knife fight:** Dimmock, "Lovejoy," 14.

p. 306   **Rock admitted:** Thompson, *Prison Life and Reflections*, 224.

p. 306   **Hope became Alton's mayor:** Norton, *Centennial History of Madison County*, 387.

INDEX

⚬⚬⚬

A

abolitionism: beginning of, 82; Birney and, 111–124, 139–147, 199–214, 297–298; censorship and, 125–127, 163; colonization and, 79; critics of, 86–89, 178–179, 287–288; as fringe movement, 9–10, 103, 298; Garrison and, 9, 15; growth of, 80; impact of Lovejoy's death on, 299–304; Lovejoy and, x–xii, 2, 5, 7–10, 83–87, 92–93, 176–182, 187, 193–194, 229–236; opposition to, 140–147, 200, 202–209; peace principle and, 292; Phillips and, 289–290; postal system and, 160–164; press freedom and, 302–303. *See also* antislavery movement

abolitionists: attacks on, 9, 87, 98–99, 210–213; Black, 154–155; Hammond and, 239–241; interracial marriage and, 173–174; from Lane Theological Seminary, 119–121; Lovejoy's view of, 76–78; mob violence against, 100–103, 275–282; public opinion on, 183–184; silencing of, 149–150; threats against, 202–209; views of, 9, 83. *See also specific people*

activism, 9, 66, 115, 118

Adams, John, 56, 301

Adams, John Quincy, 25–26, 167, 176, 299

Adams, Samuel, 49

Alabama, 114–115, 142, 159

Albion, Maine, 13

alcohol, 102–103, 177

Alien and Sedition Acts of 1798, 56, 301, 302

Alton, Illinois: clashing social values in, 44–46; condemnation of, in North, 291; economic decline in, 169–172, 177–178, 295; growth of, 42–46, 59–61, 128–129; moving of *Observer* to, 1–7, 41–42, 92; Northeast transplants in, 29–37; *Observer* in, 46–48, 62–64, 235–236, 246–247, 266–268; opposition to Lovejoy in, 178–182, 188–192, 221–222, 247; tensions in, 191–192, 245–257, 259–268; trials in, 293–295, 305–306

Alton Colonization Society, 249–250, 253

amalgamation, 173–174

American Anti-Slavery Society, 81, 83–85, 100, 118, 123, 130, 160, 161, 165, 175, 297–298

American Bible Society, 60, 66, 85, 107, 115

American Colonization Society, 76, 78, 115–118, 130, 150, 220–221

American society, changes in, 18–19

American Sunday School Union, 60, 66, 115

American Tract Society, 66, 67, 115

anti-Catholic sentiment, 105–110

antislavery movement, 174; in Alton, 62–63; Birney and, 111–124, 135–147, 199–214; censorship and, 125–127, 158–160, 163, 302–303; divisions in, 9–10, 83, 298; free Blacks and, 154–155, 158; impact of Lovejoy's death on, 299–304; Lippincott and, 32–33;